Interpretation and Obedience

OTHER FORTRESS PRESS BOOKS
BY WALTER BRUEGGEMANN

The Land: Place as Gift, Promise, and Challenge
in the Biblical Faith (1977)

The Prophetic Imagination (1978)

The Creative Word: Canon as a Model for
Biblical Education (1982)

David's Truth in Israel's Imagination and Memory (1985)

Hopeful Imagination: Prophetic Voices in Exile (1986)

Israel's Praise: Doxology against Idolatry and Ideology (1988)

Finally Comes the Poet: Daring Speech
for Proclamation (1989)

Proclamation 4: Aids for Interpreting the Lessons of
the Church Year: Series A: Easter (1989)

Interpretation and Obedience

From Faithful Reading to Faithful Living

WALTER BRUEGGEMANN

FORTRESS PRESS   MINNEAPOLIS

INTERPRETATION AND OBEDIENCE
From Faithful Reading to Faithful Living

Biblical quotations, unless otherwise noted, are from the Revised Standard Version of the Bible, copyright © 1946, 1952, and 1971, by the Division of Christian Education of the National Council of Churches, and are used by permission.

Excerpt from *The Accidental Tourist* by Anne Tyler is copyright © 1985 Anne Tyler and reprinted by permission of Alfred A. Knopf, Inc. and Russell & Volkening, Inc.

Excerpts from *The Grapes of Wrath* by John Steinbeck are copyright © 1939, renewed © 1967 John Steinbeck and reprinted by permission of Viking Penguin, a division of Penguin Books USA, Inc.

The essay "Land: Fertility and Justice" is copyright © 1987 by The Order of St. Benedict, Inc. Published by The Liturgical Press, Collegeville, Minnesota. Used with permission.

Cover design by Lecy Design
Interior design by Publishers' WorkGroup

Library of Congress Cataloging-in-Publication Data

Brueggemann, Walter.
    Interpretation and obedience : from faithful reading to faithful living / Walter Brueggemann.
        p.   cm.
    Includes bibliographical references and index.
    ISBN 0-8006-2478-5 (alk. paper)
    1. Bible. O.T.—Hermeneutics.   2. Ethics in the Bible.
3. Obedience—Biblical teaching.   4. Bible. O.T.—Criticism,
interpretation, etc.   5. Christian ethics—Lutheran authors.
I. Title.
BS476.B72   1991   90–19231
261—dc20   CIP

The paper used in this publication meets the minimum requirements of American National Standards for Information Sciences—Permanence of Paper for Printed Library Materials, ANSI Z329.48-1984.   ∞™

Manufactured in the U.S.A.   AF 1-2478

95   94   93   92   91   1   2   3   4   5   6   7   8   9   10

For Hilda M. Brueggemann
in Memory of Dorothea Pflug

In Gratitude

Contents

PART 3.   Obedience as an Act of Interpretation

PART 4.   A Cosmic Context for Interpretation and Obedience

Foreword

THESE LECTURES AND ESSAYS, almost without exception, were prepared in response to *ad hoc* invitations. As I reflected on what I had been doing over recent years, their coherence dawned on me. I believe the rubric of "interpretation and obedience" which I have used as an organizing principle reflects the actual evolution and shaping of my own thinking; nonetheless, that general rubric fits only loosely what I have done.

I have drawn these materials together not in response to any request but because editing, consolidating, and rewriting has been important for me by way of clarifying and sorting out crucial issues now facing the community of faith. I hope that some who read will find my clarifying and sorting out useful for their own work in doing the same.

It will be obvious to the reader that I have been decisively influenced by Norman Gottwald's thesis concerning tribes and state. Since Gottwald's programmatic 1979 work, *The Tribes of Yahweh,* he and his colleagues in the sociology of early Israel have made important refinements to his thesis. Specifically, they suggest that the discontinuity between early Israelite retribalization and the subsequent monarchy should not be drastically stated because at the inception of Israel's "social experiment" there were already present forces committed to a concentration of power to serve their social advantage. (This argument is made by Frank S. Frick, Norman Chaney, Norman Gottwald, and Robert Coote and Keith W.

Whitelam in *Semeia* 37 (1986), and in Robert Coote and Keith W. Whitelam, *The Emergence of Early Israel.* See also Frank S. Frick, *The Formation of the State in Ancient Israel* [Sheffield, Eng.: Almond Press, 1985], and David Noel Freedman and David Frank Graf, editors, *Palestine in Transition: The Emergence of Ancient Israel* [Sheffield, Eng.: Almond Press, 1983].) I have adjusted neither my argument nor documentation to take account of these recent arguments. While this refinement of hypothesis is important, it does not substantively affect the argument I have made, though it might in time to come lead to a less absolute contrast in the articulation of my argument.

There are a host of people to thank, including a number of persons who have invited, supported, and responded to me in various settings. There are colleagues, friends, and family who have been responsive along the way. I am grateful to Donna LaGrasso, who has been unfailing in skill, patience, and generosity as a typist. In turn, Roland Seboldt, then of Augsburg Publishing House, John A. Hollar of Fortress Press, and Marshall Johnson of Fortress Press have given their editorial encouragement. Finally, it has been Stephanie Egnotovich who has done the hard, detailed work in turning these materials into a workable manuscript, and my debt to her is enormous.

The dedication of this book is to two "mothers of Israel." My own mother, Hilda M. Brueggemann, stands in my life as an unfailing source of fidelity, a fidelity that has not waned with her growing fragility. She does not know the word, but she has been and is no mean hermeneutist. Dorothea Pflug has been a mother to many of us. I celebrate the continuing power of her life and person. In my last (telephone) conversation with her before she died, we talked of "relinquishing and receiving." She was endlessly relinquishing so that many of us could receive, grace upon grace. I am indeed fortunate to have had more than one such mother in graciousness.

Introduction

THE SUBSTANCE AND STRUCTURE of this book are an argument that liberated, imaginative interpretation and disciplined, committed obedience depend upon and require each other for faithfulness. Interpretation that seeks to let the old word be the live, authoritative word, if it is faithful to the material interpreted, must be an act of obedience. *Obedient interpretation* in the social context of the Western church is to see how the Bible authorizes, evokes, and permits a world that is an alternative to the deathly world of our dominant value system. This question of an alternative world is intrinsic to our affirmation of biblical authority.

Conversely, obedience that seeks to act according to the covenantal intentionality of the God of the Bible, attending to Yahweh's nonnegotiable demands, must be an act of interpretation. *Interpretive obedience* is an act of imaginative construal to show how the nonnegotiable intentions of Yahweh are to be discerned and practiced in our situation, which is so very different from the situations in which those intentions were initially articulated.

The convergence of obedient interpretation and interpretive obedience is not merely a formal matter but has a persistent substance. It will be clear that the obedient interpretation I have sought to articulate concerns how God's sovereign will for peace, justice, and mercy destabilizes our conventional, settled perceptions of reality and invites our visioning of an alternative which can be practiced. It

will be equally clear that the interpretive obedience I have explicated concerns how the issues of power and fidelity are practiced in
many different social transactions. Interpretation that destabilizes
and envisions, and obedience that cares about power and fidelity
bring us very close to our own primary crisis, as a church and as a
society, and very close to the core of our faith. The twin dangers we
face are that our interpretation will become autonomous and cease
to be obedient, and that our obedience will become "mere" and
cease to be interpretive.

I have been encouraged, energized, and aided in my thinking on
these questions by two important writers. The first is Paul Ricoeur
who, in his studies of the emancipatory power of biblical texts, has
shown how the biblical text can redescribe and resignify life in
evangelical ways.[1] Ricoeur understands that our obedience is shaped,
authorized, and limited by our imagination. Therefore if we are to
have changed obedience, we must have transformed imagination.
That, it seems to me, is precisely correct in the day-to-day life of the
church. Such a focus invites the artists in the community of faith
who discern so much and the moralists who care so passionately to
attend to each other much more than they have in the past.[2] It is a
sorry business in the community of faith that aesthetic, artistic, and
liturgical energy and moral, ethical, and social passion are not more
attentive to each other, and in some cases are not even "in communion" with each other. The nurturance of "the poem" as an act of
imaginative construal is indispensable for the formation of a community of sustained, radical obedience.

The second writer, Michael Walzer, has proposed that the preferred and most effective mode of moral philosophy is interpretation that is sustained, critical, subversive reflection on the moral
world that is already available to us and is already our home.[3]
Because we disagree on our moral code and have no consensus on
its meaning, "there is nothing to do but go back to the text—the
values, principles, codes, and conventions that constitute the moral
world—and to the readers of the text."[4] Walzer explicates his thesis
by showing how the prophets of ancient Israel in general and Amos
in particular did poignant, passionate social criticism by interpreting
the torah and by summoning Israel to live actively in the moral

world it presumed to inhabit.[5] The tension between the governing text (memory, tradition) and the situation that cries out for transformation creates an *imaginative moral restlessness* in a community that has a serious moral home.[6] It is this restlessness that summons Israel to new obedience and that permits and requires new interpretation. Walzer catches the concrete urgency of that restlessness well: "Social criticism is less the practical offspring of scientific knowledge than the educated cousin of common complaint."[7] Israel's moral discernment is rooted in a common, pathos-filled complaint which was first sounded against Pharaoh (Exod. 2:23–25) and which reverberates all through the life of Israel. That common complaint drives Israel to social criticism in the restless, resilient conviction that the world could be other and better, more joyous, more glorious, and more humane than it is.

In an attempt to follow the suggestive proposals of Ricoeur and Walzer, I have placed my chapter on preaching the ten commandments at the structural center of this book. I have sought to understand the ten commandments as both the deep base of Israel's covenantal existence and also as the warrant for liberated reflection. Israel (Moses) insists that no one shall add to or subtract from this simple, terse code (Deut. 4:2). Having said that, Israel (Moses) proceeds to add reams of additional commentary and exposition (speeches and sermons) to the commands. This expansive derivative literature is an odd but faithful way in Israel of "adding nothing."

The commandments are utterly nonnegotiable. They constitute Ricoeur's elemental obedience, Walzer's moral home. The commandments, it is clear, are also endlessly negotiated. This is Ricoeur's act of imagination, Walzer's work of interpretation. The commands must not be negotiated, but necessarily they are negotiated. A community with such a memory as Israel has, has no alternative but to probe the memory and to trust the future proposals of the memory that push beyond itself. Such a dynamic treasure by Israel invites us to an odd, interpretive vocation of obedience. That vocation is urgent in a society that on the one hand wants to retreat into a moral memory and refuses the hard work of venturing to the edges of the moral memory or, on the other hand, is so embarrassed by the memory that it believes we can start fresh and do better. Refusing the renovation or leaving home are two ways to guarantee that our children will be orphans, homeless, without sanctuary, and with no buoyant future. Such a fate for our children may be the outcome of our present inept, timid home-making.[8]

We cannot interpret or obey our way into a new world, but the new world is promised to us. It is coming. That promised, coming new world is the terribly destabilizing, wondrously reassuring context for our life of freedom and discipline. The connection between interpretation and obedience, as Ricoeur repeatedly insists, is imagination. Imagination led by God's spirit could break our stubbornness and permit us to receive the world of God's new righteousness.[9] Our autonomous interpretation and our dulled obedience are perhaps ways to resist that new world that frightens us before it heals us. Our story, however, asserts that neither our autonomy nor our dullness can finally defeat God's resolve for a newness. We shall indeed be frightened—and then healed.

Finally, of course, the command that orders our life is derived from our story. In the end it is not mandate but recital that is context for both obedience and interpretation. Walzer can conclude that "it is better to tell stories,"[10] that is, better than "elaborating on existing moralities."

It is for that reason that I have concluded this manuscript with a sermon. The sermon does not much urge obedience and does not much engage in interpretation. Rather, it seeks to contextualize our work of interpretation and obedience in the largest context available in biblical faith, the context of God's world-ending and God's new-world-making. In the Old Testament, the events around 587 B.C.E.—exile and homecoming—became decisive for Israel's moral reflection. In those events Israel learned and continued to learn that Yahweh is morally serious and will not be mocked (hence the loss) and that God is faithful and powerful beyond moral categories (hence the homecoming).[11] It takes no great imagination to transpose Israel's paradigm of exile and homecoming into the Christian story of crucifixion and resurrection.[12] The exile and the crucifixion are the painful tales of our incapacity to sustain the world we treasure. But that pain, real as it is, is overridden by this second moment of God's new world given in homecoming and resurrection.

NOTES

1. Paul Ricoeur, "Testimony to the Parables of Jesus," in *The Philosophy of Paul Ricoeur*, ed. Charles E. Reagen and David Steward (Boston: Beacon Press, 1978), 245, writes, "And it is in the heart of imagination that we let the Event happen, before we may convert our heart and tighten our will." Obedience concerns "tightening our will." But that depends on what happens in the heart of imagination.

2. On the cruciality of artistic awareness in the community of faith, see the passionate comment by Theodore A. Gill, "Barth and Mozart," *Theology Today* 43 (1986): 403–11.

3. Michael Walzer, *Interpretation and Social Criticism* (Cambridge: Harvard University Press, 1987), 18–20 and passim.

4. Ibid., 30.

5. Ibid., 69–94.

6. See Herbert Schneidau, *Sacred Discontent: The Bible and Western Tradition* (Baton Rouge: Louisiana State University Press, 1976). While Schneidau deals with literary matters, his title is suggestive of the kind of restlessness that concerns us.

7. Walzer, *Interpretation and Social Criticism*, 65.

8. The metaphor of home is crucial for the interpretive task. Walzer, ibid., 15–16, speaks of a home as a "dense moral culture." Negatively, Edward Farley, *Ecclesiastical Reflection: An Anatomy of Theological Method* (Philadelphia: Fortress Press, 1982), 165–68 and passim, speaks of the collapse of the "house of authority." While Farley speaks of "house" rather than "home," the usage is parallel. Perhaps Farley's use is a religious version of Peter L. Berger's *The Homeless Mind: Modernization and Consciousness* (New York: Random House, 1974). I suggest that our interpretive responsibility is not just to accept the "house" already there, but that the house will stand only if there is attentive "homemaking."

9. See Walter Brueggemann, "Imagination as a Mode of Fidelity," in *Understanding the Word*, ed. James T. Butler, Edgar W. Conrad, and Ben C. Allenburger, JSOTSup 37 (Sheffield, Eng.: JSOT Press, 1988), 13–36.

10. Walzer, *Interpretation and Social Criticism*, 65.

11. The disclosure of God made in the poem of Job asserts at the same time that God is morally serious and that God is powerful and faithful beyond moral categories.

12. Jacob Neusner, *Understanding Seeking Faith* (Atlanta: Scholars Press, 1986), 115–49, has used the language of crucifixion and resurrection for the Jewish account of exile and homecoming. I do not suggest the terms are exclusively Christian. Neusner's use of them helps us discern the commonality of the two stories that shape and mandate Jews and Christians in common ways.

INTERPRETATION AS AN ACT OF OBEDIENCE

1

The Third World of Evangelical Imagination

THE FAITHFUL PRACTICE of ministry in the church is rooted in the abiding claims of the gospel. But that faithful practice is also in part shaped by and responsive to the particular social setting of the church. In this chapter, I will reflect on the practice of ministry, which is increasingly squeezed between greedy secularism through which we become brutalized and reactive religious fearfulness that provides alternative grounds for the same brutalization. At issue in this squeeze play between secularism and fearfulness is the integrity of ministry itself.

PSYCHOANALYTIC THEORY AND THE IMAGINATION

I take as my initial conversation partner Paul Pruyser, a clinical psychologist who has paid great attention to the role and responsibility of pastors. I do not understand all of the psychological subtleties he articulates in *The Play of Imagination*, but I find suggestive hints for the task I have set myself.[1]

Pruyser's analysis is a shrewd linking of the work of D. W. Winnicott on object-relations theory and the work of Sigmund Freud. The classic psychoanalytic theory of Freud, so Pruyser asserts, posits two worlds, an *autistic world* in which the reality of the self looms large, indeed exercises complete domination, and the *"realistic" world*, the world of social expectation and performance, inhabited by demands, requirements, definitions, quotas, and the powerful interests of other people.[2] In this dual world, health means arriving at some provisional relationship between the "self-world" and the "real world," when the power of the latter may be oppressive. Freud's judgment is that the world of self is not derived from the realistic world, because the self is a unit all its own, without regard to that larger world. The development of self-world is the only serious alternative to the real world that crushes.

From the classic psychoanalytic theory of two worlds, Pruyser moves to the work of D. W. Winnicott, a British practitioner, who observed the early and formative interaction between young babies and their mothers. Winnicott took this interaction as the paradigmatic relation for the emergence of the human self. He observed, in an important corrective to Freud, that the baby's self is formed by relating to the mother as a real object, hence the term "object relations." The baby is not, as Freud would have argued, simply a sealed-off organism but takes clues and receives life precisely in its relation to its mother.[3]

Winnicott's theory is remarkable for us in one important respect. He has concluded that the very young baby, in order to form a healthy sense of self, must have an experience of omnipotence in relation to the mother, must experience the mother as existing completely in response to and for the sake of the child. If the mother is not completely responsive but takes excessive initiative, the child will very soon learn that the mother's will is absolute, and that the way to get along in the world is to please mother. There soon develops a false self which in fact is only a set of calculating responses to the will of the mother.[4]

The two worlds of classic psychoanalysis receive new contours in the light of object-relations theory. There is the real world of the mother. This is the uncompromising world of food, attention, and caring, where the mother or some other strong adult controls all of these needed resources. In order to get along, the child must live in that real world. The older the child becomes, the more she learns that this is a real world. The other world is the self-world of the child, called by Pruyser "autistic." The shape of this world is determined by the child's self-willed and self-asserted needs, wants, fears, and hopes which the child generates, manages, and protects and to which no one else has primary access. Maturation (health) is finding a workable interface between the real world and the autistic world.

Winnicott offers one other important insight. In the normal process of growing up, the child has a "transitional object" which belongs wholly neither to the autistic world nor to the real world, but stands between them and is the paradoxical combining of the autistic and real worlds.[5] The term refers to some special object—a doll, teddy bear, or security blanket—which clearly has special force and significance for the child and is respected by the family.

Pruyser, building on Winnicott's insights, concludes that this object is "an emblem of the nascent self" that the child is becoming and is crucial in and of itself beyond the other two worlds.[6] This transitional object and the transitional sphere, which the family respects, are "a product of active imagining on the part of the child, reinforced by the family's participatory creation of a transitional sphere which has all the features of play."[7] The transitional object and space are evoked by the transformative power of the imagination.

Pruyser uses Winnicott's work about transitional objects to make a discerning and powerful suggestion about "the play of imagination." The conventional issue of psychoanalysis (an issue much supported by binary thinking, such as masculine-feminine, right brain–left brain) is, Do you remain autistic or will you become realistic?[8] Into this discussion, however, a third world can be posited. This third world of health is transitional, not in the sense that it is a move from the one world to the other, but in that it stands apart from both and permits the processing of experience and the formation of life in an alternative, liberating, generative way. Following Freud, Pruyser uses the term "illusionistic world" for this process, meaning an imaginative construct of the world out beyond self and other (mother) that comes to be through imagination, evocation, articulation. This imaginative process, says Pruyser, can be shared, institutionalized in social ordering, and culturally transmitted, upheld, and valued.[9] Pruyser then probes various dimensions of social life through which illusional worlds are explored and practiced. His thesis is that the practice of the illusional world is decisive for a healthy self or a viable community. In what follows, I will explore this proposed third world in relation to our evangelical, pastoral responsibility in the church.

RELIGION IN AN ACQUISITIVE CULTURE

Freud, Winnicott, and Pruyser focus on the psychoanalytic dimensions of personhood. Here I will explore the hints they offer concerning the social dimensions of this insight. It is, of course, hazardous to move from the personal to the social, but I believe it is warranted. My thesis is this: the locus of the church's ministry in the United States is a situation in which the third world of illusional processing is denied, rejected, and dismissed. Faithful ministry is to engage people in that imaginative process which is largely resisted but upon which hangs our future as a viable society.

The "real world" of American society is powerful and easy to identify. It is the dominating mother (in Winnicott's language) which denies to the person initiative enough to be. It is the social ideology of success, competence, adequacy, and certitude. Its core in our society is probably economic—the capacity to get a job, to be an adequate producer and consumer, not to be poor, not to be lazy, not to be on welfare, not to embarrass your family. To be an economic success, a person must work hard in school and get good SAT scores in order to get into the right university. And because college admission is so competitive, good grades are not enough; one must also have diverse interests. So the "real" world drives one to activities such as sports, campus politics, and a kind of social life, all for the sake of making it in the real world.

The "real world" likely begins in economics, but it readily extends to religion and morality. The dominant religious voice in American society is the voice of conformity, centered in a proper morality reinforced by a fixed dogmatics in support of an ideological patriotism. The real world is a world of monolithic truth, one book, one lord, one nation (under God), one morality, one arms race, one God and Father of us all. The real world of production and consumption is translated into retributive theology which is theologically intolerant.[10]

The alternative, for those who tire of this insisting and weaken under its crushing certitude, is to drop out into a world of privatism.[11] The word "autism" here is not clinically precise but rather refers to a world organized only for the sake of one's own desires, needs, and fears. When I tire enough of the strenuous rule of the others, my self-world seems serene. The self-world may also be understood economically. It is a world of cynical indifference that is geared to indulgence, aimed at satiation, and powered by greed. In political language, it is called "opportunity," but the ideology of "yuppies" (and most of their parents from whom they learned) is to get all one can, live an uninterrupted life of well-being without respect to others, pay as little tax as possible (none for the public welfare), join nothing, make no commitments, and let others get along and get ahead as best they can.[12]

While I believe the central marks of the autistic world are economic, the religious counterparts are obvious. Such values yield a religion of warm, cozy embrace and affirmation that speaks no word of cost, judgment, responsibility, or accountability. Religion becomes the voice of uncritical approval, endorsing selfishness in the name of grace, reinforcing the world of self for whom God becomes simply a predictable supplier of what is needed.[13]

Some may charge that I have drawn a caricature of our situation, but I think not. The frantic movement between the self-world and the real world, between self-indulgence and pleasing mother, is an act of agility. In economics, this "movement between" requires competence in the world of the marketplace. We must be productive, either because getting ahead is an end in itself or because it is a prerequisite to withdrawing from the ratrace in satiation and self-indulgence. What is lacking in this dual picture of economics are (1) a sense of the social fabric that gives humans significance over market transactions, and (2) the awareness that competitors are in fact partners in whose lives we are enmeshed.[14]

The same agile movement occurs in cultural religion, which moves back and forth between tyrannical orthodoxy and absolute morality on the one hand, and therapeutic indulgence and satiation on the other. The dominant religious alternatives among us are a forceful urging to "get with the program" of patriotism and ideology and a soapy reassurance that we all are OK. What is lacking in that dual picture of religion are the recognitions that holiness dwells precisely in ambiguity, that brothers and sisters who are such a troublesome inconvenience to us are in fact the means and shape of life for us, and that life with, from, and for sister and brother is the only life God gives us.

We are set, then, in a costly and dangerous place. Some of us have a propensity for the "real world" of "truth," imagining that we know and wanting simply to announce it. Some of us have a propensity for grace that comes too cheaply, because we know how much hurt there has been and we want to reassure. But truth that knows too much ends by crushing. And grace that assures too easily is a lie because the world is more costly and truth is more demanding than our religious self-indulgence. The practice of religion that is both truthful and gracious, that evokes new worlds beyond the first two, is a hard task, but one essential to both our present circumstance and our tradition of faith. It is this tradition of certitude crucified and death overridden by love which lets us be human and guards against our deep brutality.

Thus far I have made use of Pruyser's analysis for purposes of a critical social comment. I want now to take this same proposal of a third world as a heuristic tool for considering the text.

THE POETRY OF JOB:
A THIRD WORLD OF TRUST

The critical problems of Job are numerous and difficult.[15] I follow convention in seeing Job first as a recognition of a world that is falling apart and in which the pain of such displacement is acute. I also take the poem of Job as a response to heavy orthodoxies that insist on the primacy of the old world even when the data do not permit it. I take the poem of Job as a near partner for us when the pain of our displacement is acute and the heavy orthodoxies insist against the data of that displacement and that pain.

The poem of Job is a conversation among three voices. While Pruyser does not specifically allude to Job, he could have used the poem of Job as a model for his thesis, for the three voices in Job sound like the three worlds of Pruyser's analysis.

1. First, and most weightily, the friends of Job are the voice of the "real world." They know how the world works, and they trust in its God-ordained processes.[16] The world works according to a firm structure of moral coherence. Those who honor that coherence will do well. Those who mock or violate that coherence will, of course, suffer. We can hear in their clear voice echoes of the book of Proverbs, and perhaps it really is an omnipotent mother who masquerades here as Dame Wisdom.[17]

The friends are not stupid or uncaring. They do not assume perfection. They know that people err and sin. And they know that God is gracious. Those who suffer for their sin can indeed be received back into God's graciousness. They need only repent and return to God. Eliphaz can ask in complete confidence:

> Think now, who that was innocent ever perished?
> Or where were the upright cut off?
>
> (4:7)

The innocent do all right, because the system works. The real world is a world of reliable equity. Even if one is not innocent, one is still not lost:

> As for me, I would seek God,
> and to God I would commit my cause. . . .
> Behold, happy is the one whom God reproves;
> therefore despise not the chastening of the Almighty.
>
> (5:8, 17)

Bildad echoes, in turn:

> Does God pervert justice?
> Or does the Almighty pervert the right? . . .
> If you will seek God
> and make supplication to the Almighty,
> If you are pure and upright,
> surely then God will rouse himself for you
> and reward you with a rightful habitation. . . .
> Behold, God will not reject a blameless man,
> nor take the hand of evildoers.
>
> (8:3, 5–6, 20)

Zophar does not differ:

> If you will set your heart aright,
> you will stretch out your hands toward him.
> If iniquity is in your hand, put it far away,
> . . . .
> Surely then you will lift up your face without blemish;
> you will be secure and will not fear.
>
> (11:13–15)

Finally, Elihu is perhaps the most convinced:

> Therefore, hear me, you men of understanding,
> far be it from God that he should do wickedness,

and from the Almighty that he should do wrong.
For according to the work of a man he will requite him,
     and according to his ways he will make it befall him.
Of a truth, God will not do wickedly,
     and the Almighty will not pervert justice.
                                        (34:10–12; cf. 36:5–12)

The utter sovereignty of God is clear and beyond dispute. One cannot fault the friends. Of course what they say is true. But their truth is all "pre-pain."[18] They have not suffered enough to have their nerve broken. They have not yet lived with pain, hurt, and loss that outdistance the system. They have not yet faced ambiguity that makes such certitude and "realism" a mockery.

The friends vouch for the real world. It is real—and one can be crushed by it. Their voice is in concert with all such religion of heavy orthodoxy. Their voice is allied with every economic and moral system that expects conformity. Their notion of retribution concerning good people and bad people is easily translated into marketplace ideology that says that diligent people succeed and unproductive people are marginal. They have not yet encountered enough raw human protest to imagine that the system may misrepresent, God may err, and the Almighty might be wrong. That the Almighty could be wrong is of course unthinkable. It is religiously unacceptable. Such a notion would begin the dismantling of all certitude, for if God today, then tomorrow parents, teachers, Dan Rather, and the CIA. One is left with the single option—submit without question, a hard-nosed version of "trust and obey." The friends could not for an instant entertain the playful notion that God could seriously enter the controversy and be at risk.

2. That God should be at risk is also more than Job wants to think. In the second voice of this reading, Job wants to be allied with the friends. He shares most of their assumptions and yearns for them to be right. There is one decisive distinction between them and him, however: Job has known pain. Whereas the friends are "pre-pain" and therefore can be religiously innocent, Job can never again be that innocent. For all his propriety, Job's voice is shrill. For all his awareness of orthodoxy and his capacity to recite the right answers with his friends, Job's pain keeps him on a short leash. He will not wander far from pain. His pain forces his mind to concen-

trate so that his speech is complaint and accusation against God, the kind of speech his friends would not tolerate and which he himself previously would not have countenanced.

As a result of his pain, however, his speech is now abrasive and challenging. He holds to his integrity (31:6). Something is deeply amiss between God and himself, but Job will not submit. To submit to the "real world" of God would violate his integrity, that is, nullify his experience. It is finally not Job's pain but his deep honesty that we notice. He has gained enough "self" so that he will not falsely submit. Deep in the argument with God, he asserts,

> Far be it from me to say that you are right,
> till I die I will not put away my integrity from me.
> I hold fast my righteousness, and will not let it go.
> (27:5–6)

In his great speech of innocence, when Job finally willingly approaches God, he approaches "like a prince," ready to meet God as an unapologetic equal (31:36–37). He will encounter, but he will not submit. Job will meet God and see whether God will submit to the reality of Job's suffering. If God will submit, the whole, coherent pattern of certitude will be broken.

It is not forced to suggest that Job has retreated from the "real world" of his friends because he no longer believes in that world. His experience has shown him that that world does not hold. He has withdrawn to his "self-world," and his own suffering, sense of innocence, integrity, and indignation are his only criteria for reality. In Winnicott's sense, Job is an autistic person, who requires that the system be broken on the anvil of personal experience, outside of which there is no compelling reality.

Our world is filled with such self-credentialed autism that requires the system to submit, that is, to cease to be. It is the voice of a wounded Catholic woman so crushed by the male hierarchy that she has nothing left but words of abrasion and defiance. It is the silent action of an older teenager who, so exhausted by his father's insistence on good grades and success, *in absentia* puts his love at best into greasy old cars. It is the despair of an anorexic daughter who cannot compete with her "perfect" sister and who disappears in California. It is the action of a suburban family who has made enough money and now lives only to itself, personal purity having displaced social connectedness. It is the rage of a terrorist who has waited so long for land and now sees that the royal system will never share it.

Strange companions. All exhausted in the sense of being right and having been wronged, no longer with moral energy to envision an alternative. The world becomes so grim that there is no capacity for playfulness, no unclaimed space where the Spirit might visit, only a wearied waiting and now an act of brutality against others or against self. There is only waiting and brutality because the only alternative—submission—is even worse.[19] The autism ends in abdication of self and Job's raging refusal:

> Thou wilt seek me,
> but I shall not be.
> (7:21)

"Not-to-be" is one way apart from the system.[20]

3. I comment on the third voice in the poem of Job only with trepidation. How dare the Whirlwind be brought within the grid of our interpretation! But that is precisely the point. The Whirlwind breaks our pattern of dispute between Job and friends, between autistic world and "real world." This voice breaks open our sense of disputed, limited options. We have been waiting a long time for this voice to sound. Indeed, that is the problematic of the poem: *This voice will not speak*, will not rescue us from the unbearable squeeze between Job's autism and his friends' realism. Is there no alternative other than Job's relentless alienation and the friends' all-too-weighty certitude?

Then comes the third voice. As James Wharton has shown, the voice of God is presented as answer to lament.[21] To that extent, this poem conforms to Israel's conventions. This insight does not go far enough, however, because the Whirlwind speech does not in fact touch the complaint of Job. The poem is largely discontinuous, incongruous in a debate between solipsism and realism, between privatism and conformity. The poem is an incredible leap beyond Israel's known world.[22]

Moving from the work of Winnicott and Pruyser, I suggest that this poem of the Whirlwind offers a third world, an illusional, imaginative, playful world.[23] God is the one who imagines and the one who is imagined.[24] My clue for this comes from Isak Dinesen, who writes in *Out of Africa*:

> [The native] faces any change in life with great calm. Amongst the qualities that he will be looking for in a master or a doctor or in God, imagination, I believe, comes high up in the list. It may be in the strength of such a taste, that the Caliph Haroun al Raschild maintains, to the hearts of Africa and Arabia, his position as an ideal ruler; with him nobody knew what to expect next, and you did not know where you had him. When the Africans speak of the personality of God they speak like the Arabian Nights or like the last chapters of the book of Job; it is the same quality, the infinite power of imagination, with which they are impressed.[25]

This third voice, this voice of God for which we have waited, is indeed "the infinite power of imagination" that conjures a third world out beyond our human map. This poem, the work of the poet, is a far stretch of exploration that invites the inhabitants of the autistic and "real" worlds to a new world of majesty, sovereignty, power, dominion, and splendor where an awful, undisciplined submitting is appropriate and gladly practiced.[26] Insofar as the poem bespeaks the heart and mind of God, it shows God brusquely moving beyond, simply bracketing out our small world of fear, our tight world of control. God moves into a world of power so astonishing that we are left utterly beside ourselves, outside ourselves, inhabitants of a new creation. God congratulates God's self like a farmer showing a prize bull, like an architect in grateful silence before her new building, like a mother or father at the gift of a child. When one flies over the African bush, Dinesen says, it is "to see the animals on the plains and to feel toward them as God did when he had just created them, and before he commissioned Adam to give them names."[27] What a crocodile, what a hippopotamus, what a world, what a God! It is not a world where my pain governs or my life is treasured in self-indulgence. It is not a world where rules govern and I am consumed in guilt or rectitude. It is instead a world of new creation, where we see God afresh, self anew, all bracketed out to begin again in doxology that is not given grudgingly.

This world uttered by God is, of course, an illusion. It is an illusion because Job's deep hurt is still there and his friends' rules still want and claim too much. It is a playful illusion of imagination that outruns reality. The doxology voiced as ultimatum is "transitional" like Winnicott's transition, not taken literally but seriously respected as a "zone of magic possibility." Through this zone, Job, who has had his categories nullified for the duration of the song, enigmatically is transformed to reenter his world of isolation and rules, submissive but not beaten. Job is transformed rather than beaten because he has submitted to neither the first voice of his friends nor the second voice of his own self. Rather he has submitted to the third voice of God, and that submission yields liberated triumph.[28] Job is on his way to being another way with God and with the world. This change is wrought by this transcendent imaginer, articulated by this awesome liturgist, positing Job freely, gladly, trustingly at a new place.

Job has been "saved"—not by a supernaturalist religious formula but by the imaginative power of this poem. Saved for God, saved for himself, saved as a creature given to praise, submission, and obedience, saved from his autism, saved from the harsh rule of his friends' morality, saved for his true life in God's world.

SECOND ISAIAH: THE WORLD OF EVANGELICAL IMAGINATION

The whole gospel is not available in Job. A poet can imagine only so much at any one time. My topic is not just any third world, but the third world of evangelical imagination. In some circles, "evangelical imagination" might indeed sound like an oxymoron. To secure the modifier "evangelical" in this proposed, imagined third world, one must, I suggest, move from Job to 2 Isaiah, a near contemporary, for Job and 2 Isaiah are surely poets moving in the same circles.[29]

In 2 Isaiah, the "real world" of Job's friends is carried by the power of Babylon, Babylonian religion and politics, Babylonian fear and hope. To live, one must conform. In that poetry, the autistic world of isolation is carried by Israel's laments, the book of Lamentation, Psalm 137 ("beside the waters of Babylon"), Psalms 74 and 79, about the charred temple. The powerful world of Babylonian hegemony and the hurt world of grieved Jerusalem are there together. Life is stretched desperately between grief and conformity, between abandonment and domination, and there seems to be no third alternative. I suggest that this way of mapping the world of exiled Israel is not unlike the religious crisis among us that is characterized by our grief over the passing of the nineteenth century, a century lost in our wistful dreams, and by our domination by the word-processing of aggressive capitalism. As in exile, there seems no third alternative, no space in which to be.

Of course there never is such third space, such a transitional sphere of transformation—unless there is a poet. But there is this poet. Second Isaiah will have no more of Babylonian domination than will the Whirlwind of Job's friends. Second Isaiah will linger no longer over Israel's grief than will the Whirlwind submit to Job's complaints. As does the Whirlwind of Job, 2 Isaiah moves on to bring a third nascent world to speech. That third world of imagination is not rooted in Israel's grief or in Babylon's domination. It is rooted elsewhere—in the playful freedom we call God's holiness. This venture into imaginative alternative is grounded in a voice heard from the holy throne. Isaiah 40:1–11 is a fantasy of the gods around the throne in earnest discussion about how to comfort exiled Israel. The word "comfort" was not yet present in the Whirlwind. Job's friends had tried to comfort him (Job 2:11; cf. Job 42:11), but comforting seems not to be an option of the Whirlwind.

In Isaiah 40 there is a discussion about how to comfort: not by grass and flowers, not by created structures, but only by an abiding, promissory word that lives beyond imperial domination and self-defeating grief. Comfort comes, as did the awe of the Whirlwind, from this other voice unfettered by our mapped worlds:

> O Zion, herald of good tidings,
>   lift up your voice with strength,
> O Jerusalem, herald of good tidings,
>   Lift it up, fear not;
> Say to the cities of Judah,
>   "Behold your God."
>
> (40:9)

God outruns our small options. God is moving ahead, heading home, creating alternatives. The power of this God is the power of the Creator God voiced in the Whirlwind speech of the book of Job:

Who has measured the waters in the hollow of his hand,
  and marked off the heavens with a span,
enclosed the dust of the earth in a measure
  and weighed the mountains in scales,
  and the hills in a balance? . . .
Have you not known? Have you not heard?
  Has it not been told you from the beginning?
  Have you not understood from the foundations of the earth?
It is he who sits above the circle of the earth,
  and its inhabitants are like grasshoppers;
Who stretches out the heavens like a curtain,
  and spreads them like a tent to dwell in;
Who brings princes to nought,
  and makes the rulers of the earth as nothing.
                                    (Isa. 40:12, 21–23)

The Whirlwind of 2 Isaiah invites timid Israel out beyond Babylonian domination and invites grieving Israel beyond grief to another world of sovereignty. What if there is a God who presides in such magnitude?

But then comes the imaginative move we know as "evangelical." This poet moves beyond the massiveness of the Whirlwind to gentle mothering:

He will feed his flock like a shepherd,
  he will gather the lambs in his arms,
he will carry them in his bosom,
  and gently lead those that are with young.
                                    (40:11)

I give Egypt as your ransom,
  Ethiopia and Seba in exchange for you.
Because you are precious in my eyes,
  and honored, and I love you,
I give men in return for you,
  peoples in exchange for your life.
Fear not, for I am with you.[30]
                                    (43:3–5)

The utterance of power breaks imperial domination among those who listen. The utterance of solidarity overrides the grief of isolation. Those life-shriveling worlds of domination and isolation are for a rhetorical moment overridden. A stunning alternative is offered by the poet. Those who hear will never again be so administered in conformity, so immobilized by loving their hurt too long and imagining there is nothing beyond themselves. There is offered a homecoming. Indeed, there is given a sense of having a home where we belong. As Job submits in glad yielding, so exiles can start again, rejoicing. All of this movement of submitting and departing homeward is wrought by a poet who speaks God's imaginative freedom and dangerous loyalty out beyond our harsh, unredeemed options.[31] The third world is imaginative, but it is imagination of a particular kind, rooted in news of a God who acts, speaks, lives, cares, and frees from and beyond our nightmarishly constructed worlds, beyond our conformity that pretends security, our loneliness that fakes a self without worth or dignity.

CONCLUSION

I have tried here to build an argument in three parts:

1. I have explored a model of transformative imagination expressed in psychological categories by Winnicott and Pruyser that speaks of health beyond realism and autism.

2. I have suggested that in religion in our cultural context the dualism of realism and autism yields a religion of harsh conformity that crushes and a religion of indulgent self interest that harbors selfishness. In America the primary religious alternatives seem to be just such conformity and indulgence.

3. I have proposed, in a brief study of Job and 2 Isaiah, that the great poets of Israel play with, propose, and offer a third world, by expressing a God who lives beyond *legalism* (in the case of Job) and *domination* (in the case of 2 Isaiah), who moves beyond all *self-preoccupation* (as in Job) and isolated *grief* (as in 2 Isaiah). That newly rendered God is the voice of the gospel that invites Israel's transition to a new way in the world, in God's world, as God's glad creation, submitting in praise, rejoicing on the way home. Both literatures, Job and 2 Isaiah, articulate a transformation wrought by God but worked only through imaginative speech. In the poem of Job, the voice of God is indeed "the infinite power of imagination" that brings Job to glad submissive trust, freed from his autistic world and the "real" world of his friends. In 2 Isaiah, the voice of

God is again "the infinite power of imagination" that wipes the tears of lament from Israel in its self-pity and that liberates Israel from the "real" world of Babylonian domination.

This three-stage analysis is intended as a thought about the faithful practice of ministry in our particular social setting. More specifically, I intend it as a contribution to the question, What ought we to be doing in theological education in our context? I mean to suggest that in every discipline in our work we must address the question, How and in what ways is the evangelical imagination of our tradition to be articulated, practiced, and set free so that men and women and communities among us may seize the promise of baptism? I submit that entrusted to the pastoral work of the church in all its aspects—teaching, preaching, education, pastoral care, and all the rest—is the distinctive act of imagination which offers and receives a new world.

It will not do for us in the enterprise of theological education to be unduly committed to conformist religion, nor to be allied with fashionable privatism. The pastoral work of the church now stands as a powerful, urgent, and lonely alternative in a society that in its conformity moves to brutality and in its isolation ends in despair. Our birthright is not to the brutality that ends in nuclear arms nor to the despair that ends in self-hatred and abuse.[32] The central things we do in the church are precisely bold, transitional acts whereby our true selves are summoned, authorized, and legitimated. We are in the image of the One who keeps imagining us. That massive imagination is odd, fragile power in our worlds of autism and "realism." It is the poem that defends us against brutality and despair. Entrusted to us is the odd practice through which we may become who we have already been but have never yet dared to be.

NOTES

This essay appeared in *Horizons in Biblical Theology* 8 (1986): 61–84, and is reprinted by permission.

1. Paul W. Pruyser, *The Play of Imagination* (New York: International Universities Press, 1983).
2. Ibid., 63.
3. On the tensions and distinctions between Freudianism and object-relations theory, see J. R. Greenberg and S. A. Mitchell, eds., *Object-*

Relations in Psychoanalytic Theory (Cambridge: Harvard University Press, 1983).

4. See D. W. Winnicott, *The Maturational Processes and the Facilitating Environment* (London: Hogarth Press, 1965), 145 and passim. See my use of his insights in "The Costly Loss of Lament," *Journal for the Study of the Old Testament* 36 (1986): 57–71.

5. See D. W. Winnicott, *Playing and Reality* (New York: Basic Books, 1971); and Pruyser, *The Play of Imagination*, 57–60.

6. Pruyser, *The Play of Imagination*, 59.

7. Ibid., 60.

8. Ibid., 63.

9. Ibid., 63–64.

10. Ibid., 167. Pruyser cites the Inquisition as the extreme example of crushing the power of imagination: "The Inquisition is perhaps the acme of the fallacy of displacing illusionistic ideas from their proper sphere in the realistic sphere and assailing them with weapon-like instructions of defense or attack."

11. Daniel Yankelovich, *New Rules: Searching for Self-Fulfillment in a World Turned Upside Down* (New York: Random House, 1981), has surveyed the social pattern of rejection of authoritarianism by embracing privatism.

12. On the power of such individualism and privatism, see the analysis by Robert N. Bellah et al., *Habits of the Heart* (Berkeley: University of California Press, 1985).

13. On the therapeutic role of religion and God as a therapeutic agent, see ibid., chap. 9.

14. On the separation of the market from the fabric of human community and its costs and religious foundations, see M. Douglas Meeks, "Political Economy and Political Theology," in *Gottes Zukunft—Zukunft der Welt*, Festschrift for Jürgen Moltmann, ed. Hermann Deuser (Munich: Chr. Kaiser, 1986), 446–55.

15. On the critical problems of the book of Job, see Brevard S. Childs, *Introduction to the Old Testament as Scripture* (Philadelphia: Fortress Press, 1979), 426–44; and the excellent commentaries by Norman C. Habel, *The Book of Job* (Philadelphia: Westminster Press, 1985), 21–73; and J. Gerald Janzen, *Job* (Atlanta: John Knox, 1985), 1–24.

16. The classic statement on the world-processes of "deed-consequence" is that of Klaus Koch, "Is There a Doctrine of Retribution in the Old Testament?" in *Theodicy in the Old Testament*, ed. James L. Crenshaw (Philadelphia: Fortress Press, 1983), 57–87.

17. It may be too much of a leap to make a connection between "Dame Wisdom," who is the embodiment of wisdom, and Winnicott's omnipotent mother, but the parallel use of imagery is suggestive. The

all-knowing woman of wisdom is contrasted with the whore folly. See James L. Crenshaw, *Old Testament Wisdom* (Atlanta: John Knox Press, 1981), 86–99 and, more specifically, Bernard Lang, *Frau Weisheit* (Düsseldorf: Patmos, 1975).

18. Dorothee Soelle, *The Strength of the Weak* (Philadelphia: Westminster Press, 1984), 90, has noted that all sound feminist theology begins in pain. That is true, however, not only for feminist theology but for all serious theology. Theology that is "pre-pain" must be treated with suspicion.

19. The brutality and exhaustion of such waiting is given powerful contemporary articulation by Vincent Crapanzano, *Waiting: The Whites of South Africa* (New York: Random House, 1986).

20. Robert Lifton, *The Broken Connection* (New York: Basic Books, 1983), has discerningly traced the connections between the will for "not being" and the social crisis of having no adequate symbols for the edges of human experience. When the symbolic connections fail, people may indeed choose not to be.

21. James A. Wharton, "The Unanswerable Answer: An Interpretation of Job," in *Texts and Testaments*, ed. W. Eugene March (San Antonio: Trinity University Press, 1980), 37–70.

22. Janzen, *Job*, 227–28, speaks of the Whirlwind speeches as subversive and deconstructive. For a shrewd and discerning articulation of the dramatic intent of this voice, see Andre Neher, *The Exile of the Word* (Philadelphia: Jewish Publication Society of America, 1981). Neher writes of the speech out of the Whirlwind: "In the story of Job, on the contrary, the reappearance of the Word of God illuminates and explains nothing. None of the words said by God in the verbal hurricane unleashed on the head of Job from the first verse of Chapter 38 concerns Job's case, his trial, or the charges against him. It is an incredible discourse wherein Job learns, with lowered head, that he cannot learn anything. It is a cosmic challenge hurled at a creature who is utterly exhausted and who can reply only by some vague mumblings. All this tempest of eloquence rests deliberately on a profound misunderstanding. When Job, after a fearful eclipse, hears the Voice of the Judge, it is not the Judge who speaks through this Voice, but some Being of transcendent dimensions who never had any connection with the Trial of Job. Into this eloquence, silence cunningly introduces itself, transforming the dialogue into a 'dialogue of the deaf.' In this Word of God, it is as if God had seen nothing, heard nothing, as if He had forgotten everything of the words spoken at the start of the eclipse" (pp. 29–30).

23. See Habel, *The Book of Job*, 533.

24. On the healing possibility present in imagining God and being imagined by God, see Elaine Scarry, *The Body in Pain* (Oxford: Oxford

University Press, 1985). Scarry shows how much imagination counters the brutal deconstruction of the world through human brutality and silent suffering.

25. Isak Dinesen, *Out of Africa and Shadows on the Grass* (New York: Random House, 1985), 24.

26. Ibid., 477. Dinesen writes of "the supreme triumph of Unconditional Surrender."

27. Ibid., 247–48.

28. See Janzen, *Job*, 257–58.

29. See Habel, *The Book of Job*, 529.

30. Peter Stuhlmacher, "Vicariously Giving His Life for Many: Mark 10:45 (Matt. 20:25)," in Stuhlmacher, *Reconciliation, Law, and Righteousness* (Philadelphia: Fortress Press, 1986), 16–29, has persuasively argued that this passage lies behind the gospel assignment of "ransom" to Jesus in Mark 10:45. Thus we are at an elemental evangelical claim. See also Stuhlmacher, "The New Righteousness in the Proclamation of Jesus," in ibid., 40–46.

31. On the kerygmatic power of such poetic speech, see Paul Ricoeur, *Essays on Biblical Interpretation* (Philadelphia: Fortress Press, 1980), 101 and passim.

32. Lifton, *The Broken Connection*, has shown in a powerful way the connections between brutality and despair, between "nuclearism" and self-hatred.

2

The Embarrassing Footnote

THE ENTERPRISE OF KNOWLEDGE—what we know and how we know it—is in crisis. Since Bacon and Descartes, we have been schooled in the canon of certitude. All of us want to be credible in both the courts of power and the judgment of the academy. To achieve this, we tend to opt either to be scientific and critical and so dispel the mystery, or to imitate those patterns of certitude in religious absolutism that crush the mystery. We are now in crisis because we are learning that not only are the certitudes we thought "objectively true" not objective, they likely are exercises in control that characteristically tilt toward domination.[1] Our exercises in knowing turn out to be exercises in domination.

Recently, we have noticed that there has always been an embarrassing footnote to this certitude. The footnote is the strange, powerful, episodic presence of human hurt and human amazement, odd experiences of human transformation that are always minority reports in our capacity to "get it right." It is only a footnote, because, though it has always been there, it is not much credited or taken seriously in those places where knowledge counts. The footnote is an embarrassment because it smacks of weakness, sensitivity, ambiguity, and uncertainty. What we have begun to notice, however (and may have known but tried to deny), is that this embarrassing footnote has a quiet, resilient authority of its own. It has staying power. It tends to heal and liberate; it does not seek to impose, subject, or dominate. It is the glad awareness that brokenness is real, that healing happens, and that such brokenness and healing have the power, generation after generation, of "abiding astonishment."[2]

If I rightly understand our epistemological situation, we are placed between *the traditions of certitude* that want to know so as to be safe, and *the embarrassing footnote of hurt and amazement* that defies the traditions of certitude and refuses to leave the world safe and unbothered. This epistemological dilemma is now powerfully at work in international politics.[3] The same dilemma is the primary, although often unrecognized, subject in most serious church quarrels. In theological education we cover over it with vague conversations about spirituality in pursuit of another certitude. We nonetheless share in the cultural crisis, struggling with what we know and how we know it.

SUBVERSIVE NARRATIVE AND PUBLIC POSSIBILITY

First and Second Kings embody the tension between the canon of certitude and the footnotes of hurt and amazement. These books, especially the post-Solomonic material, proceed on a theory of certitude in which a remarkable amount of historical data, presumably factually correct, is arranged in a sober, predictable manner. The data are arranged according to a canon of certitude in which we can indeed know the age of the kings, the length of each reign, the names of the kings' mothers, and, most interestingly, a clear, terse verdict about each king.[4]

The Deuteronomic portrayal of Israel's past, then, is an exercise in certitude. The reporting of royal history is routine, predictable, and symmetrical, because the Deuteronomist had a set of criteria about which he was quite sure. Such certitude enabled these theologians to read history clearly, even if, with their selective data before us, we sometimes wonder how they could have known. Moreover, it is clear that their certitude was not disinterested but was committed to a particular social arrangement.

There is an oddity, however, about this literature, this account of royal history. At important points in the recital there are breaks in the relentless inventory. Specifically and most extensively in the middle of the Omri-Ahab dynasty, the theologians break away from the royal recital to give voice to a very different historical memory, expressed in a very different idiom—the stunning narratives concerning Elijah, Elisha, and Micaiah. These narratives are extended accounts of the embarrassing footnote of hurt and amazement which the weighty royal report was unable to censor. While the narratives are embedded in the royal tradition of certitude, they concede nothing to that royal tradition. Moreover, this alternative portrayal of human history is expressed in a radically different mode—that of legendary narrative that focuses on particular transformations which refuse to be routinized or generalized and are never predictable.

In terms of the question of knowledge, what must be appreciated is that *what is known* in these prophetic narratives is intimately and inextricably linked to *how it is known*.[5] Israel could not know about these particular transformations by a routine, predictable, royal recital of what is already in hand; it could know only through narratives that are specific, unique, fanciful acts, and that stay very close to the concreteness of human hurt and human amazement.

These stories are placed in the midst of the royal recital, which is where narratives of transformation must always survive. Elijah must always live his faith in a world where a decree goes out from Ahab (or Caesar Augustus); Elisha is always one who suffers under Jezebel (or Pontius Pilate). When the prophet acts, Ahab (or Herod) is sent into a furious rage. The narratives, however, concede nothing to Ahab or Jezebel (or to Caesar, Pilate, or Herod) because they are alternative accounts of history to which those royal figures have no access and in which they have no important role to play. Indeed, one of the purposes of such narrative is precisely to delegitimate the kings, who are taken much too seriously in the main narrative and who take themselves much too seriously. By being given minor parts in these old narratives, the kings are made marginal.

In the royal enterprise of certitude by which the kings make the world safe, they and all practitioners of certitude have no patience with human hurt, take no notice of human amazement, credit no human transformation. Indeed, it takes a different epistemology, articulated in a different idiom, treating a different subject, and likely set in a different sociology, in order for this *other* portrayal of human history to be available, heard, received, and embraced. Let us pursue one single episode in this embarrassing footnote in greater detail.

ELISHA'S TRANSFORMING NARRATIVE

The narratives of Elisha have suffered in critical assessment. They are sometimes thought to be legendary derivatives from the Elijah narratives, which themselves are legendary. They are thought to be of little historical value. That judgment, however, is itself an assessment made by the canon of certitude which seeks to recover the world "behind the text." The practitioners of such a footnote as the Elisha narratives, however, who generate such texts, are not much interested in "the world behind the text." They are not interested in knowledge that records, controls, and chronicles. They are interested rather in the world "in front of the text." They ask, What does this narrative give us in order that we may survive? Are there alternatives for us in the face of royal power?

The Elisha narratives, as with all narratives of amazement, are told not to preserve past miracles but to generate present awe and to anticipate future astonishment among people not excessively subservient to their rulers. The narrative does not just remember a world that was. It creates a world that could be—even though the kings wanted to insist that such a world is not possible. The narrative playfully probes to see what kind of world might exist were the canon of control, the authority of kingship, and subservience to established power not taken too seriously.

In 2 Kings 6:8–23 we watch the construction of an alternative world.[6] This text is a strange portrayal of public, royal history into which there decisively intrudes the uncredentialed but irresistible power of Elisha, carrier and embodiment of another world. The narrative occurs in four scenes, two preliminary and two which articulate the main action.

In vv. 8–10, the first preliminary scene, we are introduced to a Syrian crisis. The Syrian king draws up a battle plan against Israel (v. 8). But we are told in v. 10 that the king of Israel avoided the danger. Verse 9 tells us how this was made possible: the "man of God" sent a word of warning to the Israelite king. The "man of God" is not named. We are not told how he knew or how he transmitted the secret. We are not even told how he got into the story between the two kings. All of that is left unexplored. We do learn, though, that the "man of God" has strange power, the power to "disclose" the closed world of military control. The narrative deftly asserts that the business of kings is placed in jeopardy by the inexplicable but nonetheless real and effective work of this "man of God." The ones who seem to be in control are not. What seemed closed is opened.

In the second preliminary scene (vv. 11–14), the Syrian king tries to stop the security leak. His advisors, however, know better. They tell the king that there are no leaks. "But Elisha, the prophet who is in Israel, tells the king of Israel the words that you speak in your bedchamber" (v. 12). Elisha's name has been uttered, and he assumes control of the narrative. The advisors to the Syrian king indicate no astonishment at this odd occurrence, because the narrative wants Elisha's power to be accepted as obvious. The advisors simply report the facts. They do not wonder out loud how the prophet has such access to secret information. The king sounds and acts like any king: "Stop the leak! Get control! Secure the borders! Seize him!" Surely the narrative intends to show how ludicrous the king is. He sends horses, chariots, and a great army to seize the prophet, the practitioner of another epistemology. He sends the sword against the word. One can hear an echo through the narrative: "Not by might, not by power, but by my word. . . . "

In vv. 8–14 the action has concerned the Syrian king. Elisha has been mentioned twice, once by name, once by allusion, but both times from a distance. He is talked about, but he is not present. We have read of his power but wait to see his odd authority in action. The narrative—as the entire book of Kings—presents such an uneven confrontation: great king versus a nobody.[7] Already we know, however, that the prophet will outflank, outwit, and finally outgovern the king. The world "in front of the text" concerns precisely the prophetic capacity to outgovern the king.

In scene three (vv. 15–19), the real action begins. Now the scene is set in the locus of the prophet. This shift of scene makes the Syrian king only a marginal participant in the narrative. And the narrative itself displaces royal power and focuses attention and interest on the real actors in the historical process. Kings are now not central actors; rather, they are acted upon. In this scene the ludicrous contrast persists: there is one lonely prophet who does nothing, yet his house is surrounded by horses, chariots, and a great army. It is an unequal match, and, that we not miss the contrast, the narrator tells us twice that the house is surrounded. We may look forward to a later but similar situation when Jesus says, "Have you come out as against a robber, with swords and clubs to capture me?" (Mark 14:48).

Elisha has a servant (v. 15), who has only a bit part, but to whom we want to pay close attention. The servant looks out the window, is startled at the sight of the surrounding army, and becomes terrified. He calculates quickly that if it has come for Elisha, he, as the prophet's servant, cannot be very safe. I suspect he finds Elisha's first assurance quite unassuring:

> Do not fear, those who are with us are more than those who are with them. (v. 16)

The boy must think that Elisha cannot count very well or that he has taken leave of his senses, for they are two against a throng— poor odds. But then the man of God prays. It is a short prayer, a prayer that refuses to accept royal definitions of reality. It is a prayer by one who knows that all serious prayer is petition. He speaks only petition, asking God to do the one thing needful, to give the servant eyes to see an alternative world free of the presumed categories and the immobilizing fear of the royal world.

The prayer is answered. We know not how. All we are told is that the boy sees. He sees as he had not seen. He sees that the reality of power in the world is not as the king had taught him to believe. He sees apart from the dominant ideology in which he had been schooled. He sees the mountains filled with horses and chariots of fire. The world behind the text is not very helpful, for then we must see this as metaphor or as hallucination. But the world in front of the text, in hope-filled imagination, is replete with powerful resources that the Syrian king cannot administer, fathom, or withstand. The prayer of Elisha has reshaped and redefined the world for the boy. The prophet has known, and now the boy knows, what is unknown to the kings.

In v. 18, the prophet prays again. First he had prayed that the boy would see. Now he prays that the Syrians (who seem to see and know everything) will be made blind—and they are! Thus the prayer enacts a great inversion. The blind see, the ones who see are made blind. The powerful become powerless, the powerless powerful. The weak turn out to be strong, the strong weak (cf. 1 Cor. 1:18–25: "For the foolishness of God is wiser than human wisdom, and the weakness of God is stronger than human strength"). Dangerous happenings are narrated against all conventional certitude. For not disinterested reasons, the strong and powerful and seeing will dismiss such stories as ridiculous and without reality.

In the final scene (vv. 20–23), the characters in the story have come to the city of Samaria. The Syrians, however, have come not as an invading army, as they had proposed, but as helpless suppliants and guests, led there blind. Elisha prays again, and they see. He is the only one who can cause something to happen. Now the Syrians are silent. They have been robbed of power and so do not speak. They are removed as threats, or even as active agents in the plot. They are only passive recipients of the actions of God through the prophet, reduced to irrelevance.

The conversation is between the prophet (who is still in charge) and the king of Israel (who is unnamed, indicating he is not very important to the narrator). Through Elisha's prayers, the king of Israel has received new power, and he wants to exploit it. He asks the prophet for permission to kill his Syrian enemy: "Shall I slay them, shall I slay them?" (v. 21). Notice that the king must ask permission from the prophet.

The prophet, however, refuses. For all his massive, inscrutable power, the prophet is a man of peace. Instead he authorizes a feast. "Set bread and water before them, that they may eat and drink and go to their master" (v. 22). So they prepare a great feast, and after the Syrians have eaten and drunk, they go home, defeated but fed. The narrative ends with the succinct but marvelous conclusion, "The Syrians came no more to raid Israel." Elisha's way led to peace, something the kings could not have devised. Elisha did not seek an ultimate triumph but opened the way for a different international world.

At the beginning of the narrative, Syria was a great threat. At the end of the narrative, Syria has gone home in peace. The intervention of Elisha, which changed everything, was unlikely. It was wrought by an unlikely agent, an uncredentialed prophet. His decisive action consisted of a prayer and a feast. It is as though in inscrutable fashion he had said to both warring kings, "I will show you a more excellent way," a way which stands outside royal definitions of reality and possibility. The prophetic narrative embedded in these royal recitals of certitude is a strange idiom. It protests against and undermines royal certitude with its power for life. Royal power could only lead to death and endless hostility. The narrative proposes another way that breaks the vicious cycle of death and hostility.

SOCIAL REALITY THROUGH PROPHETIC ARTICULATION

"A more excellent way" has been given us in narrative mode, the only mode available outside royal rationality. Only stories lie beyond royal reason. The narrative has appealed to and practiced a different epistemology. In order to know something different, Israel must know differently. The more excellent way is about human hurt, under threat from Syria. It is about human amazement, mountains filled with horses and chariots of fire that Israel did not know were there and cannot explain. It is a tale of transformation in which the enemy is transformed into a festival partner who goes peaceably away. The transformation is worked as the sighted ones become blind, the blind sighted (cf. John 9:29–41: "That those who do not see may see, and that those who see may become blind"). This is a transformation that permits new patterns of conduct and policy; it is a more excellent way because a vicious cycle is broken. This more excellent way, present in this embarrassing story, has several characteristics:

1. The key action is *petitionary prayer*. Elisha, the central actor, has no power of his own but refers the action beyond himself to the One who has power. While kings imagine they have authority, this narrative asserts that human history concerns submission to its true Governor. Those who submit find themselves with strange power, even in the royal enclosure.

2. The decisive power that results from prayer is *the power to perceive the world differently*, to perceive the world according to the reality of God's rule.[8] To perceive the world differently means to reject and be freed from conventional portrayals of reality which are characteristically ideological constructs of the king. Without the gift of alternative perception, the servant boy thought there were

only "two of us" and legions of them. But that turned out to be a contrivance and a fantasy that could not withstand the power of faithful, obedient perception.

3. The narrative as a whole concerns *the real shift of power in the world*. This is not an exceptionally religious narrative, nor does it deal with spiritual matters. It is about the real world, real armies, real threats, real possibilities. The actions of the story have to do with rebalancing military-political, public power in the world, so that the Syrians become less powerful and are unable to threaten. Conversely, the company of Elisha (and with him the king of Israel) receive power they did not have at the beginning of the narrative. The one with arsenals as defined by the "real world" is not the one who has serious power at the end of the story. This is power that the world can neither give nor take away.

4. The narrative is *a partisan, delegitimating narrative "from below."* The action occurs precisely among the ones who are weak and jeopardized and have no other recourse. Insofar as the story is paradigmatic, it is not an assurance that anybody who wants to pray for power can pray and receive it. We misunderstand the way of knowing given in the story if we miss the social reference of the narrative. The action in this narrative is a model "from below." The marginal ones are the ones authorized by the narrative to perceive the world differently and to act on that difference. The others, the ones who have power when the story begins, are, by its end, delegitimated and reduced.

5. The narrative causes *a transformation by way of empowerment and delegitimation.*[9] The power of the Syrian king has been delegitimated by the narrative, made ineffective, pitiful, and ludicrous. The community, powerless, exposed, and vulnerable, has been empowered to bold and effective action. The relations between the two have been transformed. Note, however, that the transformation is not simply inversion whereby the weak are made strong. The transformation is much bolder. The Israelite king wants to kill now that he has power, but the prophet restrains him just as he has immobilized the Syrian king. The narrative proposes that a festival is better than a war, that feeding one's enemies is better than killing. The hostility at the beginning of the narrative is transformed into amazement.

Every facet of this prophetic proposal of social reality is subversive of royal notions of reality.

1. Kings do not believe that prayer is powerful because they are preoccupied with and mesmerized by weapons, in which they have placed idolatrous trust.

2. Kings are so committed to their own perception of the world that they scarcely know freedom and are not willing to perceive the world differently. Indeed, to perceive differently is for the rulers of this age to be delegitimated, for it means the surrender of our carefully devised ideology.

3. Kings neither believe that real power can be redistributed nor want it to be. Thus the royal consciousness could assign prayer merely spiritual functions that are removed from the arena of real power.

4. Kings are accustomed to moving "from above" and are not likely to credit the prayers for power that emerges "from below," for those below are scarcely reckoned as serious social agents.

5. Kings generally resist the transformation from war to festival, from killing to feeding, for such a transformation appears not as change but as diminishment of royal significance.

A "more excellent way" is possible among us if we can see with the eyes of Elisha and not with the eyes of kings. In personal and in public life, to be able to see the working of God that unfaith cannot see is what permits the overpowering conclusion that "we are more than conquerors through him who loved us." If we are unable to see the horses and chariots of Yahweh which overwhelm the enemy, then in fact we have nothing important to say in the face of death. The alternative to such daring seeing is to be defeated, to abandon the subversive dream, to nullify our baptism, and to settle for a royal reading of reality. That leaves the king and his army finally in charge. This text calls us to reexamine how and what we see.[10]

THEOLOGICAL EDUCATION:
A REVISED AGENDA

As teachers of the church, we have been entrusted with this text and with its embarrassing footnote. Theological education is not about reasonableness, skill, or management, despite their importance. It is about power, insight, vision, courage, and freedom of another kind, wrought precisely against the rulers of this age. It is now a question in the church whether faith and resources are available for a radically different reading of reality.

A community of faith or of learning that practices conventional certitude will not easily entertain such stories as Elisha. Whether the certitude takes the form of political control, economic domination, theological orthodoxy, or moral correctness, the narrative witnesses against them all and hosts the prospect of transformation with which they stand in tension. Not only our knowledge but our way of knowing are jeopardized when we must listen to such tales from below which so disrespect our reasonableness. We are assaulted in our power, in our knowledge, and in our certitude.

The boy, the servant of Elisha, plays a minor role in the narrative. He is a creature of fear when he sees that Elisha's house is surrounded. He is the object of Elisha's astonishing prayer. He completes his role in the narrative when he is granted sight. Receiving sight is the dramatic trigger for the entire subsequent transformation.

Only a few are summoned to be Elisha, but all of us have minor roles in the narrative of transformation. We are all invited into the narrative to watch while the scandalous "man of God" works his odd power. We watch the narrative, the narrator, the central actor in the narrative. Our watching is theological education, spiritual formation, nurture, conversion.

To be drawn into this new and different way of knowing the real world around us involves a radical reeducation that teaches us

- the *cruciality of prayers of petition* which resubmit life to the One with life-giving power, to be weaned from the promise of kings;
- to *perceive and experience the world differently*, apart from royal ideology and slogan;
- to *watch, expect, and participate in the shift of power* which the gospel works in the world, shifts of power toward women, blacks, the poor, and all the other marginal ones whom royal modes of life have declared to be nonexistent;

- to *be present, as we are able, with the communities from below* who treasure such subversive narratives, who know differently, who are special recipients of God's gift of power for life in the world;
- to *participate in the transformation to a more excellent way* in which our wars may turn to feasts, our killing becomes feeding, and we enact the feeding of the strong, who do us in, and the "least," so that vicious cycles of hostility should end.

That sets an odd agenda for theological education. It is an agenda, I suggest, that is faithful to our tradition, and responsive to our setting, an agenda large and dangerous enough that every part of the curriculum has fresh and urgent work to do. It all begins in a relinquishment of our old certitudes that lead to domination.

I have been wondering what Elisha said to the boy-servant at the end of this episode. I imagine it was not unlike what that other "man of God" said to his apprentices:

> Blessed are the eyes which see what you see! For I tell you that many prophets and kings desired to see what you see, and did not see it, and to hear what you hear, and did not hear it. (Luke 10:23–24)

NOTES

This essay appeared originally in *Theology Today* 44 (1987): 5–14, and is reprinted by permission.

1. The basic critique of "objectivity" has been made by the Frankfurt School. Concerning exegesis, see Donal Dorr, *Spirituality and Justice* (Maryknoll, N.Y.: Orbis Books, 1984), chap. 3; and Elizabeth Schüssler Fiorenza, *Bread Not Stone: The Challenge of Feminist Biblical Interpretation* (Boston: Beacon Press, 1984).

2. This phrase is used by Martin Buber, *Moses* (New York: Harper & Row, 1958), 75, to characterize a miracle.

3. The epistemological settlements and certitudes on which we have counted are now seen to be at least in part arrangements of Euro-American politics. As the hegemony of Euro-American power is jeopardized, so also the intellectual certitudes of that arrangement are placed in question. The monopoly of power and intellectual certitude are mutually reinforcing, and so are together placed at risk. That is why

the "challenge of the Third World" relates both to epistemology and to political-economic power.

4. On the critical questions related to the Deuteronomic literature, see Brevard S. Childs, *Introduction to the Old Testament as Scripture* (Philadelphia: Fortress Press, 1979), 229–38; and, more popularly, Terence E. Fretheim, *Deuteronomic History* (Nashville: Abingdon Press, 1983). A formidable critique of the consensus and an alternative proposal are offered by Anthony F. Campbell, *Of Prophets and Kings*, Catholic Biblical Quarterly Monograph Series 17 (Washington, D.C.: Catholic Biblical Association of America, 1986).

5. The best articulation of this interrelation known to me is that of Gail R. O'Day, *Revelation in the Fourth Gospel: Narrative Mode and Theological Claim* (Philadelphia: Fortress Press, 1986), who demonstrates the way in which the "how" of the text is decisive for the "what" of the message.

6. See the fine literary analysis of the text by Robert LaBarbera, "The Man of War and the Man of God: Social Satire in 2 Kings 6:8–7:20," *Catholic Biblical Quarterly* 46 (1984): 636–51.

7. In his exposition of John 18:33–40 and 19:1–16, Paul Lehmann, *The Transfiguration of Politics* (New York: Harper & Row, 1975), 48–70, has provided a normative discussion of the interplay of real power in the form of weakness and presumed power which is in fact powerless. That same interplay is at work in these narratives of the ninth-century prophets.

8. To perceive the world differently is the aim and intent of serious kerygmatic language. On the capacity of such language to "redescribe," see Paul Ricoeur, "Biblical Hermeneutics," *Semeia* 4 (1975): 31, 127, and passim.

9. LaBarbera, "The Man of War and the Man of God," has seen the powerful social intent of the text. However, when he labels it "social satire," I am not sure he is radical enough in his understanding of the function of the text. Its purpose, I suggest, is not simply to expose or make fun of the royal arrangement, but to subvert its authority. The outcome of the narrative is that the royal claims should be completely nullified for the listeners of the narrative.

10. On scripture as re-seeing, see Gail R. O'Day, *The Word Disclosed: John's Story and Narrative Preaching* (St. Louis, Mo.: CBP Press, 1987).

3

The Legitimacy of
a Sectarian Hermeneutic

2 Kings 18—19

THE DRAMATIC ENCOUNTER between the Assyrians and Judah in 701 B.C.E. is described in 2 Kings 18:1–27 (cf. Isa. 36:11–12). Jerusalem is under siege. The Assyrian army is at the gate, ready to negotiate or, rather, to receive a surrender. The context is a mismatch between an imperial power and a tiny kingdom without visible resources. Assyria has sent its negotiating team in the person of the Rabshakeh. The Assyrian strategy is to evoke a surrender so that a forceful invasion will not be necessary.

The drama takes place in two parts, or places, which will suggest a way to state our problematic.

1. *There is a conversation at the wall of the city.* The Assyrian negotiator stands at the city wall and shouts the terms of surrender. In part, he makes an offer (18:31–32). But mostly he taunts, arguing that Judah has no real alternative to surrender; certainly, Judah's trust in Yahweh is not an alternative, for imperial reason makes clear the falseness of such reliance. The negotiator likens Yahweh to all the other pseudo-gods of the Near East who have failed, and he understands that this one also will fail.

The agents of King Hezekiah respond to this public negotiation by saying,

> Pray, speak to your servants in the Aramaic language, for we understand it; do not speak to us in the language of Judah within the hearing of the people who are on the wall. (18:26).

Speak to us in the language of international diplomacy. Speak to us in the language of sophisticated, public, imperial negotiation, which the common folk do not understand. Because if you speak in Hebrew, they will understand, and we cannot have confidential negotiations. The common people will hear what you say, and you will persuade them, because they will be terrified. The Assyrian negotiator understands this point well, and he deliberately answers "in the language of Judah" (18:28). He goes over the heads of the leaders and engages in an act of intimidation that makes negotiation impossible.

2. *There is also a conversation behind the wall.* Behind the wall, inside the city, a different language is spoken by a different set of people with a different agenda. Here the Judeans speak only to each other. Here Hebrew is spoken, not Aramaic, for not everyone understands Aramaic. The leadership is baffled by what went on at the wall. Upon instruction from King Hezekiah they do not answer the Assyrians directly (18:36).

Then, behind the wall, out of sight of the Assyrians, the king does grief work. He goes to the house of the Lord (19:1). The leaders summon the prophet Isaiah to pray for the king and for the city. The invitation is based on the fact that Assyria has *mocked* Yahweh. Yahweh will surely rebuke and repudiate such mocking. In this conversation behind the wall (unlike the conversation on the wall) no one doubts the power of Yahweh, even against the power of the empire. The very God whom the Assyrians liken to other gods is here singled out as "the living God" (19:4), utterly unlike those other gods.

Isaiah's response is in 19:6–7: "Do not be afraid of the empire." This is the word of Yahweh. It is a remarkable word, surely a word that would not have credibility on the wall. It is a terse word; and it is followed by more Assyrian taunts (19:8–13), a prayer by Hezekiah about mocking (19:15–20), an oracle of response from Isaiah (19:21–28), and a narrative reporting that the city was saved (19:35–37). The actual report of deliverance at the end of the narrative is linked to the initial oracle of Isaiah in 19:6–7. The saving of the city vindicates the prophet, relieves the king, and asserts that Yahweh is more powerful than the imperial threat. The characterization behind the wall of Yahweh as the living God is in fact more discerning than was the conversation at the wall which dismissed Yahweh by analogy with other failed gods.

Dramatically, it is important to note that these two conversations occur simultaneously. The Assyrians on the wall have no access to the conversation behind the wall. They do not know it is going on; if they did, they would not believe it. The conversation behind the wall nonetheless turns out to be decisive for relating to the empire.

THE NEED FOR
AN INTENTIONAL LANGUAGE OF COMMUNITY

In moving from this text, three qualifications are in order:

1. The critical problems of this text and its parallel in Isaiah 36—37 are acute, as noted by Brevard Childs.[1] I do not presume that this is flat historical reporting, but simply that it is a text that proposes a reading of reality. That much can be discerned in the text without sorting out all the historical difficulties.

2. I do not read the text with simplistic fideism, as if prayers to God are a direct way by which to refute the empire. The hermeneutical issues are much more complicated. I do not wish, though, simply to abandon the faith claim asserted here, any more than I wish to affirm it simplistically. I take the text as one mapping of the question of sectarian hermeneutics.

3. Obviously in moving from this text, I have chosen a certain model for discussion. Other texts that offer other models could have been chosen. In this text as model, I suggest that people of faith in public life must be *bilingual*. They must have *a public language* for negotiation at the wall. And they must have a more *communal language* for use behind the gate, in the community, and out of sight and range of the imperial negotiators. Such a view may seem harsh or unfair to the imperial negotiators as a type. Perhaps they are not always so hostile, and perhaps more common ground can be found. But the truth is that they speak a language which is for the community behind the wall not only a foreign language but a secondary language in which serious matters are not primally expressed.

In this text, Aramaic is the public language. When that language is spoken, this believing community has no privilege or advantage.

On the other hand, Hebrew is the community language, the language in which members of this community of commitment speak to each other. This different language permits a different conversation. Now this talk is to Yahweh (in prayer) and about Yahweh. In Hebrew Yahweh is reckoned as a live force, as a real character in dramatic reality. Indeed in Hezekiah's prayer, Yahweh is referred to as "the living God," the God who has power to make a difference (19:16, as in 19:4). And the conversation is carried on by different characters, especially Isaiah, who never, as far as we know, speaks Aramaic and who confines himself to conversation behind the wall. That is remarkable, for Isaiah is commonly regarded as the most urbane and cosmopolitan of the prophets. Yet even he stays behind the wall in this sectarian conversation. The conversation behind the wall, not the one at the wall, as the story has it, is the decisive conversation.

Christians should be nurtured to be bilingual, to know how to speak the language on the wall in the presence of the imperial negotiators, but also how to speak the language behind the wall in the community of faith, where a different set of assumptions, a different perception of the world, a different epistemology are at work. The conversation on the wall is crucial, because the Assyrians are real dialogue partners who must be taken seriously. They will not go away. But unless there is another conversation behind the wall in another language about another agenda, Judah on the wall will only submit to and echo imperial perceptions of reality. When imperial perceptions of reality prevail, everything is already conceded. If the conversation with the empire at the wall is either the only conversation or the decisive one, Israel will decide that Yahweh is indeed like all the other impotent gods and consequently will endorse imperial policies as nonnegotiable realities. The ground for any alternative will have been forfeited.

In 2 Kings 18:27 the Assyrian negotiator seems to have no respect for those who speak Hebrew:

> Has my master sent me to speak these words to your master and to you, and not to the men sitting on the wall, who are doomed with you to eat their own dung and to drink their own urine?

So in v. 28 he addresses them in their own language. But they do not answer (v. 36).[2] I suggest they are able not to answer the Hebrew of the Assyrian, not to submit, not to concede Assyrian perceptions of reality because they understand his Hebrew is fake Hebrew, spoken with an odd accent by one who knows neither the nuances of the language nor the nuances of the conversation behind the wall. The language behind the wall is dysfunctional on the wall. Any attempt to use it there misunderstands and betrays the power and claims of that alternative language that is not to include the outsiders.

While an argument should be made about both languages, my concern here is to examine the function and implications of the second language, the one behind the wall, the language of sectarian hermeneutic.

SOME TERMS FOR ALTERNATIVE COMMUNICATION

Now we must consider the title of this chapter. The terms are heavily freighted, yet not unambiguous.

Hermeneutic. This term requires us to acknowledge the depth of ambiguity and relativity in every process of reading reality. There is no obvious, clear, or unambiguous reading of reality. Neither the conversation on the wall nor the conversation behind the wall can claim to be simply descriptive. Both conversations construct reality as much as they receive it. Both are imaginative and work from a vested interest. Put simply, interpretation theory[3] is the lens, perspective, or bias through which experience is processed.

In this narrative, interpretation is going on at the wall, in public language, and behind the wall, in communal language. Quite clearly these are vastly different interpretive situations and processes. Not only are the languages different but so are the subject matter and the participants. On the wall, the empire does the speaking. The agenda is the imperial system. That system has nullified every other truth claim. In this conversation no prophet speaks, for a prophet is by definition excluded from imperial talk. Also excluded is Yahweh, not a force to be reckoned with. Behind the wall, the agenda is the delivering God of the exodus who is a decisive figure in the drama, the mortal culpability of mocking, and decisive prophetic interpretation. No imperial voice is sounded here.

While the two conversations scarcely overlap, they are about the same reality. The issue hinges on which is the true conversation. Is it true that a serious agenda must include the prophet and the living God because they really matter? Or is it true that they are imaginary characters in a drama that has no contact with reality? What constitutes social reality? Without deciding which is the true conversation, the text knows only that there are two conversations and that Israel must participate in both interpretive enterprises. Israel, like us, does not want to choose between the two conversations— and perhaps cannot. The narrative as we have it makes a twofold claim:

1. The conversation behind the wall makes a difference in what one says on the wall.
2. The conversation behind the wall has a prior claim. It permits one to be suspicious of the conversation on the wall and, indeed, to have some freedom in that conversation, even though the reality of Assyrian power is not nullified or disregarded. But the absolute claims of the empire are handled with unintimidated naiveté, a fact made possible by this other conversation.

Sectarian. This term often conjures up a sense of narrowness and provincialism. Following the governing definitions of Ernst Troeltsch[4] (and, derivatively, H. R. Niebuhr),[5] a sect is a community that does not share in or participate in the commonly accepted definitions of reality. It operates out of a different practice of perception, epistemology, and language. It holds to a set of alternative values which it regards as the truth. That is, it seeks to construct for its members an alternative life-world.[6]

Based on this understanding of the word "sectarian," three points must be made:

1. The breakdown of Western, scientific "globalism" may invite us to reexamine this definition of "sect," which is generally scorned by liberals, and to see its positive role. The recovery of ethnic rootage and special histories of pain (as in various liberation movements)[7] may help us see that an alternative perception of reality is not simply a defensive measure but may be an act of identity, energy,

and power. Moreover, such specificity, we are learning in painful ways, exercises an important critical function, showing that the large claims of the dominant reality cannot be taken at face value.

2. The danger in sect-truth is not its claim per se. The danger is that the "truthing community" regards itself as having a monopoly on truth and thus that the truth must be kept from the larger community in order to keep the truth pure. Such defensiveness reflects a concern not for truth but for control, and also a fear that in submitting the claim to larger scrutiny, the sect-truth will not hold.

But sect-truth as alternative need not be a protected, monopolized claim. It can be a proposal to the larger community,[8] a proposal of an interpretation (a reading of reality) in which the larger community can share and which will bear that community's scrutiny. So in our text, Israel's particular discernment of truth is made available to the empire, even though that truth implies an assault on the dominant imperial truth. The sect does not *accommodate* its truth. But on the other hand, it need not *monopolize* its sense of truth. It may share it in unaccommodating ways, knowing that such an alternative truth inevitably has an impact on dominant truth.

3. I am not interested in making a formal, general case for sect-truth. No doubt there are sect-truths which exploit and abuse. I mean only to attend to the action of Israel and its reading of reality. So we must move from the formal to the substantive claims of Israel. The substantive claim of Israel's truth is that Yahweh, the God of the exodus, is the living God (2 Kings 19:4, 16).[9] It is not argued that this living God is alive only in Israel, only behind the wall, only for Israel. Rather, it is a large claim intended to impinge upon public, even imperial, perceptions of reality. The claim flows from Israel's special history of pain and rescue, which dares to say that the power toward life, justice, and righteousness will override every power of domination. I take this as a "sectarian interpretation," but it is an interpretation in which the empire is invited to participate, albeit at great cost.

Thus, by the term "sectarian hermeneutic" I mean the conversation behind the wall that is conducted in the language of the community, in which the prophet participates crucially, and that is rooted in the memory of this community which intends to create a different discussion on the wall. The purpose of such a sectarian reading of reality is to transform the conversation with the empire on the wall.

Legitimacy. This is the difficult term in the title. One can understand "legitimacy" as reflected in the question, Does it hold water? and this may be adequate. However, a more critical understanding is available in the work of Jürgen Habermas.[10] There is some danger in using his categories, first, because they are difficult and convoluted and, second, because using them with a premodern text may be an objectional anachronism. But his insights are of such value that I shall try.

Habermas characterizes the crisis of legitimacy as the separation of instrumental functions of administration from expressive symbols that evoke assent.[11] By "instrumental functions" he means the autonomous, secularized, scientific modes of managing people, means of production, and the supportive ideology. The crisis, he suggests, is that such administrative claims rest on appeals to power, deception, and pragmatism, because the claims are largely cut off from the symbols that genuinely authorize. So the loss of energizing symbols must be compensated for by more consumer goods, diversionary activity, or the fabrication of false symbols.[12] Such a way is illegitimate because it does not touch the actual lives of people. While the deception may prevail, it cannot be compelling at bottom and therefore is illegitimate.[13]

In the discussion on the wall, we may wonder about the legitimacy of the imperial presentation of reality, the royal hermeneutic. Is it legitimate in the sense that Assyrian military and political claims cohere with Israel's expressive symbols? As it is presented in the text, I think not. In 2 Kings 18:31–32, the illegitimacy of the imperial claim is evident. The speaker knows enough of Israel's root dream of "vine and fig tree" to use the code words, which surely are words of primal legitimacy because they encompass the most passionate yearning of Israel. But then the imperial mode denies Israel's dream, showing that the dream is not really understood, by offering a substitute vine and fig tree in another part of the empire. The speaker assumes that one land is as good as another and seeing one vine and fig tree is seeing them all. Such a predictable, instrumental reading of reality is utterly alien to the expressive symbol of Israel.[14] The empire seeks to *use* the expressive symbol that shapes Israel's imagination but misunderstands it and so employs it in illegitimate ways. This imperial use violates Israel's central passion. The violation is probably not calculated or even recognized by the Assyrians. It is simply the way empires proceed. But every Israelite who hears the imperial offer knows immediately that it is a fraud, because it does not cohere with the root symbol.

But what about the counterproposal and its legitimacy? What of the discussion behind the wall? Does the sectarian reading of reality hold together the reality of experience, the necessary functions of administration, and the expressive symbols which claim assent and generate energy?

My answer is twofold. Insofar as the conversation behind the wall holds to its primal language and its generative reference, it is indeed legitimate. Israel's conversation goes deep into its own peculiar experience, where it has found energizing symbols. This is articulated in Isaiah's word in 19:6 with the primal speech, "Do not fear,"[15] in Hezekiah's certainty that Yahweh is a living God not to be mocked (19:6), and in the prophetic response of Yahweh's self-assertion against the mocker (19:22–24). All of this speech (1) stays very close to the primal language of Israel; (2) focuses singularly on the reality of God, and (3) refrains from policy formation, which is not the function of sectarian interpretation. So far so good.

But the conversation behind the wall departs from legitimacy when it enters into policy formation that ignores primal language, shifts its focus from God to the Jerusalem establishment, and makes a concrete political claim. In 19:32–34, the Jerusalem ideology seems to me to usurp functions from the proper conversation. In that claim, I suggest, the text makes sounds that are as self-serving as those of Assyria, so that now the conversation behind the wall becomes like the one on the wall. It is no longer legitimate because it is not a proposal that can be offered and received in public discourse. It is now self-serving and must be rejected. In contrasting the assertions made in 19:1–6 and 22–24 with those in 19:32–34, I make a distinction that I trust is faithful to the Protestant principle. A sectarian interpretation is valid so long as it clings to the singular holiness of God. When the singular holiness of God is assigned to historical structures, such domesticated religious power has become self-serving ideology.

The purpose of such sectarian interpretation as offered in Isaiah 18—19 is to authorize those who join the public conversation on the wall to be present freely, imaginatively, and critically. Had there been no conversation behind the wall, I believe the conversation on the wall would have been preempted by an Assyrian reading of reality that appeared to be absolute, accounted for all the recognized evidence, and faced no serious criticism.

Similarly, church education is properly and legitimately sectarian if it nurtures an alternative reading of reality that can interface with the dominant reading of reality freely, imaginatively, and critically. Without this "other conversation," the dominant reading of reality (which in our time I would call "consumer militarism") will have its way, unfettered and uncriticized. The dominant rationality of the empire must be criticized because its power actions are distinct from the truth of human suffering and human hope and are therefore illegitimate. Sectarian rationality must also be criticized when it falls into the same trap, as indeed much sectarian conversation does. But a sectarian conversation kept open to its own language, its own experience, and its own proper reference is not only legitimate but essential to serious public discourse. Without the conversation behind the wall, the conversation on the wall will surely become a totalitarian monologue.

COUNTERING "OFFICIAL" TRUTH

I do not believe that the Bible serves very often or very well in direct participation in the public discourse at the wall. That is not its intent, purpose, or character.[16] Rather, it intentionally nurtures the conversation behind the wall that then makes an urgent contribution to the public conversation at the wall. The biblical conversation is largely in the dialect of the community, only rarely in the common language of the empire. That does not make it less relevant or urgent, but only relevant and urgent in a certain kind of way.

Some of the elements of this "conversation behind the wall" become the Bible's offer to the public conversation. First, the story of Israel *originates as a counterperception of reality*.[17] If one agrees that it is the Moses narratives (rather than the Genesis narratives) that are decisive for Israel's reading of reality, then the "counter" thrust of the text is unarguable. The text itself seems to presume this, because the pervasive metaphors and allusions are those of exodus-wilderness-land.[18] The primal narrative assertion of Israel's faith is of an oppressed people yearning for and receiving emancipation from an oppressor empire. This is the historical claim of the text. This is the liturgic reenactment of the Passover.[19] This is the intention of Israel's education to its next generation (cf. Deut. 6:4–10, 20–24).[20]

The foundational word Israel entrusts to its young is a critical analysis of dominant social reality as inhumane and to be rejected. Gerhard von Rad correctly argues that the pivot of this offer of a life-world is that "the Egyptians treated us harshly."[21] That foundation of social analysis establishes for time to come the main elements for the conversation behind the wall. The Egyptians hoped that their harsh treatment of slaves would not be noticed, felt, or brought to public expression, or that it would be accepted docilely as necessary to the state. But the sectarian hermeneutic of Israel tended to notice and to bring it to speech. The "sacred discontent" of Israel derives from this beginning point of pain brought to speech.

The exodus story is initiated and powered "from below," from the articulation and public processing of pain. So the second aspect of the credal formulation is, *"We cried out"* (Exod. 2:23–25). Note that the memory does not say simply, "We hurt," but "We found voice." The voice is a harsh, hostile, subversive voice filled with revolutionary chutzpah. We are not told how or why there was energy and courage for the cry. Perhaps it simply belongs to this odd people that it is a people that does not lose its voice. And not losing its voice, it never accepts the word of the empire as an absolute voice, because it always knows about another voice that is incongruous with the sure, unhesitating voice of the empire.[22]

Conformity, docility, subservience, and depression are not served by this exodus story. The empire—Egyptian or Assyrian—does not mind oppressed people being hurt, so long as there is no public outcry. But there is outcry here. Indeed, this is what Israel's sectarian conversation is about—a cry of pain that destabilizes, assaults, and delegitimates every absolute imperial claim. Israel insists that the voice of pain brought to public speech is a decisive social reality always to be taken seriously. That is the tradition in which the sackcloth of Hezekiah stands in 19:1–4.

It is remarkable that this sectarian conversation proceeds so far without reference to God. While I tremble about the implications of that fact, the first topic in the conversation is a critique of dominant reason ("The Egyptians treated us harshly"). Only then is it affirmed that the critique and the voice of pain reach and mobilize God. God the liberator is not contained by the dominant reason and therefore can be impinged upon from below. But not by docility, only by harsh, impatient, irreverent assault. This sectarian conversation with God perhaps models and gives warrant for the subsequent conversation with the empire. Unless there be the permit of experience in the community, however, the public conversation will never happen.

The second spin-off from the critical analysis of the dominant social reality is constructive. It is the covenant, the emergence of the metaphor "kingdom of God,"[23] and the derivative torah as an alternative social practice. To be sure, there are more critical questions connected with the covenant as social theory and religious construct than we can undertake here. But with Martin Buber (before Mendenhall),[24] it is clear that the covenant and its torah are not only a religious meeting and relationship but a serious proposal for an alternative way to organize social power. Norman Gottwald has shown how the torah may be understood as a social experiment of an egalitarian kind. Many examples may be drawn from Deuteronomy, and we can also refer to the decisive proposal of the year of Jubilee. Paul Hanson has further demonstrated that the early laws of Exodus 21—23 seek to reorganize social life in ways that break with the conventions of exploitation and domination.[25] In each case, the new social proposal is closely linked to the concrete memory of pain and emancipation. What I most want to stress, however, is that the torah, while it no doubt largely borrowed from a common legal tradition in the Near East, is framed essentially in a sectarian conversation of Israel as an alternative to imperial reality. It is true that the torah of Israel is a proposal and offer made to the nations. But its first function is to provide a basis for organizing this community in an alternative way that distances social practice from the ways of the dominant rationality.

Only in its earliest period could Israel hope to form a social organization of its own. And that only for a brief time in a limited area.[26] What the prophets and, indeed, the entire tradition indicate is that Israel continued to draw its main impetus from this sectarian conversation, even as it participated in and contributed to public discourse. Israel, of course, knew that social organization must reckon with Assyria. Hezekiah knew that. Isaiah knew that. But persistently Israel met Assyria with counteroffers generated by its own sectarian conversation. It persistently moved against the dominant rationality, refusing to accept its definitions and values, refusing to be assimilated into this consciousness. Three elements may be identified as decisive for Israel's sectarian reading of reality which it offered to the nations:

1. A suspicion of all dominant definitions of reality, because they embody a harshness.
2. A readiness to make pain an inescapable public reality by bringing it to speech.
3. An imaginative proposal for ordering society in an alternative way.

It appears, by the terms proposed earlier, that Israel's offer is legitimate: it stays close to experience, it bespeaks energizing symbols, and it acknowledges administrative necessity. The conversation behind the wall is most vulnerable to criticism on this last point. It may be suggested that this conversation is never "realistic" about power realities. Certainly from the point of view of Assyria or Egypt, that would appear so. From the provisions of Deuteronomy where administrative elements are most clearly articulated, one can conclude that administrative reality is accounted for, albeit in ways alien to the empire.[27]

The focus of all three elements, of course, is Yahweh, the one regarded as *living* by those behind the wall and as *impotent* by the empire at the wall. It is the claim of Yahweh that makes the counterproposal so problematic for the empire. It is problematic because Yahweh does not appear to be such a force, and because if Yahweh is such a force, Yahweh is a force not conducive to systemic management. So Israel must go to the public conversation without insisting on the key actor in its own story. Israel must make its case at the wall in other language. But the sectarian conversation is all about Yahweh who becomes the invisible but powerful legitimator of this counterproposal in public discourse. Faithful Israel is never so taken in by the dominant consciousness that it forgets who it is that gives the courage and authority to counter official truth.

SECTARIAN CONVERSATION AS CRITICISM

Israel's sectarian conversation functions especially as a *critical* agent in the public conversation. This narrative of critique/cry/alternative keeps Israel from ever accepting the dominant consciousness as absolute. Israel's elemental suspicion regularly notices that what appears to be *rational* is in fact *interested*, that what appears to be *objective* is in fact *self-serving*. The empire wants its claims to appear rational and objective. Yahweh's critical presence enables Israel to notice the reality of Assyria's self-interest. Israel's alternative memory notices that what passes for public discourse is in fact a new sectarian proposal of an ideological kind.

In its heady season of origin, the "sectarian narrative enterprise" that was Israel had no failure of nerve. But there is historical evidence that when Israel had to exist amidst worldviews and rationalities that seemed successful and comprehensive, its own narrative enterprise was inadequate and an embarrassment. At the beginning of the monarchal period, there is evidence that Israel yearned to be "like the other nations," even if it meant abandoning its notion of Yahweh as king (1 Sam. 8:5, 20). At the end of the Old Testament period, the clearest example of such feelings occurs when the Maccabean generation, embarrassed at circumcision, devised surgery to remove every sign of having been circumcised (1 Mac. 1:15). Israel repeatedly experienced the conversation partner at the wall as having a more fully adequate hermeneutic, rationality, or way of experiencing the world. Clearly, the seduction of the dominant culture is the most persistent problem facing a sectarian community.

The insistent conversation behind the wall asserts that the conversation partner at the wall (1) is seductive; (2) does not have the final hermeneutic; (3) should not be taken at face value; and (4) is in fact acting in narrow self-interest under the guise of the general, common interest. In 2 Kings 18—19, for example, the Assyrian negotiators at the wall under such a guise are pursuing Assyrian policy at the expense of all those behind the wall. The dominant conversation partner acts and speaks in fact only from its own narrow, sectarian interest. We are not accustomed to thinking of the voice of the empire as sectarian, but so it is when it serves only a narrow interest. "Empire as sect" is a theme worth pursuing in our own situation; it may be suggested, for example, that the voice of U.S. power, which claims to be the voice of general well-being, is in a number of cases only the voice of a narrow range of economic and political interests.

The ideological guise behind which self-interest hides is effective if large numbers of people can be kept from noticing the narrow base of real interest. That will happen unless there is conversation behind the wall to give critical distance and standing ground for an alternative assessment. In ancient Israel, the prophets were the ones who regularly exposed the voice of the empire as sectarian, rather than comprehensive or disinterested. The prophetic critique against the rationality of the empire is consistent.

In Isa. 10:5ff., Sennacherib is no doubt an instrument of Yahweh. But he oversteps his mandate and imagines that his own strength and wisdom have accomplished his works (cf. vv. 13–14).

Consistently in Jeremiah, Nebuchadnezzar and the Babylonians are agents of Yahweh (cf. 25:9; 26:6), but by Isaiah 47, mistress Babylon is condemned for having acted not as means but as end (see also Jer. 50—51).

For Ezekiel, first Tyre (28:2) and then Egypt (29:3, 9) make statements of autonomy, and so are sure to be destroyed.

In Ezekiel 38—39, the enigmatic reference to Gog and Magog concerns the same overreading of the permit given by Yahweh.

In Daniel 4:33, Nebuchadnezzar becomes like an ox eating grass because he has not properly deferred to the rule of Yahweh.

Admittedly, these are extreme cases. The subject, however, requires such an accent. This way of presenting the public process of imperial history functions as a massive critique of an imperial reading of reality. It is critiqued because it is autonomous, that is, it is not

addressed to the governance of Yahweh. The quarrel could have
been one of ideologies and an argument about which name to use
for God. But the insistence behind the wall is that in the imperial
rationality there is an absence of restraint and limitation proper to
creatures of Yahweh. The Assyrians exhibit unbridled aggression
and self-interest, and a lack of humaneness and compassion. The
argument, then, concerns not only religious language but social
policy as well. The critique made by this sectarian perspective is
that the rationality of the empire lacks the social vision that must
be practiced by any power congruent with Yahweh. This critique is
characteristically not made *in principle*, but with reference to specific situations.

Such a critique in extreme cases (such as a dismissal of the
imperial conversation partner at the wall) might lead to a retreat
back into the community that has made the critique. Such a judgment has the capability, if not the probability, of resulting in a kind
of isolationism and particularism that not only critiques the voice
at the wall but also pretends there is no such voice and imagines
that the only serious conversation is the one in the sectarian language behind the wall. Then the sectarian tradition itself becomes
idolatrous and in turn must be critiqued. The most remarkable
thing about this tradition of "sacred discontent" is that it contains
within itself the sources from which to critique its own practice.
Just as this sectarian conversation can identify and assault empire-
become-sectarian, so it can also identify and assault the temptation
of the sect to make too much of itself. I mention now a number of
such critiques made from within the tradition, though others could
be cited.

The Yahwist

The Yahwist tradition in the Pentateuch articulates the election tradition of Israel with reference to a new internationalism.

1. Hans Walter Wolff has seen that the programmatic formula is
"By you shall the families of the earth bless themselves" (Gen. 12:3;
18:18; 22:18; 26:4; 28:14).[28] That is, by a theology of blessing, Israel's
well-being is somehow linked to that of other nations. There is no
blessing that can be monopolized without reference to the others.
Israel exists in the world for the sake of the nations, as a means and

not as an end. Put another way, the conversation behind the wall is for the sake of the partners *at* the wall. While it may come from elsewhere, one evidence of this line of argument is found in Jeremiah's well-known promise-threat: "In the welfare of the city will be your welfare" (29:7). The future well-being of Israel is intimately linked with the well-being of Babylon.

2. Though critical problems exist, it is plausible that some form of the Joseph narrative (Gen. 37; 39—50) belongs in the world of the Yahwist. Gerhard von Rad was the first to notice a very different perspective on faith in this literature, in which the usual priority of Israel is not acknowledged. The central figure is an Egyptian power agent, and the modes of faith and knowledge are extraordinarily "cool." Indeed, one can imagine that Joseph would have been uncomfortable if he had ever been caught in a conversation behind the wall. Or, perhaps that is what the private conversation with the brothers is about (Gen. 45:1–3). Compared with the public function of Joseph, his meeting with his brothers is a hidden, private meeting in which the vulnerability of the man is articulated as it never would have been in the public arena. It becomes clear that for Joseph this is a very different kind of conversation, emotionally freighted in a way the public conversation is not, for it is here that the providential care of Yahweh is articulated. Joseph is perhaps a model for keeping two distinct conversations going that seem not closely related to each other.

Amos

1. In the oracles against the nations (Isaiah 13—23, Amos 1—2, Jer. 46:51, Ezek. 25:32), there is a pervasive assumption of Yahweh's governance.[29] There are clearly ethical expectations from Yahweh that operate both at the wall and well outside the wall. Yahweh's governance is not coterminous with Israel. As a literary genre, the oracles make a distinct point. Yahweh does work at the wall that has no reference to Israel behind the wall.

It is in Amos 2:6–16 that the theology of "Yahweh and the nations" functions as a critique of the sectarian tradition. Amos accomplishes this odd turn of the norm by the shrewd move of incorporating Israel among the nations and thereby treating Israel like the other nations, subject to the same expectations. The result is that Israel is judged not by its covenantal understandings but as one of the nations without privilege or priority. By this move, Amos nullifies Israel's hermeneutical privilege. Israel must answer like all the others.

2. In at least two other places, Amos continues this critique. In 3:2, the claim of election is reversed (see Gen. 18:18–19). In 9:7, the claims of the sectarian narrative are affirmed and made inclusive:

> Are you not like the Ethiopians to me,
>   O people of Israel? says the Lord.
> Did I not bring up Israel from the land of Egypt,
>   and the Philistines from Caphtor and the Syrians from Kir?

The exodus is affirmed. Then it is also affirmed that what seems to be the peculiar property of the community behind the wall is not theirs alone because Yahweh characteristically causes exoduses for many peoples. This is a remarkable intellectual claim, for the normative claim of the sectarian narrative is at the same time affirmed and exploded.[30] It is not argued that the normative claim of the exodus recital is anything but true and normative, rather that it may not be monopolized. The paradigm may not be kept safely behind the wall.

Isaiah

1. The most remarkable criticism of a monopolized claim is found in Isa. 19:19–25. It is an eschatological vision. On the face of it, the oracle is a source of hope for a genuinely new thing. Behind that, less obviously but more poignantly, the oracle may be a critique of the hope so fervently held behind the wall. The promise is that the day will come when the theological map of the Near East will have a different look:

> In that day Israel will be the third with Egypt and Assyria, a blessing in the midst of the earth, whom the Lord of hosts has blessed, saying, "Blessed be Egypt *my people*, and Assyria *the work of my hands*, and Israel *my heritage*. (vv. 24–25, italics added)

The ones outside the wall will be reckoned equally with Israel. The monopoly will be broken. Again it is worth noting that the new inclusive vision can only be articulated in the language of the sectarian community: "my people/work of my hands/my heritage." Even this most inclusive vision in Israel holds to the language and vocabulary of the sect in order to make the point.

2. In this, as in all matters concerning Isaiah, the Isaiah tradition is notoriously difficult to assess.[31] The critical problems are acute, because Isaiah 1—39 seems to include a great variety of theological claims.[32] The problems are tradition-critical because it is exceedingly difficult to determine which memories nurture Isaiah, if indeed we could locate the words of that prophet. It seems likely that Isaiah is especially informed by the Zion tradition,[33] perhaps more especially those of the enthronement festival (cf. the psalms) which seem reflected in his call vision. He is nurtured in that tendency to assign to the Israelite tradition imperial scope of the most ambitious kind.

But, of course, Isaiah not only transmits that uncriticized tradition. He also *criticizes* it. In 1:21–26, the history of the "protected city" is summarized. There are three stages. The poem begins with an initial dream of justice, righteousness, and faithfulness (v. 21). Then it envisions a dismantling (vv. 24–25). Finally the poem promises renewal (v. 26). The intent of the poem turns on how drastic the second phase is, how deep the judgment cuts. My own evangelical bias is that it cuts very deep; but that is a judgment not required by the text. Even if not read with such an accent on discontinuity, what is clear from the entire chapter is that the city behind the wall is not safe and is subject to the rigorous norms of Yahweh. Any eighth-century Zionist who imagines this city with a guarantee of safe conduct from Yahweh has skewed the tradition, as Isaiah understands it.

3. The other noteworthy text is Isa. 6:9–10, in which it is clear that this people with special access is utterly unresponsive. Anyone who prized the tradition or imagined that it gave special insight or sensitivity is uninformed. The judgment leads, in vv. 12–13, to a vision of termination as harsh as the uncreation in Jer. 4:23–36. There is no special privilege.

Certainly it is true that the sectarian tradition is not everywhere or consistently critiqued. It is often simply trustingly embraced. But there is evidence that not only is it critiqued, but it is critiqued precisely by those who have been, in one way or another, engaged in this other tradition at the wall. In the cases of the Yahwist, Amos, and Isaiah, it is the experience at the wall, with the nations, beyond the community, that leads to criticism.

PRACTITIONERS OF A SECOND LANGUAGE

A series of provisional conclusions may be drawn about this bilingual enterprise before making some derivative judgments.

1. The heart of the matter is the sectarian narrative. The primal conversation in the Old Testament is behind the wall, and this does not change in the New Testament. The tradition is one of suspicion against the dominant rationality. It is the witness of the whole tradition, I believe, that this posture of suspicion is the source of vitality and passion, and, I dare say, of compassion and humaneness.

2. This sectarian narrative tradition provides the best critical vantage point from which to assess the dominant rationality. This is true not only in the text but also as the text has made its way through history. The text stands resiliently in tension with dominant rationality. It is this scandalous text of particularity that has persistently raised questions about the preemptive claims of absolute ideology. It is a topic for another day, but I submit that it is the *materiality* of this sectarian tradition (mediated by Marx and Freud) that has critiqued every absolutism that is legitimated by ideology and covered over by spiritual mythology and idealism.[34]

3. The dominant voice at the wall is not the only one tempted to absolutism. When the conversation behind the wall ignores the other conversation and imagines it is the only conversation, it also becomes ideological and idolatrous. This characteristically happens through an exaggerated attention to chosenness (see Matt. 3:7–10).[35]

The sectarian tradition thus needs also to be critiqued. What I have found telling is that the critique is based on two curiously juxtaposed matters. The critique comes from *the awareness of the others*, who must be taken seriously on their own terms. But the terms of the critique are found *within the tradition itself*. Indeed the imperial tradition is no reliable basis for critique, because it is inherently autonomous and is therefore aimed away from Yahweh and the accompanying social vision. But apparently the various critiques have had no trouble in using the tradition against the tradition.[36] That is a formal observation about what is done in the text. What is decisive and definitional in this tradition is its *aniconic* capacity against both conversations, including the one where the tradition itself is the subject under discussion.[37]

4. All of this leads to the unavoidable conclusions that both conversations are important and that Christians must be taught to be bilingual. Moreover, both conversations must be critiqued on the basis of the claims of the sectarian tradition.

The liberal temptation, felt by those embarrassed at the sectarian narrative, is to believe that the conversation at the wall is the only conversation and that all needs for conversation can be met there. That, of course, is not countenanced by any of the Judean voices in our textual encounter with Assyria. None of those in the story seem like very good liberals. They all know there is another conversation.

The conservative temptation, held by those enamored of the sectarian narrative in its uncriticized form, is to imagine it is the only conversation and to conclude that anyone who wants conversation must join this one.

The conversation at the wall, conducted according to imperial rationality, is a poor, perhaps impossible, place in which to do the night work of dreaming and visioning, remembering and hoping, caring and fearing, compassion and passion. For there the subject is about battalions, quotas of horses and riders (cf. 2 Kings 18:23–24), deadlines, and performance. Many burned-out and cynical liberals have succumbed to this conversation as though it were the serious conversation when, in fact, it cannot by definition be serious about some matters.

Conversely, the conversation behind the wall is probably not a suitable or effective place for policy formation. Policy cannot be formed in a vacuum, despite recent U.S. behavior. Nor can it be formed out of a community which only tells stories about its hurts and fears.

Our valuing of the sectarian hermeneutic of the Bible depends on our understanding its function in other conversations. I am convinced by Ricoeur's judgment that change of obedience comes from changed imagination.[38] The language of imagination, ambiguity, hurt, and discontinuity are all part of the conversation. Such talk is not irrational, but it is a rationality which grows out of hurt processed, cries heard, bread multiplied, sin forgiven, the dead raised, debts canceled, and outcasts come home (cf. Luke 4:18–19; 7:22).

It is the intent of the community that not only those on the wall will speak, hear, and decide differently but that the others on the wall who do not speak this language (Hebrew) or share the communal imagination of the Israelite narrative will by the foreign accent used on the wall be permitted to go back and engage in a conversation behind their wall. There is nothing so impossible on the wall as to have a conversation partner (it matters not from which side) who has no conversation going on elsewhere that processes the sordid and surging realities of humanness. If the conversation at the wall is one's only conversation, that conversation becomes too serious and one-dimensional,[39] with too much at stake and nothing left for negotiation or disclosure. If one is not involved in a conversation of criticism and freedom, then the public discussion must inevitably be marked by an absence of self-criticism, freedom, and a sense of humor. Very quickly everything becomes necessary.

CONTEMPORARY IMPLICATIONS

1. It is clear that a hermeneutic is not only necessary but inevitable. There are no uninterpreted events.[40] There are only events shaped and discerned through a community of perception. The options available here, though, are limited to the perception of those on the wall, which absolutizes the dominant rationality, and an interpretation from those behind the wall, which is porous and contains the capacity for self-criticism. A hermeneutic there must be; and without intentionality, the dominant rationality will claim the field at high cost to our humanness.

2. We must ask if the conversation behind the wall is legitimate. Does it hold together the reality of *experience*, the necessary functions of *administration*, and the expressive *symbols* which claim, assert, and guarantee energy? The answer in the text itself is Yes. We do not presume to go behind the text to "what happened." What the text presents as having happened is that the conversation behind the wall (consisting in penance, prayer, and oracle) completely changed the conversation on the wall. That conversation behind the

wall did touch real public experience, did cope with administrative crisis, and did generate newness. We can agree that this is a very "odd" text,[41] and this is surely no way to conduct foreign policy. Indeed we might say it was a "miracle" and policy cannot be built on miracles. In response I would make four points.

First, we are studying a text and not an event behind the text. If we take the text as text, it carves out for us a moment to "re-read" reality differently.

Second, it is always a "miracle" when the conversation behind the wall decisively impinges on the conversation at the wall, when the imagination of the community can break the dominant rationality. Miraculous turns are, in fact, what church education is about.

Third, I intend, in terms of legitimacy, that this conversation behind the wall be judged not by its power to form policy, but by its capacity to transform imagination, which makes a differently textured policy possible. Our scientific, objective, historical-critical ways find it difficult to let the text do its proper work without demanding that it do some other work, perhaps more palatable to our rationality.[42]

Fourth, the text is an oddity. Indeed it is such an oddity that the tradition of Israel included it twice. I do not suggest that its impingement on imagination should be treated as routine, normal, or capable of replication. It does seem, however, that the notion of an "oddity" is of crucial substance for our faith community and its educational processes.

On all these counts, I regard the conversation behind the wall as legitimate, as having decisively changed the other conversation which appears to the world to be the decisive one.

3. The sectarian character of this story is evident: it belongs to this language group with this memory. Two dimensions are important. First, that it belongs to this minority community is definitional. It cannot be any other way. Imperial regimes do not tell tales of slave escapes. Roman governors do not jest at resurrections (cf. Matt. 28:14); Jerusalem kings do not bow down at mangers (cf. Matt. 2:13). So unless we are to abandon the substance, we must accept the fact of sectarianism. It belongs to the genre and subject matter to be sectarian. But second, the nerve of this tradition behind the wall is to insist that this tale is "porous" enough that it will touch the experience of others if they will climb down off the wall

to tell stories in their community of hurt and passion. The governing miracles are common to all persons in all communities, even though some long ago opted for imperial ideology.

I conclude then that the sectarian interpretation is legitimate, because it offers a reading of reality that claims assent, and because it provides an alternative to an imperial rationality that nullifies the very subject matter of this interpretation.

The Practice of Interpretation

As I noted earlier, Christians must be nurtured to be bilingual, to be able to speak both the language of policy formation and the language of transformative imagination. There is merit in seeing these as distinct educational tasks but dependent upon each other.

When I consider our particular social situation and the church constituency we address, I conclude that the conversation behind the wall with its capacity for self-criticism needs particular attention: It is the church constituency of middle America that most vigorously supports the inhumane policies of our government. Our educational access is not to government leaders who form policy, but to the public which permits, authorizes, and embraces policy. Education for such a constituency needs to concern not so much the technicalities of policy questions (what should be said on the wall) as a transformed imagination, informed by hurt, ambiguity, and discontinuity.

The self-critical capacity of that tradition is urgent when a goodly portion of church constituency on the right handles the sectarian interpretation of tradition without a shred of suspicion. I do not believe that it is education in conversation at the wall that is needed, but address to the frightened assembly that holds these close narratives one-dimensionally.

There is a confusion and collapse of the two stories now sadly evident in civil religion generally. Neither story has any integrity, for the reasons of state are all intertwined with affairs of the heart, and neither can be critiqued or discerned clearly.

In the liberal church, so captured by laudable goals and imperial methods, the story which has lost power is the one behind the walls. We end up with more knowledge about what to do, but without the will, courage, energy or self-knowledge to act. What is required here is a sectarian tale that gives us freedom against our perceived vested interest.

This is not a plea for withdrawal or obscurantism, or a disregard of conversation at the wall where policy must be formed in the presence of the wielders of power. My argument grows out of my sense of the real crisis among us. It is a crisis of legitimacy. At the moment, my sense is that we have forgotten our primal language. Other languages take its place. Aramaic sounds a lot like Hebrew, but only the Assyrian ambassador thought it was equivalent. The folks who know both languages could identify the foreign accent and could recognize the difference.

NOTES

This essay appeared originally in *Horizons in Biblical Theology* 7 (June 1985): 1–42, and is reprinted by permission.

1. Brevard S. Childs, *Isaiah and the Assyrian Crisis* (Naperville, Ill.: Alec R. Allenson, 1967). See his later summary of the general issues in *Introduction to the Old Testament as Scripture* (Philadelphia: Fortress Press, 1979), 318–25. See also the important work of Ronald Clements, *Isaiah and the Deliverance of Jerusalem*, JSOTSup 13 (Sheffield, Eng.: University of Sheffield, 1980).

2. One of the freedoms exercised at the wall by those who have another conversation elsewhere is the freedom not to answer and so not to enlist in the dominant rationality. See Dan. 3:16–18; John 18:8–11. On the latter, see Paul Lehmann, *The Transfiguration of Politics* (New York: Harper & Row, 1975), 48–70, esp. 68.

3. See the most helpful summary by Anthony C. Thistelson, *The Two Horizons* (Grand Rapids: Wm. B. Eerdmans, 1979). In what follows, it will be evident that I am influenced particularly by Paul Ricoeur.

4. Ernst Troeltsch, *The Social Teachings of the Christian Churches* (New York: Macmillan, 1931). Troeltsch's summary statement is: "The sect is a voluntary society, composed of strict and definite Christian believers bound to each other by the fact that all have experienced 'the new birth.' These 'believers' live apart from the world, are limited to small groups, emphasize the law instead of grace, and in varying degrees within their own circle, set up the Christian order, based on love; all this is done in preparation for and expectation of the coming Kingdom of God" (2:993). In what follows, I have taken important liberties with this characterization. It remains to see if my improvisations completely distort the question under discussion.

5. H. R. Niebuhr, *The Social Sources of Denominationalism* (New York: Henry Holt, 1929), esp. 17–21.

6. The language, of course, is derived from Peter Berger and Thomas Luckmann, *The Social Construction of Reality* (Garden City, N.Y.: Doubleday & Co., 1967). But, see esp. Berger's earlier book, *The Precarious Vision* (Garden City, N.Y.: Doubleday & Co., 1961). His analysis there is about a protected construction of reality jeopardized by more expansive experience. The theme is not unrelated to "sectarianism."

7. See Elizabeth Schüssler Fiorenza, *In Memory of Her* (New York: Crossroad, 1983), for a history of pain that has been almost completely lost to us, due to a censored reading of the text. See also Stanley Hauerwas, "Will the Real Sectarian Stand Up?" *Theology Today* 44 (1987): 87–94.

8. Eric W. Gritsch and Robert W. Jenson, *Lutheranism: The Theological Movement and Its Confessional Writings* (Philadelphia: Fortress Press, 1976), chap. 1, have suggested, e.g., that the Lutheran Confessions are an offer made by the Lutheran community to the whole church. When it is no longer a *proposal* but an ultimatum (which, of course, Jenson does not intend), then it becomes a destructive monopoly.

9. On "the living God," see Siegfried Kreuzer, *Der lebendige Gott* (Stuttgart: Kohlhammer, 1983); and Hans Joachim Kraus, "The Living God: A Chapter of Biblical Theology," in *Theology of the Liberating Word*, ed. Frederick Herzog (New York: Abingdon Press, 1971), 76–107.

10. The original sociological work on this subject is that of Max Weber. But Habermas has considerably advanced the discussion. See Jürgen Habermas, *Legitimation Crisis* (Boston: Beacon Press, 1973), esp. part 2, chap. 6. See also Peter Berger, *The Sacred Canopy* (Garden City, N.Y.: Doubleday & Co., 1967), esp. 32–39.

11. Habermas, *Legitimation Crisis*, 70.

12. On false symbols as ways of social control, see Jacques Ellul, *Propaganda: The Formation of Men's Attitudes* (New York: Alfred A. Knopf, 1965). On the failure of symbols, see Robert J. Lifton's various analyses of the "symbol gap."

13. See Alvin Gouldner, *The Coming Crisis of Western Sociology* (New York: Basic Books, 1970), which concerns failed objectivity in the social sciences as an illegitimate enterprise. See also Berger, *The Sacred Canopy*, 90–92; and Habermas, *Legitimation Crisis*, 73, 93. Gary A. Herion, "The Social Organization of Tradition in Monarchic Judah" (Ph.D. diss. University of Michigan, 1982), 59 and passim, has shown that only conformity is required, not assent, by the administrators of the dominant rationality.

14. On bureaucratic use of an expressive symbol, see Walter Brueggemann, " 'Vine and Fig Tree': A Case Study in Imagination and Criticism," *Catholic Biblical Quarterly* 43 (1981): 188–204.

15. On the power of such primal speech to change worlds, see Peter L. Berger, *A Rumor of Angels* (Garden City, N.Y.: Doubleday & Co., 1970), 54–56.

16. Wayne A. Meeks, *The First Urban Christians* (New Haven: Yale University Press, 1983), has shown how the Pauline corpus in the New Testament is almost completely concerned with the internal ordering and symbolization of the community, or, in our terms, with the conversation behind the wall.

17. See the very shrewd discernment of this factor by Herbert N. Schneidau, *Sacred Discontent* (Baton Rouge: Louisiana State University Press, 1976), and the ongoing social, cultural function of that critical dimension.

18. The social analysis of Norman Gottwald supports this. See his *The Tribes of Yahweh* (Maryknoll, N.Y.: Orbis Books, 1979).

19. See Johannes Pedersen, *Israel*, vols. 3–4 (London: Oxford University Press, 1940), 728–37.

20. Michael Fishbane, *Text and Texture* (New York: Schocken Books, 1979), 79–83, has observed the problematic dimension of this transmission from generation to generation.

21. See Walter Harrelson, "Life, Faith and the Emergence of Tradition," in *Tradition and Theology in the Old Testament*, ed. Douglas A. Knight (Philadelphia: Fortress Press, 1977), 11–30.

22. For a remarkable analysis of the pathology of totalitarian voices and the way of recovering healthy speech, see Eugene Rosenstock-Huessey, *The Origin of Speech* (Norwich, Vt.: Argo Books, 1981).

23. The seminal study by Martin Buber, *Kingship of God* (New York: Harper & Row, 1967), anticipated much of what has come later with regard to the political power of this metaphor. In some ways, Buber has anticipated the entire development of Mendenhall and Gottwald, though not, of course, expressed in those terms.

24. See Mendenhall's summary of his analysis in "The Conflict between Value Systems and Social Control," in *Unity and Diversity*, ed. Hans Goedicke and J.J.M. Roberts (Baltimore: Johns Hopkins University Press, 1975), 169–80.

25. Paul D. Hanson, "The Theological Significance of Contradiction within the Book of the Covenant," in *Canon and Authority*, ed. George W. Coats and Burke O. Long (Philadelphia: Fortress Press, 1977), 110–31.

26. One can argue that as the early period tended to be capable of such an intentional social organization, which may be regarded as sectarian, so in the later post-exilic period the same possibility emerged. Thus the social reform of Nehemiah in Neh. 5 bears many of the same marks as the initial intentionality of Moses. It is clear that even in the earliest, most radical social organization of Israel counter-voices continued which were attracted to the concentration of urban power and

resistant to the egalitarian revolution. These voices eventually prevailed in the monarchy. See the papers in *Semeia* 37 (1986): Marvin L. Chaney, "Systemic Study of the Israelite Monarchy," 53–76; Norman K. Gottwald, "The Participation of Free Agrarians in the Introduction of Monarchy to Ancient Israel: An Application of H. A. Landsberger's Framework for the Analysis of Peasant Movements," 77–106; and Robert B. Coote and Keith W. Whitelam, "The Emergence of Israel: Social Transformation Following the Decline in Late Bronze Age Trade," 107–47.

27. Norbert Lohfink, *Great Themes from the Old Testament* (Edinburgh: T. & T. Clark, 1982), 55–75, has indicated that the legal materials of Deuteronomy are in fact intentional about administrative reality, and he finds traces of a "constitution" for a social organization.

28. Hans Walter Wolff, "The Kerygma of the Yahwist," in *The Vitality of Old Testament Traditions*, ed. Walter Brueggemann and Hans Walter Wolff (Atlanta: John Knox Press, 1975), 41–66.

29. The best critical study of these texts is Norman K. Gottwald, *All the Kingdoms of the Earth* (New York: Harper & Row, 1964).

30. Walther Zimmerli, *I Am Yahweh* (Atlanta: John Knox Press, 1982), has shown in a series of articles that the authoritative base for Yahwism is found in the self-disclosure of Yahweh in a formula that belongs in the sectarian community. The intent of Yahweh's actions is that "the nations may know." But the formulas that comment on the acts are formulas that have their setting and sense in the closer community.

31. Gary Herion, "The Social Organization of Tradition in Monarchic Judah," 312–21, has shown how the tradition of Isaiah is a remarkable "blending" of the voices we are seeking to identify.

32. On the complexity of the Isaiah tradition as it came to contain many voices, see Ronald Clements, *Isaiah 1—39*, New Century Bible Commentary (Grand Rapids: Wm. B. Eerdmans, 1980), who is especially influenced by the hypotheses of Hermann Barth, *Die Jesaja-Worte in der Josiazelt* (Neukirchen-Vluyn: Neukirchener, 1977).

33. See Gerhard von Rad, *Old Testament Theology II* (London: Oliver & Boyd, 1965), 147–75.

34. This is what makes Gottwald's proposal so important. See Gottwald, *The Tribes of Yahweh*, 592–607, on the problematic of an idealist reading. More positively on a materialist reading, see Kuno Fussel, "The Materialist Reading of the Bible," in *The Bible and Liberation*, ed. Norman K. Gottwald (Maryknoll, N.Y.: Orbis Books, 1983), 134–46; Fernando Belo, *A Materialist Reading of the Gospel of Mark* (Maryknoll, N.Y.: Orbis Books, 1981), esp. the introductory materials; and Walter J. Hollenweger, "The Other Exegesis," *Horizons in Biblical Theology* 3 (1981): 155–79.

35. It is a pervasive judgment that in recent Old Testament theology too much attention has been paid to the more sectarian traditions to

the neglect of more comprehensive claims. A number of scholars have made proposals to redress that one-sided approach, including Paul Hanson, Samuel Terrien, and Claus Westermann. See my article, "A Convergence in Recent Old Testament Theologies," *Journal for the Study of the Old Testament* 18 (1980): 2–18.

36. See Walther Zimmerli, "Prophetic Proclamation and Reinterpretation," *Tradition and Theology in the Old Testament*, ed. Douglas A. Knight (Philadelphia: Fortress Press, 1977), 69–100; and, more programmatically, Herbert N. Schneidau, *Sacred Discontent: The Bible and Western Tradition* (Berkeley: University of California Press, 1976).

37. On the aniconic character of the tradition, see Dominic Crossan, *Finding Is the First Act* (Philadelphia: Fortress Press, 1979), 93–122.

38. Paul Ricoeur, "Toward a Hermeneutic of the Idea of Revelation," *Essays on Biblical Interpretation*, ed. Lewis S. Mudge (Philadelphia: Fortress Press, 1980). That judgment has been worked out in some detail as concerns education by Craig Dykstra, *Vision and Character* (New York: Paulist Press, 1981).

39. See Herbert Marcuse, *One Dimensional Man* (Boston: Beacon Press, 1968), esp. chap. 4, where he describes the dominant language as becoming so narrow and coercive that it no longer permits serious communication.

40. See the judicious way in which Amos N. Wilder, "Story and Story-World," *Interpretation* 37 (1983): 353–64, has sorted out this matter. He places major stress on the creative power of narrative construction, but in a way that is not subjectivist.

41. On the "oddity" of the text as a way of revelation see Paul Ricoeur, "Biblical Hermeneutics," *Semeia* 4 (1975): 122–29. Such "oddity" belongs to its revelatory power.

42. See my brief consideration of this problem in "The Text 'Makes Sense,'" *The Christian Ministry* 14 (Nov 1983): 7–10.

For ASSYRIA, READ U.S.

4

The Transformative Potential of a Public Metaphor

Isaiah 37:21–29

IN CHAPTER 3 I EXPLORED Israel's life of prayer, worship, and ethical reflection as "a conversation behind the wall." In that conversation, Israel, without explanation or apology to anyone else, engages in conversation about its own fundamental loyalty to Yahweh and its derivative, distinctive identity in the world. I noted that this unexplained, unargued conversation is essential to Israel's faithful life in the world. Israel could not exist without such a distinctive conversation.[1] Moreover, I suggested that in our Euro-American context of moribund Christianity, such a conversation behind the wall is now crucial for the church, in order for it to recover and reconfess its foundational loyalty and distinctive identity in the world.

I used the term "sectarian" to describe that conversation and intended to affirm that the community of faith must have its own speech and cannot articulate its loyalty or its identity in speech that is immediately available to and assessed by outsiders. It is that community that is so crucial in the biblical community and so neglected in the established church.[2] This "prior conversation" is a main concern of the contemporary educational, liturgical, and proclamatory enterprise of the church as it seeks to recover faithful vocation.[3] Such a "prior conversation" permits the community of faith to begin with an alternative epistemology, distinct from the governing rationality of our culture.[4]

To be sure, the notion of "sectarian" is not without cost. The term suggests a withdrawal into a private sphere of social reality. In

70

this chapter I will explore the way in which such a prior conversation may contribute to a "second conversation" on the wall, that is, a conversation faithful people have with others, a conversation in which the sectarian categories of conversation have no special claim or privilege.

THE PUBLIC POWER OF COVENANT

Isaiah 36—37 (2 Kings 18—19) characterizes an encounter between the Assyrian negotiators and the intimidated Judean king, Hezekiah.[5] They meet at the wall of Jerusalem. Then Hezekiah retreats into the city behind the wall to pray to Yahweh and to consult with the prophet Isaiah.

1. Israel's conversation "behind the wall" is shaped by and in the service of the "public metaphor" of *covenant*. Two generations of scholarship, derivative from Mendenhall and Baltzer,[6] have shown that covenantal language in ancient Israel is not expression in a religious idiom but is, rather, akin to the language of international relations in the ancient Near East. Israel seems to have decisively broken from conventional religious language, and prefers a political mode of discourse. Its primal speech of covenanting (rooted in Sinai) concerns governance, sovereignty, public order, public policy, public possibility, and the sanctions that go with such social transactions.[7] Thus the dominant metaphor of Israel's faith is from the outset public and not narrowly Israelite.[8] At the same time, though, this metaphor, even if borrowed, is given concrete substance by Israel from its understanding of the distinctiveness of Yahweh, the Lord of the exodus. Israel's discernment of public issues is derived from and informed by Israel's peculiar discernment of who Yahweh is, remembered from the exodus narrative and articulated in covenant language.[9] Thus, while the dominant metaphor is profoundly public and not the property of a sectarian community, it is public in a very specific way, because the metaphor is filled with Israelite experience. I shall argue below that Christians must be nurtured in this peculiar public metaphor.[10]

In the idiom of this public language of covenant, the preferred metaphors for Yahweh are king, judge, and warrior.[11] Israel conversely is cast in the roles of vassal, suppliant, or accused, and of recruit or beneficiary of Yahweh's power. These metaphors govern and shape Israel's "rules of speech."[12] This is Israel's foundational speech. Israel has no prior speech that is religious, private, or spiritual; its speech is always public, political, and social. This preferred speech shapes the conversation behind the wall.

2. This speech has a *transformative potential* for the conversation on the wall. That is, the peculiar political claims and implications of this speech are not confined to Israel's in-house conversation; they necessarily and powerfully spill over and have impact upon the public arena in which Israel participates but in which Israel's faith and language have no preferred position. The immediate potential of the governing metaphor of covenant which Israel brings to the wall is to insist that the conversation on the wall be a genuinely political conversation, that it talk about power and order among competing, conflicting claims. The transformative potential of this speech is found in the accompanying affirmation that there is a governance of public life that is not at the disposal of or administered by any party on the wall, least of all those who have a monopoly of power.

This covenantal notion of Yahweh's governance of public life has two functions. First, it *deabsolutizes* every claim made on the wall, even those made by the imperial monopoly. While this deabsolutizing formally and theoretically works against every claimant, in fact and in practice it works especially against the voice of monopoly, in Isaiah 36—37 the voice of the Assyrian empire. Second, while this metaphor deabsolutizes, it also *legitimates* the political conversation as a real and serious conversation that takes place under a governance that is not controlled by any of the parties who actively participate in the conversation. Yahweh's governance of public life assures that each voice in the conversation is invulnerable to intimidation and not open to preemption by any of the parties involved.

The twin functions of deabsolutizing and legitimating keep all parties in the conversation from imagining either that some voice at the wall has a better claim than the others or that there is a more important conversation somewhere else in which more significant matters are under discussion and being decided. Deabsolutizing asserts that Assyria may not control the discussion because Yahweh governs. Legitimation asserts that even Israel's voice, in all its frailty, is an important one on the wall. The covenantal metaphor intrudes the holy governance of Yahweh even into the conversation on the wall. Without this intrusive governance, the conversation at the wall inevitably becomes a unilateral decree of imperial domination. It is the covenantal sovereignty of Yahweh, so Israel discerns, that keeps Assyria's voice from dominating and being absolute and keeps the voice of Israel (and all the other vulnerable ones) from being dismissed.

Deabsolutizing and legitimation give rise to a *critical awareness* and a *constructive affirmation*. The critical awareness is that no party in the conversation has a prior claim to truth. There is no source of priority outside the conversation, because all parties are children, subjects, creatures, servants (wittingly or unwittingly) of the God who governs at the wall. Members of the conversation are not who they imagine themselves to be, not autonomous, not detached agents, either in pride or in vulnerability. The constructive affirmation is that the conversation at the wall is real, serious, and legitimate—with all parties having a legitimate voice, because there is a context of governance that provides ordered space for conversation. Thus, chaos will not overwhelm during the risky conversation the Israelites have with Assyria. This affirmation provides legitimacy for every voice to be heard, because every speaking partner is a valued citizen of the same governance.[13]

It is not Israel's right or intent to claim that the conversation on the wall is to be an Israelite conversation. But the peculiar contribution of Israel's faith and language is to transform the shape, character, and possibility of that conversation into a real and serious conversation, rather than the false conversation that the empire will conduct if there is not another governance in the midst of the conversation. Moreover, all conversation at the wall is about power and access, that is, about matters of justice. It is a legitimate conversation because the God who governs at the wall is a "lover of justice" (Ps. 99:4; Isa. 61:8) and entertains no secret conversation elsewhere that will override this conversation. The conversation about justice is always the ultimate conversation. The subject of power, access, and justice that inevitably comes up at the wall is the subject to which the Holy One gives primal attention.[14]

I suggest that Israel's primal metaphor of covenantal sovereignty holds potential for transforming the conversation at the wall into a conversation out of which may come genuine human possibility. But that outcome requires all parties at the wall to be seriously available for real political conversation. Israel's confession that the justice-working God Yahweh has displaced the absolute gods in heaven is the ground for a serious human conversation on earth that may permit human life to be transformed.[15]

THE ENTHRONEMENT LITURGY AS
SUBVERSIVE CLAIM

This proposal that in the public conversation the metaphor of covenant serves to deabsolutize and legitimate requires textual specificity. The texts to which I will give primary attention are in the tradition of Isaiah. I access the Isaiah tradition, however, through the enthronement liturgy on the assumption that the tradition of Isaiah has its foundation very close to the liturgies of the temple.[16]

The beginning point for considering Israel's "public metaphor" is in the enthronement liturgy, reflected in the enthronement psalms. Israel either regularly enacted an enthronement of Yahweh or imitated such an enthronement.[17] For our purposes, the distinction is not important. This liturgy is reflected in Psalm 96 which no doubt was enacted "behind the wall" but which spills over beyond Israel in its imaginative thrust.[18]

The political rhetoric of governance is found throughout Psalm 96. Indeed there would be no poem or liturgic act without the political rhetoric. Israel's worship is relentlessly political. Verses 1–6 are a general summons to praise, on the basis of Yahweh's defeat of the idols, that is, the false claims of other peoples in their ideological commitments (v. 5). Verses 11–13 characterize the world derived from Yahweh's new rule. It is a rule characterized by righteousness and truth (v. 13). This newly ordered world evokes from all of creation glad rejoicing (vv. 11–12). Between the summons (vv. 1–6) and the characterization (vv. 11–13) is the actual enthronement formula, "Yahweh reigns," or as Sigmund Mowinckel might have rendered, "Yahweh has just become king" (in this moment of liturgical enactment). The liturgy asserts, enacts, and celebrates a new governance that has concrete and specific significance.

For our purposes, it is crucial to observe the scope of the psalm, which in principle moves beyond Israel, beyond Israel's conversation behind the wall. The glory is to be declared "among the nations, among the peoples" (v. 3). The summons is to "the families of the peoples" (v. 7); the whole earth is to "tremble" (v. 9). The enthronement formula of v. 10 is to be said "among the nations." "The peoples" are to be judged with equity (v. 10). The earth, the world, the peoples are to be judged with righteousness and truth (v. 13). It is amazing that there is no reference to Israel, election, David, Jerusalem, or temple. While the Jerusalem establishment is surely the context for the poem, it will not be contained in that context or in that conversation. It pushes beyond Israel to its real addressees, the nations, who are the ones who must know, who are summoned, and who are reassured. The ones behind the wall are given no privilege or acknowledgment but must participate in the claims of the poem only as one of the peoples and with the other peoples, all of whom are at the wall together. They are all there, under the governance of Yahweh that is now freshly proclaimed. This liturgic enterprise serves to place Israel among the nations, without preferential position. The temptation to sectarian privilege is overcome!

Yahweh's kingship and comprehensive governance concern the world of the nations, not especially Israel. All are judged by the same norms. The book of Isaiah in its canonical form gives the most sustained and effective articulation of this theme of enthronement over the world of the nations.[19] It is a commonplace that the Isaiah tradition pays no great attention to the covenantal traditions of Moses but is primarily grounded in the Jerusalem traditions of Zion and David. The current two-stage canonical reading of the traditions of Isaiah affirms that Yahweh judges and rescues, certainly in Israel, but finally among all the nations.[20] The dramatic use of the enthronement formula in Isa. 52:7 deabsolutizes Babylonian claims and invites a new possibility for Israel. The Isaiah tradition specifies the claim of sovereignty made in the enthronement liturgy of Psalm 96. Indeed, it is likely that the Isaiah tradition takes up the liturgical tradition of the Jerusalem psalms and appropriates them for prophetic use. In the prophet as in the liturgy, the text focuses on Yahweh's governance over Israel and the nations. With this background, we can now turn to the text of Isaiah 37.

ISAIAH 37:21–29: A MODEL
FOR CONVERSATION

Hezekiah has made a petition through Isaiah (Isa. 37:16–20). In this responsive oracle from the prophet, King Hezekiah and Israel (and even Isaiah) are no longer pertinent characters (Isa. 37:21–29). The characters who have been important behind the wall have disappeared in the rhetoric of this passage. Now there is only Yahweh who speaks at the wall, who undertakes a one-sided conversation directly with Assyria. This development in the exchange is intentionally ironic. The Assyrians had thought there was no one at the wall with them except the frightened Judean king whom they could intimidate (Isa. 36:4–10, 13–20; 37:10–13). Assyria had failed to reckon with Yahweh as a serious voice and presence at the wall. Indeed, the Assyrians had mockingly treated Yahweh as though Yahweh were at the most a feeble party behind the wall in the sectarian imagination of Israel, but not a serious, present party on the wall (Isa. 36:18–20). Now, however, in the oracle Yahweh speaks.

It is immediately clear that Yahweh will not be intimidated or banished by Assyria's harsh rhetoric. As Yahweh now speaks directly to and with Assyria, in a dramatic sense the conversation has a changed venue. Israel is not even present, and as Assyria quickly notes, it has overestimated its own importance and miscalculated about one other voice at the wall.

Thus Isa. 37:21–29 offers clues and a model for conversation at the wall. Verse 22 asserts that Zion/Jerusalem "despises"/"scorns"/ "wags [its] head" at Assyria. The empire, which takes itself so seriously, is dismissed even by this modest adversary. The poetry serves to dismantle Assyrian claims to preeminence. Even little Judah now dares to despise and dismiss self-impressed Assyria, who is on the way down. But notice that Israel does not voice its scorn until that scorn can be put in the more formidable mouth of Yahweh.

The poem falls into two main units: vv. 23–25, a taunting indictment, and vv. 26–29, a counterassertion by Yahweh. The first part (vv. 23–25) toys with the arrogant claims of Assyria, the second (vv. 26–29) celebrates the legitimate claims of Yahweh. The poem is structured to present a one-sided contest to determine whether Assyria or Yahweh is the more powerful.[21] The contest is one-sided not because Assyria does not act but because Assyria is never even permitted to speak, except through the quotations of Yahweh.[22] Israel is completely absent and has no status, no claim, no presence, no voice. And Assyria is not much better off. Assyria is the addressee but is never permitted an initiative. To be reduced to silence is to be eliminated from the flow of power. In the drama of the poem, the speaking of Yahweh now dominates all the action at the wall. All others are reduced to silence in the presence of Yahweh. It is a silence of deference and intimidation. Yahweh is thereby acknowledged as sovereign.

Claim

Verses 22–24 respond to the accusatory prayer of Hezekiah (v. 16) who said that Assyria had "mocked" Yahweh. Yahweh can vividly remember what Hezekiah has said behind the wall but makes no allusion to it, neither quoting Hezekiah nor proceeding with accusatory hearsay from behind the wall. It is nonetheless clear that what Yahweh says on the wall is responsive to what was said by the king behind the wall. The conversation continues to focus on Assyrian self-importance (cf. 10:12–14), which imagines the empire autonomous, absolute, self-sufficient, and in charge at the wall.

The conflict between Yahweh and Sennacherib is clear in v. 23, a question in two parts:

> Whom have you mocked and reviled?
> Against whom have you raised your voice and haughtily lifted
> 　　your eyes?

The answer is immediate and uncompromising: "Against the Holy One of Israel." Against anyone else, Assyria likely could have made a legitimate case. Indeed, Assyria was used to making a compelling case against the gods who are no gods (Isa. 36:19). The problem in this instance is that Assyria reckoned Yahweh to be like the others. Assyria and the other powerful nations always misunderstood, always failed to reckon with the distinctiveness of Yahweh before whom every imperial claim is destabilized. The question (v. 23a) and answer (v. 23b), both from Yahweh, admit of no negotiation. Assyria is indicted. More important, the empire is delegitimated in the eyes of all the nations. Its special claims have been shown to be fraudulent.

The mocking done by the empire was in order to claim absolute-ness, a claim with which Hezekiah could not cope and Yahweh will not tolerate. Yahweh dismisses the absolute claim. Assyria is not driven from the wall by Yahweh, but is now required to be at the wall in a very different tone and posture.

Verses 24–25 are words allegedly spoken by Assyria that give particulars to the indictment of v. 22. The words are now spoken by Yahweh. Assyria has mocked Yahweh by making outrageous, ill-founded claims for itself at the expense of Yahweh's distinctive and unrivaled claims. Assyria's dismissive statement quoted by Yahweh is dominated by first-person references:

> You said, . . . my chariots,
> > I have gone up,
> > I filled,
> > I entered,
> > I dug,
> > I drank,
> > I dried up.

In Assyria's speech of self-congratulations, no one else is significant or taken into account, not even Yahweh. Assyria is an autonomous self-starter and imagines it holds the initiative in the world process, even daring to govern the Nile (cf. Ezek. 29:3). More than only an arrogant speech, this is enormously intimidating to others who come to the wall for conversation. At the wall, Judah could hardly answer, because Assyria seemed to have done all that it claimed. And if Assyria could do all that it claimed, clearly Judah could do nothing and dare not speak. The conversation at the wall is finished before it begins, ending in overriding domination.

This conversation at the wall, if governed by Assyria's language and not by the language spoken behind the wall, is open to two distortions. First, the conversation may be distorted if the major party (Assyria) claims an absolute priority so that while justice is ostensibly under discussion, it is a distorted justice in which key power questions are already settled. This is a distortion of *political absolutism*, and it precludes any serious conversation.[23] The second distortion is one of trivialization.[24] Here, the lesser party (Israel) is so positioned that its only modes of functioning are deference and docility; serious exchange is again precluded.

The oracle of the prophet, as a countervoice to these distortions, serves to assert that the conversation at the wall never involves only the voice of Assyria with all other voices intimidated into silence. Yahweh is decisively present in the conversation at the wall, and this holy presence changes all talk and reshapes the conversation. In the presence of Yahweh, Assyria must speak differently, if at all. As a result, we may imagine that the frightened participants such as Judah may regain something of their courage and their voice. Indeed Yahweh at the wall permits genuine conversation. Yahweh has broken the power of the fearful, imperial monologue.

Counterclaim

The second half of the oracle (vv. 26–29) is a counterclaim in which the claims of Yahweh (here fully held to be legitimate) displace the claims of the empire. The central assertion, uttered mockingly, is, "I have done it." Assyria may not mock Yahweh, but Yahweh may and does mock Assyria, for Assyria is a derivative power and a dependent party. Yahweh claims to have ordered, planned, and decreed all of Assyria's powerful acts (v. 26). It is acknowledged that Assyria has done all those acts, but not of its own initiative, not under its own authority, and not out of its own imagination. Assyria could not do what it does without Yahweh's authorization. Assyria is reduced to a secondary cause; Yahweh is the only primary cause. Assyria awaits Yahweh's initiative and good pleasure.

Yahweh asserts, "I know" (v. 28). I know all you do, all you intend, all you think. Yahweh's "I know" is a partner to "Have you not heard?" (v. 26). I know—did you not know (cf. Isa. 40:21)? Yahweh knows, has always known. Assyria has not yet caught on. Assyria is operating without all the necessary data. Indeed, Yahweh operates on a "need to know" basis. Assyria did not need to know and therefore does not know. And because Assyria does not know, the empire is not omnipotent.

Assyria imagined it knew more than it did. As a result of that misinformed imagination, Assyria was too pretentious, too dismissive of Yahweh (vv. 28b–29a). Now Yahweh judges Assyria and turns the empire back from its intimidating, arrogant, self-serving invasion. Assyria runs precisely against the overriding will of Yahweh—and must yield.[25]

In both form and substance, this is an extraordinary poem. In form, it is remarkable because it is speech directed from Yahweh to Sennacherib. Israel is no party to the conversation. Yahweh, to be sure, is referred to as the "Holy One of Israel" (v. 23), but beyond that, the reality of Israel is of no moment. Yahweh is the God who governs Assyria, whom Assyria will need to acknowledge. If that acknowledgment is not made willingly, then it will be made painfully. In substance, roles are reversed by the poem. The one who mocked is now the one mocked and reduced to a subordinate status. Yahweh presides at the conversation on the wall. The conversation at the wall will therefore need to be conducted from assumptions very different from those made by the empire and from those made by the frightened Hezekiah. Kings in Israel take the empire too seriously. A prophetic oracle is indispensable in order that both Assyria and Israel may rightly discern the true character of this conversation. Without that prophetic clarification, the conversation likely will be distorted either toward absolutism or trivialization.

NATIONS AT THE BEHEST OF GOD

The critical problems related to the oracle of Isa. 37:21–29 are difficult and complex.[26] In its rhetoric, scope, and daring, the oracle is sufficiently congruent with the tradition of Isaiah, however, that we may legitimately consider other Isaiah texts in relation to it. More than any other prophetic literature, the Isaiah tradition attends to the conversation at the wall, the public conversation outside the community of faith.[27] In the tradition of Isaiah, Yahweh deals directly with the other nations, without Israel as mediator. According to the Isaiah tradition, Yahweh's treatment of the other nations, especially Assyria, involves agentry, judgment, and anticipated election.

1. Assyria (and Babylon and Persia) are *agents of Yahweh* whose purposes are worked out among the empires. This agentry is not intentional, willing, or knowing on the part of the empire and its leaders but is nonetheless definitional for the way these nations are understood in the international process. Thus Yahweh dispatches Assyria, who is said to be Yahweh's razor, to shave the head of Judah (Isa. 7:17–20). The most familiar statement of the use of Assyria as Yahweh's agent is in Isa. 10:5–19, which contains a com-

plete philosophy of history about the relation of God and the nations. A single couplet from this unit is enough to demonstrate that Assyria is Yahweh's agent:

Rod of my anger,
Staff of my fury. (10:5)

Yahweh summons the nations, even the empires, by a whistle, and they do Yahweh's bidding (7:18). The empire is "on call" from Yahweh. Assyria is summoned to enact Yahweh's will "against a godless nation" (10:6).

2. The very imperial nations that are recruited and mobilized by Yahweh are *subject to Yahweh's will and judgment*. When the nations violate that will, it is as if they violate torah stipulations and receive covenant curses. In the world of *Realpolitik*, we may say the empire has no awareness of Yahweh's will or of covenant conditions, certainly not of limits. Clearly the nations do not understand themselves to have bonded themselves willingly to such conditions. In the world of prophetic imagination, however, these nations are not free beyond Yahweh's governance. Thus the arrogance so poignantly presented in 37:23–25 is anticipated in 10:13–14, again in a first-person decree of arrogance placed in the mouth of Sennacherib, again asserted with intimidating self-assurance:

By the strength of my hand I have done it,
By my wisdom . . .
I have removed, . .
I have plundered, . .
I have brought down, . .
my hand, . .
I have gathered.

I have done it all! The language parallels Yahweh's in 37:26. The question now joined is, How has Assyria "done it"? In Isaiah 37, Yahweh, not Assyria, has done it. Here, in Isaiah 10, the point is somewhat different: Assyria has indeed done it—but without legitimacy or authorization.

Assyria has claimed too much and has imagined autonomy. But imperial autonomy is not true and will not be tolerated. In Isaiah 47, an oracle against Babylon, an ethical criterion for assessing the nations is introduced: "You showed no mercy." But here, the claim is not ethical but theological. Assyria imagined autonomy but is not autonomous. Therefore Assyria stands under massive judgment (10:16–19). Again, Judah plays no role in the transaction between Yahweh and Assyria. Indeed the only apparent reference to Judah is in 10:6:

> Against a godless nation . . .
> against the people of my wrath . . .

It is remarkable that through the rhetoric of this poem, Judah is dismissed. Judah has no status at all, and Assyria is not condemned for not being generous to Judah. What counts is only the acknowledged sovereignty of Yahweh, which Assyria cannot outflank.

3. Assyria, the one summoned as a useful agent (10:5), the one held under judgment as excessively recalcitrant (10:13–14), is finally anticipated to become *God's chosen people*:

> In that day there will be a highway from Egypt to Assyria, and the Assyrian will come into Egypt, and the Egyptian into Assyria, and the Egyptians will worship with the Assyrians.
> In that day, Israel will be the third with Egypt and Assyria, a blessing in the midst of the earth, whom the Lord of hosts has blessed, saying, "Blessed be Egypt my people, and Assyria the work of my hands, and Israel my heritage" (Isa. 19:23–25).[28]

Yahweh will stay with Assyria through all these early, troubled dealings for the sake of a promised outcome—a time when Assyria will be peculiarly beloved of Yahweh. To be sure, Assyria is not to be the only chosen people. It is anticipated not that Assyria will have a monopoly or a special relationship with Yahweh, but, rather, that Assyria will share this status with—of all peoples—Egypt and Israel! Verses 23–25 take three terms traditionally reserved for precious, beloved Israel and apply two of them to Judah's worst threats and Yahweh's greatest nemeses. We have seen that with Assyria as agent of Yahweh and object of Yahweh's judgment, Judah has played no part. But Israel is present with Assyria as a chosen people—as an equal, however, not in a preferred status. It is anticipated that all of these peoples will become chosen peoples of Yahweh, that all the peoples in the conversation on the wall will become Yahweh's preferred partners. When that happens, the family conversation behind the wall will become unnecessary because the conversation at the wall will be open, honest, responsive, and respectful of all parties, for all parties are among the chosen.[29]

Thus the public conversation between Yahweh and Assyria is not a conversation fixed in a certain posture. It is a conversation that has a history to it, and this history has an end-goal. The end-goal (and the sure outcome) is that even the empire will be a beloved partner and creature of Yahweh. Yahweh does indeed articulate and enact wrath and judgment against the empire, but Yahweh's actions do not culminate in hostility. Yahweh hopes and promises that even recalcitrant Assyria will come to its true identity and will conduct itself accordingly in the conversation on the wall.

The public metaphor of covenantal sovereignty has the potential of transforming the conversation at the wall. It has that potential because (1) Yahweh has a long, ongoing relation with Assyria, and (2) Yahweh has a firm hope and intention for Assyria which is sovereign and covenantal. This resolve of Yahweh intends that, in the end, the conversation at the wall will be conducted with covenantal sensitivity toward the will of Yahweh and toward the reality of others (Judah) at the wall. This will happen when Assyria comes to its true status and identity as one of Yahweh's chosen peoples, chosen for well-being and obedience.

YAHWEH'S LARGE GOVERNANCE

The rhetorical transaction that Yahweh has with Assyria, proposed by the poet in Isaiah 37, is complex and subtle in its intention.

1. Within the drama, it is Assyria who is addressed. The oracle moves from behind the wall, where there is a "sectarian" conversation, to the wall, where there is a "public" conversation. Israel/Judah is scarcely a presence in this conversation. The text indicates that Yahweh is capable of and appropriate to public discourse. The intention of the oracle is to position properly even Assyria as a creature and servant of Yahweh, albeit a recalcitrant and unwitting one.

The practical effect of the oracle is to draw Assyria into the public metaphor of Israel's speech, to require Assyria to participate in and be shaped by the Israelite metaphor of covenantal sovereignty. As a result, Assyria's pretended autonomy and daring absolutism are theologically denied and rhetorically dismantled. The dramatic result is to force Assyria to participate on the wall in a new and appropriate posture. This requirement is so demanding that to meet it, the empire must give up most of its characteristic claims and postures at the wall. Now Assyria knows that there is a governance that permits and requires a genuine political conversation in which Assyria—as other conversation partners—is subject to and cared for by Yahweh.

2. When the oracle is appropriated critically, it is clear that the oracle is addressed to Israel and not to Assyria. We have no reason to think Assyria ever heard this poem or that Isaiah or the canonical process ever intended Assyria to hear it. The poem is intended for Israel, who is invited to "overhear" what Yahweh has said to Assyria.[30]

Given that "overhearing," we may ask, What is the poem intending to communicate to Israel? Most likely the purpose of the poem is to permit and authorize Israel to be "at the wall" with a different perception of reality and therefore with a different voice. It is important that Assyria be deabsolutized so that someone else may speak. It is even more important that Judah experience and perceive Assyria to be deabsolutized. Judah can then participate at the wall with a new kind of legitimacy and courage. Without this oracle, Assyria seemed inordinately powerful, even as it claimed to be (cf. Isa. 36:8–9). More than that, Assyria's dominating role seemed ordained of the gods (Isa. 36:10). It would be easy to conclude then that the conversation at the wall is no real conversation, because the empire has preempted all decisions. There will be no serious and free political exchange if one power practices totalism.[31]

The intent of the oracle, I suggest, is not to give Judah any false assurances, not to pretend that Judah will prevail on the wall, for no such "sectarian" claim is made. Appeal to the sovereign reality of Yahweh must no more foreclose the conversation on behalf of Judah than Assyria is permitted to foreclose the conversation in its own interest. Rather, the oracle creates an arena of imagination in which there is no preferred partner in the conversation. The oracle legitimates Judah's agenda of justice and precludes excessive submission to the empire or excessive despair in the face of the empire. Notice that the oracle legitimates not Judah, but Judah's normative passion for justice. The governance of Yahweh so dramatically asserted in the oracle does not resolve the problems to be discussed at the wall, but it creates a context in which new settlements must be boldly pursued. The oracle precludes any imperial preemption by Assyria and any religious preference for Judah. The governance of Yahweh intends to guarantee a serious concern about urgent human matters shared by all parties at the wall, and to deny any voice at the wall self-serving veto power over the conversation.

3. The oracle addressed to Assyria and overheard by Judah authorizes a specific conversation by working two dimensions of destabilization. First, Assyria's grand claim of autonomy and self-sufficiency is destabilized, for even Assyria is seen to be a creature and agent of Yahweh and not more. In 10:5ff., the attempt to act beyond Yahweh's mandate and imagine something is done "by my strength, . . . by my wisdom" meets with sharp and harsh nullification. Not even Assyria is free beyond these mandates from Yahweh.

Second, by relating the oracle of 37:21–29 to the promise of 19:23–25, it is clear that Israel's special claim is also destabilized. It would be simpler to say that Yahweh is allied not with Assyria but with Israel. That ideological claim is not in the text, however. Neither in 10:5ff. nor in 37:22–29 is any transfer of preference made from Assyria to Israel. The argument is made on grounds of sovereignty over all, not election for some. This represents an important check on any sectarian claim, for the sovereignty of God is not intrinsically associated with Israel's historical significance or well-being. All parties on the wall must face Yahweh's sovereignty and speak free of their ideological claims of empire or sect, of the arrogance of power or the arrogance of religious preference.

The promise of Isa. 19:23–25 goes further in its specificity about Yahweh's peculiar sovereignty. It is an electing sovereignty. We know it is an electing sovereignty through Israel's peculiar experience and language of election. But Israel's peculiar language and experience move beyond Israel. Yahweh wills to govern at the wall as well as behind the wall, over Assyria as well as over Judah. What is known of Yahweh's character and governance is known from transactions behind the wall. The language spoken behind the wall concerning election is not abandoned when the conversation moves to the wall, for what is learned behind the wall is pertinent to and definitional for the wall. The categories (which might be termed "sectarian") are retained, even at the wall.

As Yahweh is not the enemy of Israel (as Hezekiah knows and trusts), so Yahweh wills not to be the enemy of Assyria. The oracle anticipates an overcoming of all such enmity. Assyria is not summoned by Yahweh to cease to be Assyria, any more than Israel is asked to give up its identity as Israel. But Assyria is expected to be the Assyria of Yahweh who is a God of justice. When both Assyria and Israel know that a governance of justice is the future of the empire, they can both enter the conversation afresh. They can both have a different sense of the other and can have a very different conversation on the wall, a conversation genuinely political and permitting new social possibilities. As Assyria, an enemy of Yahweh, is to become "the work of my hands," so Israel is "a godless nation" (10:6) but nonetheless "my heritage" (19:25). All parties at the wall are invited to their true identity, an identity in each case yet to be embraced.

4. It is curious and important that the poem pays no attention to Israel except for identifying Yahweh as "the Holy One of Israel" (37:23). That identifying formula may be only a convention, and perhaps more should not be made of it.[32] But for our purposes, the phrase is important. Yahweh's identity is linked to Israel. Yahweh is the God of Israel known by the nations as one who has special transactions behind the wall with Judah (cf. Num. 14:13–16). The nations may not know that Yahweh will regard Egypt as "my people" or Assyria as "the work of my hands," but Yahweh is everywhere surely known as One who claims Israel as "my heritage." That peculiar identification means that Yahweh is known inalienably as One who makes covenantal commitments and practices solidarity.

But this one allied with Israel is "the Holy One." Yahweh is not mere patron and ally to Israel or to any covenant partner. The entire identifying formula of Isa. 37:23 asserts that Yahweh's identity is too restless and free to be held in captivity to that one sectarian conviction; it will break out beyond that conversation where Yahweh can be the Holy One of Assyria and the Holy One of Egypt, as well as the Holy One of Israel. Thus the phrase of 37:23 suits well our notion of a bilingual conversation with Yahweh as present for, central to, and involved in all dimensions of conversation. The conversation with Israel has priority and gives the categories for all of Yahweh's other conversations. All of these conversations, with Israel and with the nations, concern covenantal sovereignty of God who is *"with,"* yet a God who will not be mocked. Assyria at the wall is invited to learn that Yahweh will not be mocked and, in due time, to learn about "Yahweh with"—even Assyria.

YAHWEH'S HIDDEN INTENTIONALITY

As Israel moves out of its sectarian conversation behind the wall to a public conversation in the midst of the empire, it knows that it must speak and be present in a different way. Israel is committed to Yahweh's covenantal sovereignty as the overriding subject of all its conversation. But Israel also knows that this covenantal sovereignty must be spoken about differently in the midst of conversation partners who have not embraced this covenant or decided about this sovereignty. All of Israel's conversation, behind the wall and at the wall, is about the rule of Yahweh. The centrality of this claim changes all transactions. Put most succinctly and directly, this claim about the rule of God is expressed in the liturgical formula "Yahweh is king."[33] That simple statement legitimates certain conversations, destabilizes some conversation partners, and critiques some assumptions about the conversation at the wall.

But Israel also knows that it cannot in the presence of others at the wall directly and blatantly operate with and appeal to this affirmation about Yahweh's covenantal sovereignty. Israel must operate with confessional reticence and critical subtlety in its public conversation for two reasons. First, not all the parties to the public conversations subscribe to this central affirmation of Israel's identity. Some will be affronted and scandalized. Some will misunderstand. Some will regard themselves as excluded by a statement that is heard as polemical. Israel cannot speak as though all the others subscribe to this language and understand this mode of discourse.

But second, and perhaps most important, it is not unambiguously clear—even to Israel itself—that Yahweh is fully king. In public places, Yahweh's rule is at best hidden, hidden in historical-political processes that can be given other, more convincing explanations, hidden in actions and conditions that seem to dispute the very claim itself. That is, imperial logic could explain the politics of the Fertile Crescent in terms of Assyrian power, without reference to the God of Israel. At the wall there are other claimants to sovereignty who can marshal evidence for their claims. (That, in fact, is what Sennacherib is doing in his triumphalist bombast at the wall in Isa. 36:4–10, 13–20; 37:10–13.)

Israel's speech and faith must assume and affirm the legitimating, destabilizing rule of Yahweh, but must be about that affirmation in ways that honor both the disbelief of others and the *hiddenness of the reality* affirmed. This way of speaking is crucial if Israel is to have a serious voice in public conversations and if Yahweh is to be seriously acknowledged in the public conversation. Such speech is found for Israel in the *voice of wisdom*, which speaks about the hidden rule of Yahweh in the normal life-processes of persons and states.[34]

1. The use of wisdom categories for public conversation precludes direct speech about Yahweh's decisive actions. Wisdom categories for faith prefer to talk about God's forceful, hidden intentionality operating in the midst of visible events.[35] That hidden intentionality (which is a mode of sovereignty) affirms that there are interrelations between cause and effect, between deed and consequence, and that these interrelations are the expression of God's sure rule.[36] These interrelations are concerned not only with the "natural," but also involve ethical and moral behavior.[37] Acts of injustice that violate the ordered reality of Yahweh's world bring hurt and eventually death.[38] Wisdom teaching as a mode of Yahwistic faith discerns in human experience the power of a righteous will that cannot be nullified, disregarded, or, as Hezekiah understood so well, mocked.

2. Wisdom as a mode of theological reflection is powerfully at work in the tradition of Isaiah.[39] Johannes Fichtner and J. William Whedbee[40] have paid careful attention to the use of the sapiential genre of speech, and Fichtner hypothesizes that Isaiah the prophet was at various times and in various ways a wisdom teacher. Indeed, Fichtner gives special attention to the use of "council" as motif in Isaiah, suggesting that the tradition of Isaiah relies greatly on the notion that Yahweh has a "plan" that is being worked out in the public arena.[41] That plan, as the tradition affirms, is hidden, relent-

less, and ethically concerned. It is hidden in the affairs of nations so that it is not self-evident that the affairs of states are actually related to the rule of Yahweh. Thus the oracle from Isaiah 37:21–28 agrees that Assyria did all of its alleged actions but asserts that Yahweh destined the empire to act. The plan is relentless, for Yahweh will not quit until it is accomplished; Isa. 14:24–27 asserts that none can annul or resist the intent of Yahweh. The plan is ethical because Yahweh will finally create a city of justice and a world of righteousness.[42]

Israel asks nations and empires not to believe directly in the rule of Yahweh but to observe the hidden, relentless, ethical intentionality that is being worked out in the processes of history. The powerful nations at the conversation on the wall may imagine that public life is a series of ad hoc decisions and technical achievements made by the powerful and the skillful. Israel, because of its conversation behind the wall, knows that life cannot be reduced to ad hoc happenings, either technical in their explanation or marked by raw power. Technology and power are not adequate ways to understand the moral shape of the historical process; it finally requires the reality of Yahweh for full understanding.

Against the "plan of Yahweh" is a counterplan rooted in the counterwisdom of the nations, which will lead to death. The wisdom of the nations is a wisdom that is marked by an astonishing foolishness. Israel knows about this foolishness in its own life (Isa. 1:2–3). Israel itself "does not know, . . . does not understand" (1:3): it does not recognize Yahweh's rule and therefore imagines it can have its own rule. Later in the tradition, the insistence of Yahweh's hidden, relentless, ethical "plan" is said to be an alternative to Israel's "wicked plan" to submit to the claims of the empire (now Babylon) (Isa. 55:6–9). Israel's foolishness is contrasted with Yahweh's plan. Yahweh's plan is to trust in Yahweh, not in the power of the empires.

As the "plan" is for Israel an invitation to trust, so it is for the others at the wall as well. Assyria imagines it is "by the strength of my hand, by my wisdom" (Isa. 10:13) that the empire has done its work,[43] but the tradition of Isaiah counters such a claim. Yahweh's counterclaim is made in two ways. First, the way of the empire is not wise but foolish. It is foolish because it imagines autonomy, and therefore it generates a plan lacking in ethical sensitivity. This plan leads to death. Second, the imperial plan cannot succeed because it has only the vaporous resolve of the empire to implement it, and that will not work in the face of the resilience of Yahweh. Thus Yahweh's foolishness overrides Assyria's wisdom. Yahweh's weakness overrides Assyria's strength.[44]

In this mode of thinking, Israel's faith does not directly speak about Yahweh's intervention. It speaks, rather, of resolve, decree, determination, plan. The visible implementation of the plan can be understood and explained in other ways. What finally counts for Israel, however, is this hidden intentionality that Israel has discerned but the nations in their arrogance tend not to notice.[45]

THE POTENTIAL FOR TRANSFORMATION

It remains now to consider what this argument implies and proposes for the church today. I urged in chapter 3 that church education must be boldly sectarian, that is, it must be concerned for the nurture of a peculiar identity that is not embarrassed in the face of the nations and does not offer explanations according to the rationality of alien epistemologies. The North American church has generally failed to address this dimension of nurture, because it views such a perspective as intellectually embarrassing. The mainline church does not want to appear to be obscurantist. As a result, the church tends to suffer from a failure of nerve and a lack of conviction about its own validity and modes of knowing.

Conversely, I would argue that nurture into an unembarrassed identity and vocation is by itself inadequate, important as it is. Along with such nurture, attention must be given to the transformative potential of Israel's public metaphor. On the one hand, the mainline church has not nurtured an unembarrassed and peculiar identity and vocation. This has made Christians susceptible to dominant cultural values and robbed us of any critical sense of the difference Christian faith may make. On the other hand, it is equally the case that the church has not effectively nurtured either an awareness of the centrality of a public metaphor of God's sovereign covenant rule or an awareness that that public metaphor has pertinence in our public life. This has made Christianity either privatistic in public conversation (and therefore irrelevant) or too ready to accept the categories of others (and therefore compliant and accommodating). Without such education for public life, Christians themselves become either irrelevant or accommodating and thus unable to be present in the public conversation in a distinctive or effective way.

I suggest that the shifted rhetoric of Isa. 37:21–29, which presents Yahweh as addressing Assyria directly without Israel's mediation, is an invitation for church nurture in public metaphors. That is, we are not addressed directly by this oracle any more than is Hezekiah. The only people directly addressed are the Assyrians, those who control dominant public power. I argue, however, that this oracle initially was not intended for Assyrian hearing. The address to Assyria is a rhetorical strategy, and we may surmise that Assyria in fact did not hear this oracle. Rather, the oracle is ostensibly addressed to the empire precisely for Israel's overhearing. Hezekiah is invited to overhear, and on the basis of the overhearing, to be present differently at the wall.

I submit that we, in our contemporary context of church education, are included as the third listener, after Assyria and Hezekiah. Our overhearing is crucial for our educational process. We are invited to hear what Yahweh says directly to the nations, those who do not share the faith but do hold power. In that overhearing, we learn that Yahweh's presence at the wall deabsolutizes the empire and legitimates lesser voices that have been dismissed as politically irrelevant. While Yahweh's presence and voice at the wall are formally evenhanded concerning all parties at the wall, in effect the speech of Yahweh is a partisan presence that serves the interests of the lesser voices by legitimating them and criticizes the dominant voice by showing that it is not absolute and should not be taken absolutely. Overhearing such a voice and discerning such a presence in the midst of the empire may instruct the church in an awareness that every dominating voice—including our own—is destabilized, and every timid, intimidated voice—including our own—is authorized and taken seriously at the wall.

In one important aspect, education is overhearing what Yahweh says in public to the nations, that is, to other claimants to ultimate power. I suggest three important educational outcomes of such overhearing, which may counteract the accommodating, trivializing propensity of the church.

1. This overhearing makes clear that *Yahweh is indeed present in and concerned for the public conversation*. Yahweh does converse with the powers of the world. This is an enormously important point, even before we ask about the subject matter of such a conversation. It is important that there is a conversation among such parties that includes Yahweh. The existence of the conversation asserts that Yahweh has a sphere of concern and influence beyond "me," beyond "us," beyond the church, beyond our conventional horizon of faith. Yahweh cares intensely about the formation of public policy and the deployment of public power. This dimension of concern is definitional for Yahweh and is not an addendum to a spiritual or private faith. To be educated in faith is to overhear this ongoing conversation and, as a result of overhearing, to have a different sense of who the parties are, how they are related to each other, and what they are saying to each other.

2. This overhearing notices that *Yahweh is present as sovereign in the public sphere*. Yahweh speaks and is present according to the liturgy which asserts that "Yahweh is king." This claim of sovereignty in the real world is ambiguous and in dispute. The other claimants in the public conversation, for example, Pharaoh, Sennacherib, and Caesar, do not readily concede the point of Yahweh's sovereignty, and indeed may never do so. Moreover, the data for deciding sovereignty is in fact quite mixed. What is important is that Yahweh, the God of exodus and exile, the one known in crucifixion and resurrection, the one who acts in relation to slavery and freedom, injustice and justice, death and life, is fully engaged in the dispute. Yahweh is not present as a lesser partner, as a chaplain or as a mascot, but as an adversary in a disputed conversation in which the stakes are very high.

It may be that those who overhear will still excessively esteem the claims of the other parties to the dispute and will give their real loyalty elsewhere. Overhearing the conversation does not automatically convince, because the data is disputed. When listening, some may judge Sennacherib to have the better case. But never again will the claim of Pharaoh or Sennacherib or Caesar be lightly and uncritically accepted. That claim will remain forever criticized, unsettled, in dispute, open to question, and provisional at best. It may be acceptable liturgically to affirm that the dispute is over and Yahweh's sovereignty is fully established. In the process of public life, however, it is less important (and we are less likely) to settle the dispute than to participate in the dispute, which is still vigorously under way. Those who overhear are no longer simply observers waiting for the conclusion, ready to applaud the winner. They are rather parties to the conversation about the dispute. Such an overhearing precludes a lesser gospel to which public issues are carried late.

3. The overhearing reminds us that God's intervention as sovereign may be celebrated directly in the liturgy. But *God's sovereign interventions are discerned in life only indirectly, in hidden ways.* That is why the conversation is always overheard and never heard directly. It is not clear that Yahweh prevails over Assyria, that Yahweh is stronger than Sennacherib. It is not clear on any given day at the wall that well-being overrides fear, that justice prevails over brutality, that peace overrides greed. The evidence is mixed. The agentry of Yahweh is not visible or convincing. Overhearing invites us to watch with subdued language, to speak less directly, to witness to God's painful intentionality but not God's direct transformation. This learning protects the ones who overhear from glib expectations and from the embarrassed fatigue that would result.

There is now a need, a yearning, and an invitation for those who are schooled in overhearing. The ones who have heard the poetic, prophetic assertion of Yahweh's rule may be invited to two fresh awarenesses, one negative, one positive. Negatively they are made aware that the language behind the wall is not insulated from disputes about sovereignty. Nor is it language that can be used directly in public discourse. Positively they are made aware that at the wall some discerning form of the language behind the wall is pertinent, even if subdued. And because some form of this language is credible, we need not embrace immediately the language of Assyria which preempts political reality and wrongly characterizes the public process of political and economic power in terms of imperial monopoly. The utilization of subdued language from behind the wall is a nervy protest against a presumed monopoly.

When Christians do not "overhear," we are tempted to do one of two things: either to hold exclusively to our language behind the wall as the only mode of possible discourse (the conservative, sectarian temptation); or to abandon our language as parochial and to conduct business at the wall in the language of the empire (the liberal temptation). Overhearing makes a second language possible for Israel. This second, overheard language must always be the second language of Israel. The first language lets faith have energy and courage, but energy and courage need tools for communication with others who have power. This is the offer of the second language.

Overhearing is a biblical mode of nurture. This second conversation is present in the Bible. The God of the Bible not only addresses Israel but also summons the non-Israelite world to faith, obedience, and well-being. This is Yahweh's "second conversation" in the Bible. In the church, this second conversation of biblical faith has been largely disregarded and has gone unnoticed. If public responsibility is to be seen as urgent and legitimate in the practice of faith, Christians across the theological-political spectrum must recover these neglected texts.

NOTES

This essay appeared originally in *Horizons in Biblical Theology* 10 (June 1988), and is reprinted by permission.

1. My understanding of and concern for this distinctive conversation has been greatly clarified by George A. Lindbeck, *The Nature of Doctrine* (Philadelphia: Westminster Press, 1984). See Stanley Hauerwas and William H. Willimon, "Embarrassed by God's Presence," *Christian Century* 102 (June 30, 1985): 98–100, for a brief, practical exposition of that distinctive conversation.

2. This distinctive language has been neglected by both liberals and conservatives. Lindbeck, *The Nature of Doctrine*, has been concerned mainly with the "experiential-expressive" alternative but also has in purview the "propositional-cognitivist" alternative. It is easy to see that liberals have neglected this distinctive language, but conservatives, in opting for scholastic certitude, are also tempted to forsake the distinctive language of the faith community.

3. See Jack Seymour, Robert T. O'Gormon, and Charles R. Foster, *The Church in the Education of the Public* (Nashville: Abingdon Press, 1984), on "sacramental imagination." Their urging is parallel to mine, but my focus is more precisely on how this community speaks and teaches its members to speak.

4. On the liturgical practice of an alternative epistemology, see Walter Brueggemann, "The Exodus Narrative as Israel's Articulation of Faith Development," in *Hope within History* (Atlanta: John Knox Press, 1987), 7–26.

5. In chap. 3, I based my study on 2 Kings 18—19. Here I am working from the parallel texts of Isa. 36—37. The shift from 2 Kings to Isaiah is made in order to have access to other Isaiah texts that extend the themes in Isa. 36—37. While Isa. 36—37 is no doubt appropriated from an earlier tradition, its incorporation into Isaiah gives it a canonical placement that requires and permits consideration of other Isaiah texts.

6. See George E. Mendenhall, *Law and Covenant in Israel and the Ancient Near East* (Pittsburgh: Biblical Colloquium, 1955); Klaus Baltzer, *The Covenant Formulary* (Philadelphia: Fortress Press, 1971).

7. See the recent and mature assessment of the covenant as a radical mode of public discernment by Ernest W. Nicholson, *God and His People* (Oxford: Clarendon Press, 1986), esp. chap. 10.

8. In this chapter I intend to juxtapose the terms "sectarian" and "public." By "public" I mean discourse and interactions that are carried on with those who do not accept the premises and presuppositions of the sectarian community. My argument in chaps. 3 and 4 is that it is the interpretive process between sectarian and public discourse that is the burden and potential of biblical faith. Israel's primary sectarian metaphor (sovereignty of Yahweh) has public dimensions that cannot be contained in the community behind the wall. For a useful example, see Ted Peters, "A Christian Theology of Interreligious Dialogue," *Christian Century* 103 (Oct. 15, 1986): 883–85.

9. Michael Walzer, *Exodus and Revolution* (New York: Basic Books, 1985), has chronicled something of the public potential in the narrative and metaphor of exodus.

10. The metaphor of covenantal sovereignty is both peculiar to Israel and public in its claims. That it is both peculiar and public means that it lives very close to triumphalist temptation, so that the sovereignty of Yahweh is equated with the sovereignty of Israel. But that is surely a distortion. The cost of this powerful metaphor, as Israel's prophets understood, is that the public sovereignty of Yahweh makes Yahweh no special patron of Israel in public affairs (cf. Amos 3:2; 5:18–20; 9:7).

11. See Patrick D. Miller, Jr., "The Sovereignty of God," in *The Hermeneutical Quest*, ed. Donald G. Miller (Allison Park, Pa.: Pickwick Publications, 1986), 129–44.

12. See Lindbeck, *The Nature of Doctrine*, 73 and passim.

13. This legitimation of marginal voices is concrete in the Sinai torah with its characteristic attention to widows, orphans, and sojourners. These are the "dispensable" people who are nullified in every imperial policy. The staggering fact of Israel's metaphor of covenantal sovereignty is that Yahweh, unlike imperial rulers, attends to the "dispensable" people and out of them summons a new community. Yahweh's attentiveness to "dispensable" people is evident in Yahweh's "address to the nations," as in Amos 1:11, 13; Isa. 47:6. Even the nations are expected by Yahweh to attend in mercy to the dispensable people. On public policy and the marginal ones, see the alarming analysis of Richard Rubenstein, *The Age of Triage: Fear and Hope in an Overcrowded World* (Boston: Beacon Press, 1984).

14. The issue is joined dramatically in Ps. 82. It is asserted that Yahweh's godness consists in attentiveness to the poor and afflicted. This assertion breaks with conventional, i.e., imperial, notions of divinity.

15. This is the liturgical assertion of the plague transactions in the exodus narrative in which Yahweh finally defeats Pharaoh and thereby breaks the power of absolutism.

16. The rootage of the Isaiah tradition in the Jerusalem establishment has been well articulated by Gerhard von Rad, *Old Testament Theology 2* (New York: Harper & Row, 1965), 155–69.

17. On the enthronement festival, see Sigmund Mowinckel, *Das Thronbesteigungsfest Jahwas und der Ursprung der Eschatologie* (Amsterdam: P. Schippers, 1961). For a sympathetic critique of the hypothesis, see Aubrey Johnson, "The Psalms," in *The Old Testament and Modern Study*, ed. H. H. Rowley (Oxford: Clarendon Press, 1951), 162–81.

18. See my analysis of Ps. 96 in terms of its liturgic offer of a world, in Walter Brueggemann, *Israel's Praise: Doxology against Idolatry and Ideology* (Philadelphia: Fortress Press, 1988), chap. 2.

19. See Norman K. Gottwald, *All the Kingdoms of the Earth* (New York: Harper & Row, 1964), 147–208, 330–50.

20. On the canonical structure of the Isaiah tradition, see Ronald E. Clements, "Beyond Tradition-History; Deutero-Isaianic Development of First Isaiah's Themes," *Journal for the Study of the Old Testament* 31 (1985): 95–113.

21. The classic form of the the contest between Yahweh and the other gods is in the plague cycle of the exodus narrative. In 2 Isaiah the contest is given a juridical cast, e.g., Isa. 41:21–29.

22. On the strategic use of quotations as a form of theological argument, see Hans Walter Wolff, "Das Zitat im Prophetenspruch," in *Gessammelte Studien zum Alten Testament* (Munich: Chr. Kaiser, 1964), 36–129. Wolff takes up this oracle on pp. 83 and 99.

23. Clearly the Assyrians practiced such absolutism (Isa. 10), as did Babylon (Isa. 47) and every great imperial power. See Donald E. Gowan, *When Man Becomes God* (Pittsburgh: Pickwick Press, 1975). For contemporary practices of the same reality, see Robert Jay Lifton, *The Broken Connection* (New York: Basic Books, 1983), chaps. 20–23, on nuclear "totalism." Joseph Lelyveld, *Move Your Shadow* (New York: Penguin Books, 1985), has provided an account of political and cultural totalism in contemporary South Africa. In a society practicing totalism, serious political conversation is precluded. Recent developments around the release of Nelson Mandela make evident yet again that finally such brutalizing totalism cannot be sustained. (The same such brutalizing totalism is evident in the collapsing repressive societies of Eastern Europe.) The biblical assertion is that Yahweh evokes and permits fresh and transformative conversation, even in contexts of presumed absolutism. The dispensable ones are permitted back into the conversation.

24. On the capacity of civility to stifle and prevent serious exchange, see John M. Cuddihy, *The Ordeal of Civility* (New York: Basic Books, 1974); and Norbert Elias, *Power and Civility* (New York: Pantheon, 1982).

25. V. 29 is the sentence concluding the speech. While it is important to complete the formal argument, it is not as important for our argument as the first two parts of the unit.

26. See Brevard S. Childs, *Isaiah and the Assyrian Crisis* (Studies in Biblical Theology 32; Naperville, Ill.: Alec R. Allenson, 1967), 94–103; and Ronald E. Clements, *Isaiah 1—39*, New Century Biblical Commentary (Grand Rapids: Wm. B. Eerdmans, 1980), 280–88.

27. Gottwald, *All the Kingdoms of the Earth*, 204, concludes: "Above all, Isaiah attempted for the first time on a broad basis to do justice to foreign nations as realities in their own right. He tried to discern their inner motivations, their guilt and deserved retribution, and their right to mutual consideration in a community of nations. . . . There is a purpose in the midst of the flux of history toward which the chaotic events of half a century have been moving in spite of appearances to the contrary."

28. On this passage, see Gottwald, *All the Kingdoms of the Earth*, 224–28.

29. Yahweh's attentiveness to the nations is reflected in a theological trajectory in the Old Testament that begins with the Yahwist and includes much of Isaiah. See Hans Walter Wolff, "The Kerygma of the Yahwist," in Walter Brueggemann and Hans Walter Wolff, *The Vitality of Old Tes-*

tament Traditions (Atlanta: John Knox Press, 1982), 41–66. In that sequence of texts, special attention should be given to Amos 9:7.

30. On the theme of "overhearing," see Fred B. Craddock, *Overhearing the Gospel* (Nashville: Abingdon Press, 1978).

31. Lifton, *The Broken Connection*, 293–301, relates totalism on the one hand to a complete loss of symbolization and on the other hand to political fascism. Psychic *numbing* and political *ideology* go hand in hand in the loss of serious human conversation.

32. See Walther Eichrodt, "The Holy One in Your Midst," *Interpretation* 15 (1961): 259–73.

33. See my exploration of the liturgical and political significance of the formula in *Israel's Praise*, chaps. 1 and 2.

34. The basic book on the theme is Gerhard von Rad, *Wisdom in Israel* (Nashville: Abingdon Press, 1972).

35. The clearest sustained statement of such hidden intentionality in the Old Testament is in the Joseph narrative, Gen. 37—50. It is disputed whether this is indeed a statement of wisdom theology. I am inclined to follow von Rad in spite of the critique by James L. Crenshaw. In any case, the Joseph narrative is a clear statement of the power of God's providential resolve. See my exposition of the text in *Genesis* (Atlanta: John Knox Press, 1982), 288–380.

36. The basic argument for this intellectual construct is that of Klaus Koch, "Is There a Doctrine of Retribution in the Old Testament?" in *Theodicy in the Old Testament*, ed. James L. Crenshaw (Philadelphia: Fortress Press, 1983), 57–87.

37. Walther Zimmerli, "The Place and Limit of Wisdom in the Framework of the Old Testament Theology," *Scottish Journal of Theology* 17 (1964): 146–58; and idem, *The Old Testament and the World* (Atlanta: John Knox Press, 1976), has made the case well that wisdom reflection is creation theology, i.e., a study of how creation functions faithfully and intentionally. On the utilization of wisdom forms as a way of commenting on the order and mystery of creation, see Isa. 28:23–29.

38. The wisdom traditions affirm that right discernment leads to life. See Roland E. Murphy, "The Kerygma of the Book of Proverbs," *Interpretation* 20 (1966): 3–14.

39. Because our oracle is both lodged in Isa. 37 and 2 Kings 19, it is important to note that the deuteronomic theology (i.e., 2 Kings) also may be informed by wisdom. See Moshe Weinfeld, *Deuteronomy and the Deuteronomic School* (Oxford: Clarendon Press, 1972).

40. See Johannes Fichtner, "Jesaja unter den Weisen," in *Gottes Weisheit* (Stuttgart: Calwer, 1965), 18–26; J. William Whedbee, *Isaiah and Wisdom* (Nashville: Abingdon Press, 1971).

41. Fichtner, "Jahwes Plan in der Botschaft des Jesaja," in *Gottes Weisheit*, 27–43.

42. On righteousness as a theme in the tradition of Isaiah, see Walter Brueggemann, "Righteousness as Power for Life," in *Hope within History*, 27–48.

43. While Sennacherib is accused of such arrogance in Isa. 10:13, in Deut. 8:17 Israel is also subject to the same temptation. In these texts there is no theological difference between the temptations facing Assyria and Israel. Both are tempted to arrogance and autonomy, which in each case will bring death.

44. I have deliberately stated the matter to contrast strength and weakness, wisdom and foolishness, in order to call attention to the evangelical inversion in 1 Cor. 1:18–25. What the nations are slow to understand (as is Israel) is that Yahweh's apparent weakness is strength and Yahweh's apparent foolishness is wisdom.

45. See esp. Gen. 50:20. In that narrative, the brothers play a role not unlike the nations. They do not notice the hidden intentionality of God that has been at work in their common life. On the text, see Walter Brueggemann, "Genesis 50:15–21: A Theological Exploration," *Supplements to Vetus Testamentum* 36 (1983): 40–53.

5

The Case for
an Alternative Reading

IN THIS CHAPTER, I make a case for theological education on biblical and theological grounds. Two preliminary thoughts
occur to me. First, such a case can be made in one sentence: the
purpose of theological education is (to stay within ecclesiological
bounds) *to reflect critically on the church's call to obedient mission.* If
this is not compelling, a more extended case will not persuade.

My second thought is perhaps more fruitful and less disconcert-
ing. The case for theological education cannot finally be made once
and for all. It needs to be made again and again, because what
theology and theological education are called to do varies in each
social setting and cultural circumstance. The case to be made very
much depends on one's judgment about the time and the points of
urgency and danger, as well as on one's hermeneutical posture about
those points of urgency. (Indeed, even to speak of hermeneutics
indicates how time-conditioned our work is.) I believe that theological education today must articulate, explore, and exposit an alternative reading of reality, because we live in a culture that in its
dominant modes is committed to a reading of reality that is false
and will finally dehumanize and destroy. As a corollary, I suggest
that the church in our cultural setting is largely contained in and
seduced by that false reading of reality so that it has little energy or
imagination, not to say courage, for its mission. And as it is with
the church, so it is likely to be with the enterprise of theological
education.

We are, in North American church life, and derivatively in North American theological education, in a crisis situation in which it is clear that the reading of reality entrusted to us in the community of faith is in profound contradiction to the dominant reading of reality. The sense of collision between *our faith story* and *the story of the North American way of life* is new because these stories, out of our Puritan heritage, have historically had a friendly relationship, even if one not without tension.

A FORMAL SENSE OF SCRIPT

As might be expected from a scripture teacher, I begin with a text. The issue is which text, and how do we read that text? Four points occur to me about the textuality of theological education.

1. When transactional analysis was in vogue, it was argued that everybody is "scripted."[1] I find the metaphor of "script" suggestive, as long as we remember that it is a metaphor. The script, or "tape," was a way to understand our various roles, tendencies, and habits to react as parent, child, or adult. The metaphor was so graphic that it was suggested that our minds were akin to tape recorders and the key factor in relations was the selection of a tape or script, which would then play out a certain pattern of behavior. It was as if a person were fated and really had no choice once he or she had yielded to a certain script. That script might come, so the argument went, out of early childhood experiences, and this child script might continue. It could be displaced only by a mature act of will. Transactional analysis has been critiqued, and rightly so. But we may linger over the notion that people have "scripts" that authorize and legitimate behavior, that define worlds for us. The key is choosing the true script and reading it well.

The critical function of theological education is to identify the script, or tape, that is now being played out in American life, in public policy, in interpersonal relations, and in the self-understanding of the church. While these spheres are mutually reenforcive and the same issues are at work everywhere, the true character of the script is most evident in public policy, domestic and foreign. The script is committed to security through power, wealth, and management. It is cynical about human community, indifferent to human need, and largely devoid of compassion, care, forgiveness, and justice. I will not here probe the roots of this script, though its political and economic legitimators can be identified. The question I raise for theological education is, Why are we so unquestioning and uncritical about this script, despite its incredible toll on human worth, dignity, and community?

2. Robert Bellah has identified and discussed the assumptions of mainstream social science—positivism, reductionism, relativism, and determinism.[2] I suggest that, congruent with Bellah's argument, these features characterize the script of the North American story. Bellah argues that Thomas Hobbes is the progenitor of this script which cancels out tradition, community, and precisely those perspectives that make a human community of care, dignity, and well-being possible. He further observes that the practitioners of these assumptions do not think of them as conflicting with the assumptions of biblical religion. That, however, is because of a largely uncritical understanding of both our dominant American script and the alternative script of biblical faith. Bellah is a most restrained observer and so does not pursue very far the costs of these governing assumptions of the modern world. But it takes no great insight or imagination to conclude that (1) such a script leads to a loss of humaneness and humanness; and (2) we are well on our way toward the full embodiment of those values.

3. The dark, practical consequences of the modern script are laid out by Richard Rubenstein. In a nearly apocalyptic book tellingly named *The Age of Triage*, Rubenstein considers the outcomes and implications of the script. He argues that by the sixteenth century in England, laws of enclosure had already been instituted in order to secure land for the dominant class at the expense of the peasants who were then legally and systematically displaced. Triage, the practice of disposing of marginal, useless, and extra people, he asserts, is a value commitment of the modern world. The laws of enclosure were an early way by which some were made marginal and useless for the sake of others. Rubenstein cites Irish famine, the Holocaust, and the Vietnam War as examples of both the disappearance of compassion in public policy and modified forms of triage. In a devastating critique of the alliance between modernity and religion, he concludes:

The related value-systems of Social Darwinism, Neo-Malthusianism, and secular Calvinism have yet to be discredited. . . . What Calvinists proclaim in the name of God, Social Darwinists assert in the name of a strangely providential nature. . . . In a time of acute socio-economic crisis, Social Darwinism could provide decision-makers with the legitimating ideology for political decisions that would spell disaster to millions of their fellow citizens. . . . Moreover, Social Darwinism is not merely one ideology among many. It is a conceptualization of the pre-theoretical foundations of the way the American middle and upper classes have tended to perceive social reality. The plausibility of Social Darwinism is enormously enhanced by its roots in both the predominant religious and scientific traditions of American civilization.[3]

While Rubenstein is more brutal and "practical" in his analysis than is Bellah, both arrive at the same urging: it is now up to religious transformation to counter the inhumane ideology that dominates public policy and the underlying value process. That religious transformation is quite pivotal. It requires imaginative liturgy and art. It requires imaginative proclamation and bold patterns of missional compassion. But none of that will have staying power unless there is hard intellectual work, both critical and constructive. Making viable a perception of reality alternative to this dominant one is the proper work of theological education.

4. Martin Marty has argued (persuasively) that the Bible is America's iconic book in that it has provided to America's public imagination the dominant images, or icons, that have shaped public policy and values.[4] Bellah has observed what an ambiguous phenomenon such a civil religion has been.[5] From the iconic book, or script, has come a civil religion that has fostered humaneness, civility, and compassion. Yet from that same book have also come images justifying colonialism and imperialism of the rankest kind.

The tricky reality then is that this biblical script has played a decisive role in forming the values Rubenstein and Bellah criticize. But I shall argue that it is also the case that this script rightly read is the ground for an alternative reading. The task of theological education then is to see if this alternative script that has been entrusted to the church and the synagogue can counter the dominant script that is leading us to inhumaneness and brutality. If we accept the analyses of Bellah and Rubenstein, we can identify few sources from which can come an alternative reading that contains the seeds of life.[6]

Such a life-giving script will not be generated out of our raw experiences or our good intentions. It will not be generated by the greedy who simply celebrate selfishness. Such a script will not come from the suspicious tradition of Marx, Nietzsche, and Freud, though much is to be learned from them.[7] Nor will it come from the modern icon-makers such as Jung and Levi-Strauss. While there is not space to argue here, a case can be made that finally it is this strange text, the Bible, entrusted peculiarly to the communities of faith, that makes available an alternative reading of reality.[8] I shall argue that unless that text receives a fresh, serious, honest hearing among us, the dominant script of brutality, selfishness, and inhumaneness shall surely have its way.

But if Marty is correct, this alternative script requires a careful reading and a change of focus: what has been America's iconic book must now be read as the *aniconic text of church and synagogue*. While the Bible may indeed offer images for the construction of public life, the key task now entrusted to theological education is to see the Bible's aniconic power, its power as a text that breaks images, critiques religion, exposes ideology, identifies hidden interest—out of which comes room for the holiness of God and the newness of humanity.

A SUBSTANTIVE HEARING OF THE ANICONIC

The Bible knows, as theologians are now discerning, that the more powerful temptation is not atheism but idolatry.[9] The hazard is not that we shall cease to believe in God, but that we shall generate and construct gods because they are more comfortable and convenient for us. The vocation of theological education in a season of idolatry is to see if this alternative text has the basis for defense against idols and the articulation of the true God who guarantees human possibility. Both Bellah and Rubenstein are clear that finally the issue is not economics or politics, but faith, a confession of who God is.

Israel understood from the beginning the powerful and unavoidable links between *the identity of God* and *public economic and social policy.* Of course Israel learned this the way we always learn most and best—painfully and through praxis. The primal experience of slavery and liberation in Egypt taught Israel best and generated the script we call the Bible.[10] The experience of enslavement and the event of liberation came to dominate Israel's imagination and to shape decisively the main claims of the text.

Israel learned through impossible brick quotas that the real human problems are power, freedom, and justice. Israel learned that those who have political power are able to determine and impose economic solutions upon those who lack political power. Through the strange events connected to the birth of Moses (Exod. 2:1–10), the violence of Moses (Exod. 2:11–22), the cry of pain (Exod. 2:23–25), and the burning bush (Exod. 3:1–14), Israel learned that what seemed to be a hopeless, closed political-economic context is in fact an arena in which the power of several gods is at issue; it is a situation that requires theological criticism. Israel learned *in a season of pain* that the Egyptian political and economic apparatus depended on the legitimacy of the Egyptian gods who sanctioned oppression and did not blink at exploitation. Israel also learned in *a season of amazement* that there is a power of freedom and justice at work in the brickyard—Yahweh—who has the will and power to end the injustice and evoke a new community of equity and compassion.[11] This God has been unknown but is disclosed precisely among the hopeless, helpless ones who had no access to Egyptian power.

This twofold accent of pain and amazement is at the heart of our script. Israel's primal insights are (1) that injustice depends on divine sanction and (2) an alternative intrusion can make justice possible. The script has discerned that social processes always operate at two interrelated levels. At one level—socio-political-economic—it is always brickyard owners versus brick-making slaves, and the owners always set the quota without negotiating. At a second level, however, equally compelling, it is the sovereign voice of freedom and justice who challenges the gods of the empire and thereby delegitimates the socio-political-economic arrangements of oppression.

This text, unlike the hopeless text of the slaves or the complacent text of the masters, urges that life always be read at the hinge— between God and social process:

the false gods (Egyptian) are created by and support false social arrangements of power and goods;

the true God (Yahweh, giver of justice and freedom) sponsors social arrangements of compassion and care.

The true God exposes the false gods as powerless idols. The "rumble" in the empire terminates the oppressiveness sanctioned by the idols and grants unutterable human possibilities.

This hinge in the text of heaven and earth, the God issue and the human issues, is the key agenda of theological education. It is possible to fall off on either side of the hinge—on the side of the liberals who abandon the God question and focus only on human arrangements, or on the side of the reactionary myth-makers who treat human arrangements with scorn and focus on religious reality. But both betray biblical faith. This text lies precisely at the connecting point. The false texts of our society want to break the connection, so that the war planners proclaim the year of the Bible because they do not see that the Bible breaks the icons that permit war and all its supportive policies. Understand me well; I am not urging liberal or conservative social policy. I am simply insisting on the key insistence of the text itself. It is this text that now needs to be explicated if "the script of triage" is to be countered in time.

THE ANICONIC SCRIPT IN A
FRESH HEARING

The formal process now required is to attend to this script that is authoritative, surprising, and subversive. The substantive claim of the script is aniconic: it intends to critique and break every religious image that yields or legitimates social practice that is ideological. This aniconic script thus is studied, proclaimed, and embraced as a critical defense against religious and social practice that is dehumanizing and oppressive.

In ancient Israel, the tradition of Deuteronomy is the practice of returning to the normative script in a later generation to address a social crisis of devastating proportion.

1. Deuteronomy is not the primal script. The primal script is the Mosaic event and the Mosaic narrative of exodus and Sinai. Deuteronomy is a "re-reading" of this ancient script, a second reading (cf.

Deut. 17:18, from whence comes the name Deuteronomy), a derivative reading done with authority and imagination. Deuteronomy thus offers a model for theological education, for it shows the community of faith returning to its script, the text of Moses, with enormous freedom and imagination.

2. The cultural crisis in which Israel returns to this script is presented as the challenge of a Canaanite reading of reality.[12] That is the claim of the literature itself. It is a series of speeches given at the Jordan just as Israel enters the land of promise, which is in fact the land of Canaanite temptation and Canaanite possibility. The Israelites pause there with Moses to inquire if the ancient script can have a decisive way in this new world.

Common critical opinion locates the text in the seventh century B.C.E., facing Assyrian religious alternatives.[13] Conservative conven tion places it in the thirteenth century. Either way, Israel is confronted and tempted by a rival reading of reality that holds peculiar promise, powerful attraction, and dangerous perversion. "Canaanite," it is now clear, is not an ethnic term. Rather, it refers to a form of social organization that legitimated and practiced certain social relationships, and a certain distribution of social power and social goods which in the end were hierarchical, oppressive, and unjust.[14]

3. The complex hermeneutical act that is Deuteronomy (which offers one model for theological education) is to permit the ancient script of Moses and the present crisis of Canaan to confront each other. This complex operation is not easy to understand or explain. On the one hand, it is clear that Deuteronomy holds to old values which some must have regarded as outmoded, for it appeals to ancient narrative and ancient law. That holding to the old, however, is not done in a dead, literalistic, or reductionist fashion. It is also clear, though, that Deuteronomy fully discerns the new situation and understands that this is where Israel must live, but that Israel characteristically enters the new situation critically and suspiciously, not prepared to embrace that which contradicts Israel's own clear identity. The old is handled freely and imaginatively. The new is received suspiciously and guardedly.

The outcome, which is the reading of reality in Deuteronomy, is something that did not exist until this moment of articulation and interpretation. Deuteronomy does not simply engage in reiterating and valuing the tradition, but participates in constructing the tradition in the present moment. The hermeneutical key in Deuteronomy, which I suggest could be our hermeneutical key, is in 5:3:

> Not with our fathers did the Lord make this covenant,
> but with all of us who are here alive this day.[15]

Deuteronomy knows that theological interpretation is an act in and for the present. We cannot parrot old theological acts nor abandon the reflective critical process; we must continue the scripting process in ways that honor the main claims of the memory and that take into account the new issues and new possibilities only now available. Unlike other parts of the Old Testament, Deuteronomy is weighted on the side of the old script. It is clear, nonetheless, that the interpretive process is open and constructive, not regurgitive and traditionalist.[16]

RELIVING THE SCRIPT

Deuteronomy 4 is one of the rich, theological resources of the tradition of Deuteronomy. No doubt the chapter has been wrought through a process of extensive and repeated editorial work.[17] As we have it, parts are probably from the exile, that is, later than the main body of Deuteronomy. I consider the chapter here as *the process of hermeneutical construction* that is the center of the theological task. I consider three points.

1. The text is grounded in and makes explicit appeal to the old script of Sinai. Thus in 4:10, the tradition makes a direct appeal to Sinai and seems to refer to Exod. 19:9 and 16. This is Sinai revisited. In appealing to this old tradition, the text makes the enormous affirmation that the old claims of covenant are the decisive ones for Israel in this and in every circumstance. And if covenant is decisive, then torah is definitional for the character and life of this community. It was surely old-fashioned in the Babylonian exile to hold to the notion of obedience to torah, but this tradition does so unabashedly.

Following the paradigm presented by Norman Gottwald,[18] I take covenant-torah to be a social proposal or experiment that intends to counter imperial shapes of reality that are hierarchal and oppressive. Reference to covenant and torah is not nostalgic, but a public assertion of a commitment to justice and freedom that marks Israel and that is to be crucial for public life. It is not only a religious idea, but a proposal of social policy and practice that grounds human dignity and human worth in the character and will of Yahweh. The old script thus is used to find standing ground against the values of the day that no longer discern human society as a covenant and no longer understand torah obedience as a well of well-being.[19]

2. At Sinai, as evidenced in this script, there is *voice but no form* (4:12). This is an exceedingly important affirmation for Israel. There was a voice. It was a clear voice. It was not doubted that it was the voice of Yahweh. The community is rooted in a moment of revelatory disclosure. The message of the voice is clear. The voice at Sinai gives no religious philosophy, no psychological assurance, no social analysis except for the ten commandments (v. 13).[20] How stark! But that is the shape of the script. There is not even any exegesis; the basic claims are known and conceded, not open to review.

In the present form of this text, however, it is the negative counterpart that receives attention: "you saw no form" (vv. 12, 15). This is not to say God has no form, only that it was not at Israel's disposal, even in this powerful theophanic event (cf. Exod. 33:17–23). The event yields a voice of command, but not a form of religious presence.[21] This tradition is theologically sophisticated. It knows that where God has an identifiable form, God's freedom will soon be lost and God will be reduced to a fixed, stable, and controllable image.[22] That is what Egyptian, Canaanite, and Babylonian religion has done, always in the interest of a social, economic monopoly. That is what every great power, secular and religious, has sought to do. Indeed, that is what the great powers today seek to do. Where images of God are authorized, there a fixed ordering of society will also come. The problem for Deuteronomy is not religious images as such, but the social ideology that seems inevitably to accompany them.[23] The domestication of God leads to social docility. In vv. 15–19, then, we are given a catalogue of the dangers of images. Then abruptly, as a sharp contrast, Yahweh is said to be the powerful, active agent who freed the slaves from the empire (v. 20). The argument is subtle and complicated, but in this theological tradition a voice liberates, a form consolidates and finally immobilizes and dehumanizes.

This relates to the theological process, because every new insight given form soon becomes a fixed shape which enslaves. Theological reflection is to criticize all fixed shapes, to be open to the voice of command that unsettles, liberates, and transforms.

3. Deuteronomy 4 reflects on the character of God, which is a proper agenda for theological education. The temptation then for Israel and in all serious reflection is finally to reduce God to a fixed formula, which may be done in liberal or conservative, religious or secular terms. This chapter remarkably narrates and articulates the vitality and dynamic of God. Perhaps the texts are arranged through redactional work, but in reading the text as it stands, we can observe a progression.

First, in v. 24, "Yahweh your God is a devouring fire, a jealous God." While this statement is certainly astonishing in a chapter on covenant, it is the last line in a long paragraph on idols and the temptation to fix, reduce, and secure. Yahweh, the key character in this script, is the enemy of all such reductionism.[24] This new generation of Deuteronomy which returns to the script, like the primal generation of Sinai (Exod. 20:20), understands the terror of this God against every social form that does not keep life open to justice and freedom.

In v. 29, theological rhetoric and Israel's possibility for faith are "from there": from Babylon, from exile, from a point of vulnerability, need, and failed power. This return to the old script of Moses lets the script take on contemporaneity by extending the story of the present generation in exile in Babylon. The new announcement "from there" asserts that God is now available and findable, as God has not been in the land oppressively organized.[25]

Finally, in v. 31, this God is a God who is "merciful and does not forget the covenant." This is a face of God we would not have expected after reading v. 24. The jealous, devouring God has become the God of mercy and covenant. The script narrates this move on God's part. It is now the womblike mercy of God that is known among the exiles.

I suggest that Deuteronomy 4 as a *live practice of old script* provides a map for the vitality of God. It traces the story of God from *jealousy*

(v. 24) to *mercy* (v. 31) by way of *exile* (v. 29). It intends to bring the listening community along with the script so that this generation can freshly experience the God of the script in new ways: Every such statement about God is, without any manipulation, a disclosure to the community about the possible shape of its own life.

4. This great text on Sinai, images, and voices, moves in v. 40 to an assurance about the land:

> Keep his statutes and his commandments, which I command you this day, that it may go well with you, and with your children after you, and that you may prolong your days in the land which the Lord your God gives you for ever.

Good theology does not stay in heaven reflecting on God's character. Good theology comes to earth. It reflects on the dangerous, anxiety-ridden materiality of life. It asserts that social well-being is linked to obedience, and that land practice, land possession, land loss, land abuse, and land sharing are proper theological concerns.[26] Any theology that runs off in a spiritualizing quest for meaning or community without attending to this reality misunderstands and betrays.

It is striking that Deuteronomy 4 ends with a provision for cities of refuge (vv. 41–43), a stunning practice of humaneness. And this same trajectory spills over into Deuteronomy 5, to the ten commandments to which reference is already made in 4:13.[27]

Working with the metaphor of "Canaanite," the text asserts that Canaanite modes of social practice will lead to land loss and exile, but that covenant modes of social power will preclude exile and land loss. Covenantal modes of social power, however, will not derive from a fixed, static god who is always too friendly with imperial monopolies of power. Thus, the theological project of Sinai and Moses, as scripted in Deuteronomy, relentlessly moves back and forth between the vitality of God and the possibility of humane social life. The two cannot be separated.

CONTEMPORARY INTERPRETIVE PARALLELS

There are no easy or simple parallels for our own situation. At some risk, I must seek to draw them because my concern in this chapter is not "a Deuteronomic hermeneutic," but contemporary theological education based in Bible and theology. So I suggest some parallels and admit that they deserve more precise nuancing than can be done here:

1. The theological task is an unending one:

Not with our fathers was this covenant made,
but with all of us who are here alive today.
(Deut. 5:3)

The community of faith is under summons to find out what this covenant claim means for the complex issues of the day. Indeed that is what Deuteronomy itself does, for it addresses the complexities of a Canaanite context. Clearly, old answers to these current issues are not adequate, which is why theology must always be done again.

2. The theological enterprise in our day consists of a reflection on the script and a critique of alternative scripts. I say this metaphorically, but refer quite concretely to this script. The reason for the urgency of the script is twofold. First, we are faced with rival scripts, especially those of Marxism and liberal capitalism, which carry the seed of our destruction. Second, the community of faith is now discovering that other appeals for authority, especially those grounded only in personal experience or the social sciences, are not adequate. When those appeals are found inadequate, there will be a turn to a script, if not to this one, then to some other. Down that road lies authoritarianism.

In holding to the script as the center of the theological enterprise, I do not mean to do so blindly or uncritically, for neither Jew nor Christian has ever handled the script in that way. It has always been done critically, even suspiciously. Having said that, however, let us not miss the main point: this script, unlike the other scripts available to us, legitimates, requires, and insists upon the key human issues among us as derived from, connected to, and pointing toward the Holy One. None but these communities of faith—Jewish and Christian—press intentionally and consistently in our society for the human issues of justice, freedom, dignity, well-being, equity, security, and hope. Theological education must include energy and will, and space and context for serious reference to the text, for facing candidly the issues of our own humanness as they are related to the reality of God.

3. As in Deuteronomy, the theological enterprise must be done in a situation of danger and crisis. The Canaanite alternative constitutes an enormous threat to the community of ancient Israel for it proposed not only that Israelites would be killed, but that the social possibility of an egalitarian community would disappear as a vision from the Near East. The urgency of Deuteronomy is to keep this social possibility available when surrounded and largely contained by hostile alternatives.[28]

If Bellah and Rubenstein are on target, as I judge them to be, our situation in Western society is of the same urgency. The practice and the script of our society will surely lead to death. I term this script the vision of "consumer militarism," which legitimates such practices. Militarism is a vigorous effort to preserve the disproportion of goods and power that we now have. Consumerism is a philosophy of greed and satiation which knows no limits and screens out all the serious human issues.

This particular parallel to Canaanite practice is evident not only in public policy, but also in our domestic and personal lives which become increasingly cynical and brutal. These rival scripts focus on the wrong issues and so entertain the wrong solutions, which leave us all diminished.

Theological education then is done to keep the crucial, reflective conversation going between the script that we hold to be authoritative and the context of American society in which other scripts are powerfully at work.[29] How that script and that context are to be related is not simple, obvious, or easy. It is no doubt the case that as citizens of this context, we are shaped in the ways we receive and handle the script. The influences are mutual, interactive, and multidirectional. We are indeed in a hermeneutical circle. While we live in this context and are assaulted by the values of consumer militarism to which none of us is immune, nonetheless this script is entrusted peculiarly to these communities of faith. The enterprise of theological education is urgent, for our society seems to have lost its central vision of human possibility. The enterprise of textual criticism and interpretation is urgent for us because we believe this script contains a peculiar and distinctive word about human possibility. Where the claim of this script is not heard in all its power and authority, we will settle for icons which enslave. We do not know the outcome of this conversation, but we are unambiguous in knowing that something crucial is at stake in the conversation. If we do not keep the conversation going with the script, we shall all be scripted in ways that are neither human nor faithful.

POSTSCRIPT

1. There are, of course, other models for theology and theological education besides this one. This one, with its emphasis upon the text, is one you might most expect from a scripture teacher. While my approach owes much to the tradition of von Rad, Zimmerli, and Noth, I believe that at two points my remarks are more germane to our own situation. First, the voice of command is presented as sociologically more radical and therefore is more problematic than much "credo theology" has allowed. This is best explained by Norman Gottwald. Second, the interpretive interaction between text and context is more complex than has often been acknowledged, as in some current modes of narrative theology. Our present situation with respect to hermeneutics is more complex than some other previous settings recognized.

The two predominant paradigms for theology now are process theology and liberation theology. Each of these labels covers many things. With both, the interplay between a scriptural text and a sociology of knowledge about the present context is central to method. Thus in broad outline, I hope my argument leaves room for such methodological alternatives.

2. I have placed critical emphasis upon the text. I do not suggest, however, that the entire theological curriculum be reduced to scripture study. In an attempt to be attentive to Edward Farley's call for coherence in the theological curriculum,[30] I suggest that all parts of the theological enterprise must attend to the interplay of text and context. Thus, for example, Ebeling's programmatic statement that church history for Protestants is a history of exegesis must be more fully considered.[31] And I suggest that the distinctive mark of practical theology, with references, for example, to pastoral care, is the clue given in the text for a specific view of reality, personal and public.[32]

3. Choosing to speak of the text over against the context does not tilt the conversation either in a liberal or a conservative direction. It

is my view that the text is so dangerous and the context is so problematic that the old divisions of liberal and conservative are largely obsolete and irrelevant. Thus, supporting this kind of theological education need not affront persons of one particular ideological persuasion any more than any other, for it is a scandal to us all. The truth is that we are now all at risk, as are our ideologies. The categories through which we have processed our experience— liberal or conservative—are now largely shattered.[33] The issue before all in the community of faith is what this text has to say in offering an alternative destiny both to the community of faith and to the public world in which that community lives.

The promise of this text is a *liberated public imagination* so that we

> know this is a land which the Lord your God cares for; the eyes of the Lord your God are always upon it, from the beginning of the year to the end of the year. (Deut. 11:12)

The summons of the text is to find a *radical public ethic* in a quite concrete memory:

> Love the sojourner, therefore, for you were sojourners in the land of Canaan. (Deut. 10:19)

The enemy of the text is a *social ideology of possessive individualism:*[34]

> Beware lest you say in your heart, My power and the might of my hand have gotten me this wealth. (Deut. 8:17)

The interplay of liberated public imagination, radical public ethic from a concrete memory, and social ideology of possessive individualism comprises, I propose, the agenda now before these communities of faith, and therefore the concern in their educational enterprise. Support for that enterprise is both urgent and honorable, indeed essential to faithfulness.

NOTES

This essay appeared originally in *Theological Education* 23 (Spring 1987): 89–107, and is reprinted by permission.

1. Eric Berne, *Transactional Analysis in Psychotherapy* (New York: Grove Press, 1961), chap. 11 and passim.

2. Robert N. Bellah, "Biblical Religion and Social Science in the Modern World," *NICM Journal for Jews and Christians in Higher Education* 6[3] (1981): 8–22.

3. Richard L. Rubenstein, *The Age of Triage* (Boston: Beacon Press, 1983), 222.

4. Martin Marty, "America's Iconic Book," in *Humanizing America's Iconic Book*, ed. Gene M. Tucker and Douglas A. Knight (Chico, Calif.: Scholars Press, 1982), 1–23.

5. Robert N. Bellah, "Civil Religion in America," *Daedalus* 96 (1967): 1–21.

6. Bellah, "Biblical Religion and Social Science," 21–22, speaks precisely of the metaphor of seedbeds: "As corruption widens it is more than ever necessary that there be demonstration communities where elementary decencies can be maintained and handed down, humanizing a bad situation as long as it exists, and providing seedbeds for larger efforts at social amelioration when that becomes possible."

7. Paul Ricoeur, *Freud and Philosophy* (New Haven: Yale University Press, 1970), has articulated the crucial importance of the "masters of suspicion"; I do not minimize their importance for the present topic. Nonetheless, the script that makes life possible must include also a hermeneutics of retrieval which is not found in such suspicion. David Tracy, *The Analogical Imagination* (New York: Crossroad, 1981), chap. 9, has shown how retrieval is to be found in the classics of the faith communities.

8. On the role of the classics in the theological enterprise, see Tracy, *Analogical Imagination*, chaps. 3–7.

9. On the temptations to atheism and idolatry, see Pablo Richard, *The Idols of Death and the God of Life* (Maryknoll, N.Y.: Orbis Books, 1983), 1–4 and passim.

10. On the cruciality of that core memory, see the splendid exposition of Walter Harrelson, "Life, Faith and the Emergence of Tradition," in *Tradition and Theology in the Old Testament*, ed. Douglas A. Knight (Philadelphia: Fortress Press, 1977), 11–30.

11. See the paradigmatic statement of Norman K. Gottwald, *The Tribes of Yahweh* (Maryknoll, N.Y.: Orbis Books, 1979).

12. Gerhard von Rad, *Studies in Deuteronomy* (Chicago: Henry Regnery, 1953); and idem, *Old Testament Theology I* (New York: Harper & Row, 1962), 69–77, has most clearly seen the dynamic of the tradition of Deuteronomy. Of course to speak of "Canaanites" in this context is to speak of a theological model and not a historical reference.

13. On the critical consensus concerning Deuteronomy, see Brevard S. Childs, *Introduction to the Old Testament as Scripture* (Philadelphia: Fortress Press, 1979), 204–10.

14. See Gottwald, *Tribes of Yahweh*, 210–19 and passim.

15. On this way of doing hermeneutics, see Martin Noth, "The 'Representation' of the Old Testament in Proclamation," in *Essays on Old Testament Hermeneutics*, ed. Claus Westermann (Richmond: John Knox Press, 1963), 76–88.

16. On the dialectic tension between dogmatism and criticism in the tradition of Deuteronomy, see Robert Polzin, *Moses and the Deuteronomist* (New York: Seabury Press, 1980), esp. chap. 2. In my judgment, Polzin has slotted the book of Deuteronomy too rigidly; I believe the dynamic he sees elsewhere has vitality there as well.

17. On the redactional character of Deut. 4, see Georg Braulik, *Die Mittel Deuteronomischer Rhetorik: Erhoben aus Deuteronomium 4* (Rome: Biblical Institute Press, 1978), 1–40.

18. See the summary by Gottwald, *Tribes of Yahweh*, 102–3.

19. On the breakdown of the model of covenant as concerns our contemporary situation, see Robert N. Bellah, *The Broken Covenant* (New York: Seabury Press, 1975).

20. On the dread power of these commands in relation to Sinai, see Martin Buber, *Kingship of God* (New York: Harper & Row, 1967); and Jon Levenson, *Sinai and Zion* (New York: Winston Press, 1985), part 1.

21. Samuel Terrien, *The Elusive Presence* (New York: Harper & Row, 1978), has well explicated the tension between the voice and form. Levenson, *Sinai and Zion*, 150, also appeals to the dialectic of eye and ear.

22. On the diminishment of God's freedom through image, see Gerhard von Rad, *Old Testament Theology I*, 212–19; and Walther Zimmerli, *Old Testament Theology in Outline* (Atlanta: John Knox Press, 1978), 120–24.

23. On the social dimensions of the prohibition of images, see Ronald S. Hendel, "The Social Origins of the Aniconic Tradition," *Catholic Biblical Quarterly* 50 (1988): 365–82.

24. On the banality of religious redactionism, see Dorothee Soelle, *The Strength of the Weak* (Philadelphia: Westminster Press, 1984), chap. 1. The intellectual counterpart of such reductionism is the "dryness" characterized by Iris Murdoch, "Against Dryness: A Polemical Sketch," in *Revision*, ed. Stanley Hauerwas and Alasdair MacIntyre (Notre Dame, Ind.: University of Notre Dame Press, 1983), 43–50.

25. On being able to find God precisely with reference to exile, see Jer. 29:13 and Isa. 55:6–7, texts belonging to the same theological trajectory.

26. On the centrality of land for serious biblical thought, see Walter Brueggemann, *The Land* (Philadelphia: Fortress Press, 1977).

27. On the policy implications of the ten commandments, see Walter Harrelson, *The Ten Commandments and Human Rights* (Philadelphia: Fortress Press, 1980).

28. On keeping this alternative social possibility alive, see Walter Brueggemann, *The Prophetic Imagination* (Philadelphia: Fortress Press, 1978). On the work of imagination as understood in the tradition of Deuteronomy, see Walter Brueggemann, "Imagination as a Mode of Fidelity," in *Understanding the Word*, ed. James T. Butler et al., JSOTSup 37 (Sheffield, Eng.: JSOT Press, 1985), 13–36.

29. Paul van Buren, *Discerning the Way* (New York: Seabury Press, 1980), has taken "conversation" as the dominant metaphor for his way of doing theology.

30. Edward Farley, *Theologia* (Philadelphia: Fortress Press, 1983).

31. Gerhard Ebeling, *Word and Faith* (Philadelphia: Fortress Press, 1963), chap. 1. His proposal on the cruciality of exegesis is decisive for the model of biblical interpretation presented by Brevard S. Childs, *The Book of Exodus*, Old Testament Library (Philadelphia: Westminster Press, 1974).

32. To focus theological categories and issues around textuality is not unrelated to the argument of George A. Lindbeck, *The Nature of Doctrine* (Philadelphia: Westminster Press, 1984). Lindbeck writes, "Finally, in the instance of religions more than in any other type of semiotic system, description is not simply metaphorically but literally intratextual. This is true in some degree of all the world's major faiths. They all have relatively fixed canons of writings that they treat as exemplary or normative instantiations of their semiotic codes. One test of faithfulness for all of them is the degree to which descriptions correspond to the semiotic universe paradigmatically encoded in holy writ. The importance of texts and of intratextuality for theological faithfulness becomes clearer when we consider the unwritten religions of nonliterate societies" (p. 116).

33. Leslie Newbegin, *The Other Side of 1984* (Geneva: World Council of Churches, 1983), has succinctly stated the intellectual crisis now facing the churches whose theology and self-understanding are wed closely to Enlightenment modes of articulation.

34. On the theme of possessive individualism, see Crawford B. MacPherson, *The Political Theory of Possessive Individualism* (Oxford: Clarendon Press, 1962).

6

Canonization
and Contextualization

THE EMERGENCE OF CANON as a serious category into theological reflection is a major and surprising gain. It has shifted the nature of our discussion in healthy ways. First and most important, it has exposed the inadequacy of historical-critical study, which is endlessly analytical and fragmentary, and has invited attention to the literature as a whole. Consideration of the canon has placed recent historical-critical study in perspective by showing that our distinctively modern modes of criticism are derivative from the Enlightenment. The study of canon has consequently led us back to an older tradition of theological interpretation which had been largely dismissed as outmoded. Attention to the canon has helped us see that historical-critical study may tell us more about ourselves than the text.

To treat canon as a formal literary category rather than a substantive theological matter is in itself not adequate. The notion of canon has long been treated largely as a problem concerning the history of the literature. The canon was understood as a secondary, literary grouping of books, resting on late, extrinsic theological decisions. It is now clear that an attempt to understand the literature historically is not an adequate approach for canonization. Reaction against critical fragmentation done on the basis of newer literary critical theory without reference to the canon is a step forward, but does not in itself move to questions of theological norm.[1] Brevard Childs's contribution has been enormously important, but some of his strictures against fragmentation could have been made on

119

grounds other than canonical. They could have been made simply on literary grounds.

Thus, I submit, that if canonicity is a useful notion for biblical theology, we do better to treat it as a theological conviction about normative literature that articulates norms.[2] I have the impression that Childs attempts to assert this *theological claim* of authoritative norm in the guise of a literary argument, and that way of arguing contributes to our confusion. It would be more helpful to claim or assert authority in the *content* of the literature (a substantive articulation of what is true) than to try to assert authority in the literary *shape* of the material. The argument from literary shape cannot be sustained in every case and even if it were, it leaves us only with thirty-nine (or twenty-four) individual canonical statements.[3] In his more recent book, *Old Testament Theology in a Canonical Context*,[4] Childs's argument is closer to a substantive theological argument than a formal literary one. The grounds on which canonicity guides his move from literary shape to theological substance is, however, not always obvious. Thus we are only at the beginning of sorting out literary shape and theological norm.

AN INVITATION TO INTERPRETATION

If canon is an affirmation of theological norming, then the canonical authority of scripture is minimal but crucial. It is minimal because canonical norm in and of itself is formal, and in speaking of canonical authority we have not yet uttered a substantive sound. It is minimal because even those of us who accept canonical authority as theological norm still have all our interpretive work in front of us. The authority of canon is also crucial because it is an assertion and agreement that these books, like no others, will receive our attention and will shape and govern our imagination. It means we will wait on this literature for whatever words of life and truth we expect to be given to us. It means that in this literature we are prepared to find the criteria by which other truth (in other literature) is to be assessed. It means our imagination is under a discipline which precludes and judges other fields of imagining.[5] This literature, we confess, is our true home, held passionately and uncompromisingly against all our homelessness.[6]

Canonical literature as normative and norming is deeply timeless and utterly timeful, which is why it receives our sustained and loyal attention. The question facing both church and academy is, How is this timeless document kept always timeful?[7] That it is timeless means we always enter this literature in a conviction of elemental certitude. This literature is God's house and God wants the children to play there.[8] Canon is the claim that the "house of authority" is intact, because it is the house of the holy.[9]

That the canonical literature is timeful and timely, however, means that it requires interpretation. David Tracy, in his discussion of the term "classic," asserts,

> [A] timeless document both demands constant interpretation and bears a certain kind of timelessness—namely, the timelessness of a classic expression radically rooted in its own historical time and calling to my own historicity. That is, the classical text is not in some timeless moment which needs mere repetition. Rather its kind of timelessness as permanent timeliness is the only one proper to any expression of the finite, temporal, historical beings we are. . . . The classic text's fate is that only its constant reinterpretation by later finite, historical, temporal beings who will risk asking its questions and listening, critically and tactfully, to its responses can actualize the event of understanding beyond its present fixation in a text. Every classic lives as a classic only if it finds readers willing to be provoked by its claim to attention.[10]

I have found the work of Frank Kermode especially helpful regarding the *crucial* but *minimal* significance of canon. Kermode is concerned with the "canon" of Western literature. He reflects on how and why literature comes to be accepted as canonical in this community of interpretation and how it is treated once it is accorded canonical status. He observes that once literature has canonical status, it is clear that it must be dealt with. It may, however, be dealt with in a variety of ways. Indeed, he writes, "Every effort of exegesis is justified without argument,"[11] because the literature is canonical and must always be freshly interpreted. Canonical literature permits and requires endless ongoing interpretation which claims always to discern new meanings. Each new effort to interpret the canon, says Kermode, "may be regarded not as modern increments, but rather as discoveries of original meaning hitherto hidden."[12] In

Kermode's judgment canon does not dictate or control interpretation. It only insists that interpretation must always be done again on this literature as on no other.

Canon is a precious conviction for us, for it invites us to interpretation once again, always again, perhaps this time to get it ultimately and for the first time right. The *crucial* character of canon requires that we will attend in this way only to this literature. The *minimal* character of canon means that canonical literature always still awaits its "right" interpretation. Along the way, canon that requires new interpretation is always and in principle destabilizing of every old consensus of interpretation.

THE AMBIGUITY OF CANONICAL INTERPRETATION

Canon perennially requires interpretation and always moves the literature from "meant" to "means."[13] The interpretive task is to find the faithful interpretation, because it has "not yet" been found—always "not yet." Canon as an interpretive enterprise is concerned with the question, How now is the norming voice of this literature present and heard among us?[14] Serious concern for canon moves us not toward canonical text but toward canonical interpretation.

The phrase "canonical interpretation" is deliberately ambiguous. On the one hand, it means the ongoing interpretation of canonical material. On the other hand, it means an agreed-upon normative interpretation. This ambiguity is my subject here. Is interpretation of the canonical material necessarily and by definition a normative interpretation?

The long-held and widely shared canonical interpretation of scripture articulates the saving, reconciling, liberating concern of God for God's world. That is, the norming claim of the canon concerns the gospel.[15] Normative interpretation is about God mending the world.[16] Patristic as well as Reformation interpretation sought to do its work in light of this thematic. Interpretation was done with great freedom, but it had an authorized center. Canonical practice has concerned the relationship of all texts to this authorized center.[17]

Two critical points may be made about that centered and autho-

rized interpretation. First, the institutional power of church interpretation monopolized that normative claim.[18] The memory became
church-sponsored and church-guarded; it became privileged and
protected interpretation.[19] This kind of interpretation leaves the
canon in an odd place, because while such interpretation articulates
the truth, it is clearly not disinterested truth. And if it is not disinterested, it is difficult to regard such interpretation as unfailingly
the truth. To trust this truth, I must trust the interpretation.

Second, Brevard Childs has seen that the historical-critical
approach has been indifferent to or negative about the normative
interpretation. Indeed criticism arose as a response to institutional
authoritarianism choosing either to ignore or to work against such
authoritarianism. Critical scholarship intended to liberate the
canonical text from controlled interpretation so that the text could
have its own fresh say. The outcome, initially unintended, was a
new institutional interpretation in the academy around "assured
results" which characteristically have no saving power. The academy, in order to fend off authoritarianism, opted for objectivity as
the norm for validity. The latent meanings in the text, however,
could not be honored and discerned by the "canonical interpretation" of academic objectivity any more than they could be made
available by the church's claim to canonical authoritarianism. True,
both the church in its authoritative certitude and the guild in its
thin objectivity are engaged in interpretation. Both, however, treat
their interpretation as a conclusion rather than an invitation. In
doing so, each violates the very power of canon, whose nature it is
to require and permit always new interpretation.[20]

IN THE MIDST OF CRISIS

Canon criticism, as we now have it is, I suggest, a response to a loss
of a normative, norming theological *habitus*. The timeless text is no
longer experienced as powerfully timeful and timely. But such an
understanding still leaves the questions, Why do we have canon
criticism just now? Why not earlier, since the old, normative, evangelical reading of the text was largely abandoned long ago? Why,
even when scholarly exegesis rejected that theological norming, was
such criticism not seriously challenged by canon before now?

I submit that canon criticism is on the agenda now because of a deep intellectual, political, and economic crisis that besets us all. Until this crisis, even the loss of the old norming process did not seem serious because we had fall-back positions in Enlightenment realities which seemed reliable. Canon criticism is a response to our recent awareness that academic objectivity offers no more satisfactory interpretation than does church authoritarianism. Canon breaks the grip of self-serving certitude in the church and the mask of objectivity in the academy so that we may see how much more open and dangerous is our interpretive task. Our loss of confidence in the canon of objectivity, as in the canon of certitude, is a new crisis for us. The failure of "objectivity" includes two distinct but related dimensions, without which canon criticism cannot be understood.

1. We face a profound epistemological crisis, because we now know that Enlightenment objectivity is no longer reliable.[21] This problem is evident in every intellectual discipline in our culture. With the loss of "objectivity" as "certitude," attention to canonical norms and canonical interpretation holds great attraction. That is, canon criticism comes now because our trusted modes of knowledge are in disarray.

2. The epistemological crisis is matched by the loss of Western political and economic hegemony, so that traditional claims of power are no more convincing than the old reliable opinions of certitude. We cannot seriously consider questions of knowledge without facing questions of power. We cannot talk about truth or truth-claims without noticing the reality of power and power claims.[22] As the hegemony disintegrates, as it surely is, new, long-silenced voices will be heard, which will now have or will insist on having power. Such voices cannot be ignored. As they speak about power, they inevitably make new sounds about truth. New sounds about power and truth force a new interpretive situation.

The loss of *certitude* and the loss of *domination* together open up new interpretive questions. The normative accepted interpretations of canon, either in church or academy, no longer prevail. We are driven back to the literature itself for norming, but that norming no longer honors or conforms to old certitudes or domination. Concerning canon, then, it makes a great deal of difference whether canon as norm is a *field of authorized possibility* in which we practice new interpretation, or a *field of certitude* for which we already know the right conclusions. It matters whether we imagine ourselves as on the way to truth or already possessing the truth. The former option commends itself, both because it is required in our situation and because it honors the restless authority and power of canon. Canon is a literature that must be taken with ultimate seriousness. Yet when we take it with ultimate seriousness as truth, we hear voices in the midst of the literature that we did not hear for a long time, because we were a party to the hegemony now waning. It is the waning hegemony of certitude and domination that requires and permits a return to the canon in all its timefulness.

The canon to which we return is the horizon for the investigation of norming guidance and a field for fresh discovery and articulation of latent meanings. The breakup of the hegemony shatters canonical interpretation which itself has become canonical, and requires a fresh entry into the canon itself for new reading. Canon asserts, even in the face of the collapsing hegemony, that these continue to be the books. They are relentlessly the books, even when we no longer have the certitude of truth and the monopoly of power which have for so long been companions of this literature. The canon permits us to return hopefully to these books, without the fellow travelers of certitude and domination.[23]

INTERPRETIVE RESTLESSNESS

The breakdown of our epistemological, political hegemony suggests that the old settlement of center and margin is now under harsh review. I further suggest that the urgent canonical question now is the relation of center and margin in the text and in interpretation. I have been stimulated by Kermode's work on literary theory, and Mary Douglas and Aaron Wildavsky's anthropological analysis.

Kermode relates the suggestive notion of center and margin to canonical interpretations. Reflecting on the theological reorientation that occurred in the Reformation, he writes,

> In disowning the authority and the tradition, Reform shows how
> it is possible to alter the relation of center to margin. . . . All such
> centralities (or centralizations) are in the nature of the case pre-

carious. Anybody can remarginalize what I centralized and centralize something else; anybody . . . can re-hierarchize the elements I was at pain to de-hierarchize.[24]

On deciding what is central in the canon, he says,

> Sometimes it appears that the history of interpretation may be
> thought of as a history of exclusions, which enable us to seize
> upon this issue rather than on some other as central, and choose
> from the remaining mass only what seems most compliant.[25]

Kermode observes that by convention and consensus certain pieces
of literature—and certain interpretations—assume a dominant,
controlling position, thereby making other literature and interpretation marginal in significance. The act of new interpretation may
rearrange this convention, so that "new literature" in the canon (or
new interpretation) takes on importance and becomes freshly
authoritative. Thus the distribution of power and attention in various
parts of the literature can and does shift, and with each interpretive
shift, the canon looks very different and takes on new meanings.

Kermode's suggestions about literature are reinforced by the
anthropological argument of Mary Douglas and Aaron Wildavsky,
who have used the concept of center and margin to analyze social
power and social relations.[26] The sociology of center and margin is
pertinent to our theme because the capacity to give authoritative
interpretation is a matter of social power, and not primarily a matter of insight or sensitivity.

Douglas and Wildavsky observe on the one hand, "The center is
complacent."[27] By the center they refer to those with expertise and
power, who are able to focus on small, specialized, technical questions because they believe and act as if the larger questions are
settled; and this center does not want those large settlements
reviewed. On the other hand, they say "The border is alarmed."[28]
Those who live at the edge are characteristically abrasive, restless,
and challenging, forcing those at the center to review the large
questions of power and certitude that they assumed were comfortably settled. The ability of "the complacent center" to fend off "the
alarmed border" is not a matter of being right but of having the
power to resist and the social consensus to claim authority. In both
church and scholarly interpretation, we are witnessing the erosion,

perhaps the collapse, of the old centrist powers' capacity to have unchallenged control of the text.[29]

Robert Wilson considers this issue in his analysis of central and peripheral prophets.[30] He discusses not the interpretation of the text but interpretation of social reality, although the issues and dynamics are much the same. Both concern interpretation determined largely by social position and social power. The more interesting prophets are those at the periphery who are voices for the marginal, who keep assailing, questioning, and hoping, and who occasionally require those at the center to review and decide again.[31] The interest in maintaining stability and the restlessness for change are evident within the text in and between those at the center and those at the periphery. What we have to discern is that the same is true in the interpretive community. It is this interchange of stability and restlessness that is now the issue for canonical interpretation.

Thus the literary question of interpretation (which is how canon has been posed among us) cannot be separated from the social questions of power, access, and certitude. Canon criticism is on our table because the "center does not hold" in its old form.[32]

The center does not hold any longer in the church because a protesting, abrasive practice of seeing anew assaults the accepted authoritative interpretation.[33] The center no longer holds in the academy for many interpreters, among them Third World and feminist interpreters, no longer wait on the historical-critical monopoly through which to discern the issues. We are led back to the canon by new voices to discern a new truth latent until now.

Thus I suggest that the urgency of canonization is itself a powerful contemporary practice of contextualization.[34] Our cultural context forces us to think about canon, about a timeless literature that has interpreted, interpreting timefulness. Our context is not simply one of pluralism, but of abrasive conflict and challenge.[35] The issue before us is how the settled centers of interpreted truth are addressed by the abrasive voices of challenge, assault, and invitation from the margin. The question is not only a literary question about heeding voices in the text that we have not noticed. It is also a sociological question of heeding interpretive voices we have not heretofore honored. The communal process of center and margin is acknowledgment that the lesser members must be honored in the interpretive process (1 Cor. 12:22–25). The wonder of canon, as Kermode asserts, is that this literature tolerates, invites, and attends to all these fresh probes unauthorized by the old occupants of the center.

THE CENTRALITY OF THE MARGINAL

Three dimensions of the canonical conversation between center and margin deserve comment.

1. The new situation of canonical awareness does not call us always to the center, but invites us to attend to voices of marginality in the text away from the center, to notice that the voices away from the center are also voices bred by the canon we are committed to honor and hear.[36] The canon does not consist only in the normative credo,[37] crucial as that normative credo is, but in the dangerous stories at the edge which protest the center.[38]

No one has done more to sound these other voices in the canon than Phyllis Trible, whose "texts of terror" are texts of unanswered pain and unresolved brutality.[39] What Trible has done is to centralize what has been at the margin and marginalize what has been at the center. Because of such work, we now take these unnoticed voices to be in some way voices for us and to us. Such interpretation from the margin reminds us that texts like these do exist in the canon; there really are people like Hagar norming in the text, and they speak a truth like that of the daughter of Jephthah. The center habitually gathers around von Rad's credo to say, "We cried out to the Lord and the Lord heard our cry" (Deut. 26:7). But Hagar and Jephthah's daughter are members of the interpreting community who have cried and not been heard, or who have been so rejected that their cry has been stifled and the text has been censored, or who simply have not been admitted to the interpreting conversation. They have boldly assaulted the centrist credo, however, and required that the center be changed and the credo heard differently. They have shifted our sense of the canon. Trible has shown us how texts at the margin may place the center in jeopardy, and all because the canon permits new truth to enter into the norming process.

2. Center and margin in the text are not unrelated to center and margin in interpreting. The hegemony of the academy is cracking,

not only because of "new method" but because of *praxis* that waits
for no authorized method. Among the poor and the marginal, in the
base communities, out of the resentment of Minjung,[40] we are
hearing new readings which are compelling and unavoidable. Thus
the story of Naboth's vineyard (1 Kings 21) can no longer be contained by questions of its date, whether vv. 27–29 are later, or whether
the Deuteronomist had to tone down the story because Ahab lived
too long. The voices at the edge run urgently past such questions
and read the text as a revolutionary manifesto about land, land
rights, and land usurpation, and about the circumstances under
which life is possible and death is decreed. Centrist interpretation
will not be able to make the "farm crisis" or the "peasant revolt"
disappear from the praxis of the text. The centrist church will not
stop these interpretive voices from letting the text touch contemporary questions of power. The canonical crisis concerns not only new
literary judgments, which Childs has so well illuminated, but new
social questions which have begun to be addressed by Norman
Gottwald.[41]

3. I cite one specific example of a canonical transaction indicating both literary and social dimensions of the interpretive act. The
center wants order and safety in the land. That is why Moses, in
Deut. 24:1–4, could announce a stringent rule against remarriage
after a "polluting" second marriage. Such remarriage would
threaten the land. Moses sounds like a "canon lawyer" who is always
situated in the center, who always gets it right, who always guards
the center.

Canon lawyers, however, cannot stop poets. In Jeremiah 3, Yahweh is articulated by a pathos-filled poet who casts an eye away
from the torah of Deut. 24:1–4 to glance at beloved, wretched Jerusalem. Yahweh yearns for Jerusalem and will take Jerusalem back—
the torah notwithstanding.[42] The poem and the poet know about
the truth of pain at the margin, and, from that pain at the margin,
they critique the certitude at the center reflected in the torah. By
articulating such a critique, the poet creates a new historical possibility. The poem of Jer. 3:1—4:4 moves to the center the pain that
had been at the margin, and thereby moves the certitude that had
been at the center to the margin.

In our particular interpretive context, where center and margin are freshly aware of each other, the presence of pain, the power of marginality, and the pathos of hurt are all heard freshly in the text and in the interpretive process. Pain and poverty have been very well kept at the margin by the excessive certitude or objectivity of classic canonical interpretation. We are seeing, however, that the marginalization of pain and poverty is not intrinsic to the canonical literature but is imposed on the text by the political process of canonical interpretation by the dominant community.[43] The text itself, under another reading, allows more voices to speak than does conventional, established interpretation. This other reading (in another context) is also seriously canonical.[44]

It is astonishing that the voices of marginality have not been crowded out of the text.[45] It is more astonishing that they are given credibility in the interpreting community.[46] The old voices of domination, enforced by military power, sponsored by oppressive regimes, legitimated by unyielding religious authorities, practiced uncritically by technicians, finally cannot stop the authoritative, authorizing cry of the poor and pained which is a voice in this text. This cry cannot be silenced because the same struggle of center and margin is present in the heart, life, mind, and will of God.[47] This canon compels us because it has insisted (as no other canon) that these other protesting, hurting, hoping voices are held to be constitutive for the life of society, as for the life of God.

Israel knows that when you come into the land, you will have a king who will get it right (Deut. 17:14–20). But Israel also knows that along with the king, a viable community must have a voice such as the voice of Moses, a prophet who will speak a different word not confined to the dominant rationality (Deut. 18:15–22).[48] That prophetic alternative in the face of Pharaoh becomes definitional for Israel and its literature. The force of the margin occurs in the prophets, in Deuteronomic abrasiveness, in the Pauline offer of justification by grace, in a theology of the cross, and in apocalyptic hyperbole of expectation, each of which crowds the center in desperate, unyielding ways. It is wondrous that the canon insists on these voices. It is sobering that much of established interpretation has made these voices marginal.[49]

INTERPRETATION AS EXPECTANT, INSISTENT CONVERSATION

I propose that there is a peculiar congruity between the odd dynamic of the text as center and margin (which we call canon)[50] and *our interpretive situation* of center and margin (which is our context).[51] I do not imagine that this tension of center and margin is the best or last interface of text and interpretation, or canon and context, but it is *our* interface. Canonical interpretation never gives an absolute grid for interpretation. It only permits us to find a reading through which we can be faithful. There is no eternal interpretation, no single "meaning." There is only timeless literature and timeful readings, and these together comprise canonical interpretation.

Our canonical work in biblical theology is to foster and participate in the conversation between center and margin. The voices at the center of the text must be honored and taken seriously. They are at the center for reasons judged good by our mothers and fathers in interpretation. To dismiss them or displace them as the center is foolish and likely a distortion. They are not, however, the only voice. There are those other voices included in the canonical literature and honored in a faithful interpreting community as they are honored nowhere else.[52] This interplay of center and margin is both a textual, literary problem and an interpretive, social problem for us. As center and margin engage each other, we shall discern something of how God's mercy and God's majesty together inhabit God's heart.[53]

The notion of the margin addressing and transforming the center suggests a different notion of canonical certitude. Douglas and Wildavsky write,

> Instead of the old recurrent imagery of knowledge as a solid thing, bounded or mapped out, we prefer the idea of knowledge as the changing product of social activity. It is not so much like a building, eventually to be finished, but more like an airport, always under construction. It has been compared to an open-minded communal enterprise, to a ship voyaging to an unknown destination, but never arriving and never dropping anchor.[54]

I submit that theological truth is like that. The canonical literature is the water in which the ship of interpretation must sail, "never dropping anchor."

The canon then is not a settled truth. It is an ongoing conversation in which the ongoingness is an epistemological decision about the character of truth. The hope is to keep the conversation going without excluding any voice or giving any voice veto. The conversation must be attentive to the role, function, gift, power, and claim of different voices.[55]

Such open-ended canonical enterprise leads finally to the notion of *canonical interpretation as a conversation* in which all members have voice, in which serious, transformative words are spoken between center and margin, in which the voice of the poor and the pained is taken so seriously as to be disruptively canonical. The canon does not permit reductionism, but opens the conversation to be "an ideal speech situation" in which all concerned parties have voice.[56] It is the failure of our dominant intellectual and political claims that makes ours a context for thinking about canon afresh. Another context would no doubt permit and require a different posture on canon or might not even face the question of canon. But we cannot postulate a context other than the one in which new voices sound, old voices are in question, old truth is in jeopardy, old power is at risk. The new conversation is on the way, and our critical task is to let all the voices be heard, in the hope that each will be changed by the presence of the others.

Paul Van Buren in his suggestive approach to Jewish and Christian transactions takes the metaphor of "being on the way together" for the possibility of serious engagement[57] and freedom from our tightly held separate and separating destinations. On the way, believers have only one business—conversation.[58] The canon is a recognition of which book we carry, how we talk together,[59] and what we talk about. Most of all, the canonical process is an honoring of all those who walk and converse with us. What is most astonishing is that on the royal road of fidelity, many walk with us whom the church and the academy have not noticed. The ones who are not noticed but who legitimately participate in the interpretive conversation are the poor, the marginal, and the powerless. The canonical project for us is to see how we all talk differently when they join the conversation, how we all walk differently when they accompany us.

In a world so enamored of power, control, certitude, and domination, we should be more amazed than we are that the voices of pain and poverty speak truthfully and powerfully in this interpretive conversation. We should not be so smitten with centrist categories that we fail to notice how odd this conversation is, how peculiar its participants, how strange its subject matter, how dangerous its possibility, how distinctly life-giving its hope in the midst of a world bent toward death. Precisely because this conversation is open and yet has a subject, obedient and free, celebrative of healing and informed by hurt, because of all of this, it is truth in this world of lies.[60]

James Muilenburg reflects on the destiny of this conversation called faith. He writes:

> The time appointed [Israel] by the grace of God never permits her the security of the present. No present is ever the consummation intended or desired by God. Every present is stamped with the seal of the "not yet." There were those, to be sure, who sought to congeal the present, but against this, the vicissitudes of time and the interior dynamic of the historical faith registered its emphatic protest. Over the whole Old Testament there is inscribed the preposition "until," and it is not without significance that its latest book, in a context of august imagery and mythological pageantry, should throb with the anticipation of the demonstration of God's final sovereignty expressed in the "until" of faith (Dan. 4:23–32; 7:1–22). So Israel's existence is always provisional, tentative, and preliminary of what is still to come.[61]

The canonical conversation is a tentative one with odd partners, as tentative as Israel's life in the world. We do our interpretation in a context in which some want to settle the conversation and silence many of the voices which shatter our truth and nullify our domination. This inescapable context makes our interpretive conversation more risky and more urgent. Entrusted to us in this conversation is a text of subverting timefulness even "until."

I submit then that canon and canonical interpretation are not and cannot be only timeless. Literarily, the canon is open literature in which "every effort of exegesis is justified without argument," as

Kermode has observed. Sociologically, our interpretive context is "the alarm of the border" pushing against the complacent center. Theologically our faithful interpretation is a provisional as "until," as Muilenburg has said so well. This interpretation is "never dropping anchor." It is, however, not rudderless. This interpretation knows the One to whom we must give answer. This One is the subject of text and interpretation; we dare say this One is the voice that haunts the text, our interpretation, and our faithful living. Attention to this haunting Voice in text and in life is the evangelical *habitus* which I believe finally concerns Childs, as it must concern us all.

NOTES

This essay was originally delivered at a "Biblical Jubilee" at Union Theological Seminary in New York, on April 9, 1987.

1. See the analysis of John Barton, *Reading the Old Testament: Method in Biblical Study* (Philadelphia: Westminster Press, 1984).

2. On the norming process, see David H. Kelsey, *The Uses of Scripture in Recent Theology* (Philadelphia: Fortress Press, 1975). Kelsey speaks of a *discrimen* rather than a norm, by which he means "a configuration of criteria that are in some way organically related to one another as reciprocal coefficients" (p. 160).

3. See Brevard S. Childs, *Introduction to the Old Testament as Scripture* (Philadelphia: Fortress Press, 1979). Such a judgment may be unfair to Childs, but at least in that book he makes an argument about canonical intentionality by reference to the shape of each book.

4. Brevard S. Childs, *Old Testament Theology in a Canonical Context* (Philadelphia: Fortress Press, 1985).

5. See Kelsey, *The Uses of Scripture*, where he speaks of "a particular *construal* of the *discrimen* in an imaginative judgment . . . imaginative characterization of the *discrimen*" (p. 167). Quite clearly the norming on which Kelsey reflects is an act of imagination, but it is not an undisciplined imagination.

6. On the modern reality of "homelessness," see Peter L. Berger et al., *The Homeless Mind* (New York: Random House, 1973). Insofar as the Christian canon was historically a response to the threat of Gnosticism, one may conclude that in the early situation of the church as well the canon is a home in the midst of intellectual homelessness, which took the form of amorphous pluralism.

7. On the interrelation of these two interpreting communities, see Brevard S. Childs, "Some Reflections on the Search for a Biblical Theology," *Horizons in Biblical Theology* 4 (June 1982): 1–12. Both communities, in very different ways, operate with accepted canonical forms of interpretation.

8. The phrase from Raymond Brown, *The Sensus Plenior of Sacred Scripture* (Baltimore: St. Mary's University, 1955) 28: "After all, in the Scriptures, we are in our Father's house where the children are permitted to play."

9. The phrase "house of authority" is from Edward Farley, *Ecclesiastical Reflection: An Anatomy of Theological Method* (Philadelphia: Fortress Press, 1982), 165–68 and passim. It is a useful phrase, even though a discussion of canon makes claims for the authority of the normative literature which Farley would not accept. The conclusion of the collapse of "the house of authority" has led to "foundational theology," but that is a theological position very different from the general claims made for canonical authority. It is interesting that in very different contexts Brown and Farley employ the metaphor of "house" for the general issue of authority and the specific matter of canon. Farley's thoughtful and discerning analysis is not to be taken lightly or answered easily. It appears to me, however, that the authority of scripture he critiques is idolatrous. I intend to argue another way of understanding canon precisely against such idolatrous certitude.

10. David Tracy, *The Analogical Imagination* (New York: Crossroad, 1981), 102.

11. Frank Kermode, *The Genesis of Secrecy* (Cambridge: Harvard University Press, 1979), 5.

12. Frank Kermode, *Forms of Attention* (Chicago: University of Chicago Press, 1985), 75.

13. Krister Stendahl, "Biblical Theology, Contemporary," *The Interpreter's Dictionary of the Bible A–D* (Nashville: Abingdon Press, 1962), 418–19, has most forcefully articulated the case for a rigorous distinction between "meant" and "mean." The discussion has moved sharply away from such a distinction, which is now commonly regarded as not sustainable. Stendahl's work came just as a fresh hermeneutical awareness dawned on scripture study which made that distinction most problematic. See the assessment of Stendahl's distinction by Ben C. Allenburger, "What Krister Stendahl 'Meant'—A Normative Critique of Descriptive Biblical Theology," *Horizons in Biblical Theology* 8 (1986): 61–98.

14. In different ways, this is the question of Kelsey, *The Uses of Scripture in Recent Theology*; and Childs, *Old Testament Theology in a Canonical Context*. However, Kelsey's approach is to observe the wide

variation in usages, whereas Childs seeks a way of "norming" that is less tolerant of variation.

15. This of course is a Christian vocabulary because the canonical discussion in biblical studies has been largely a Christian discussion. The same general claim might be made in a Jewish conversation about the torah. See James A. Sanders, "Torah and Christ," *Interpretation* 29 (1975): 372–90. For a carefully nuanced discussion of the issue from a Jewish perspective, see Paul van Buren, *A Theology of the Jewish Christian Reality* 2 (San Francisco: Harper & Row, 1987). See also M. H. Goshen-Gottstein, "Tanakh Theology: The Religion of the Old Testament and the Place of Jewish Biblical Theology," in *Ancient Israelite Religion*, ed. Patrick D. Miller, Jr. et al. (Philadelphia: Fortress Press, 1988), 617–44.

16. See the remarkable and daring treatment of the theme by Emil Fackenheim, *To Mend the World: Foundations of Future Jewish Thought* (New York: Schocken Books, 1982).

17. Edward Farley, *Theologia: The Fragmentation and Unity of Theological Education* (Philadelphia: Fortress Press, 1983). He characterizes the embrace of this center for interpretation as "*habitus*," a "cognitive disposition and orientation of the soul" (p. 35). Farley's portrayal of the loss of such a disposition and orientation may be a critical counterpart to the sociological analysis of Robert Bellah et al., *Habits of the Heart* (Berkeley: University of California Press, 1985). Though applied to very different spheres, both Farley and Bellah are concerned with the loss of foundational gestures of healthy and faithful humanness as habit, *habitus*. On the "Rule of Faith" as an interpretive framework, see Roman A. Greer in James L. Kugel and Roman A. Greer, *Early Biblical Interpretation* (Philadelphia: Westminster Press, 1986), 155–76.

18. Kermode, *The Genesis of Secrecy*, 123, refers to "those doorkeepers." See more fully Frank Kermode, "Institutional Control of Interpretation," in *The Art of Telling* (Cambridge: Harvard University Press, 1983), 168–84.

19. The monopoly of interpretation has such power that it is synonymous with the claim that "there is no salvation outside the church." A monopoly of interpretation leads to and entails a monopoly of salvation.

20. My misgiving about Childs is that he seems to regard canon as a conclusion rather than an invitation. While I do not resist the drawing of interpretive conclusions, I believe we must self-knowingly take responsibility for our interpretive conclusions and not imagine they are simply there in the text. Childs seems to believe that an objective, enduring conclusion can be drawn. I regard that as implausible and

believe that Kermode's general understanding of canon as a literature that justifies new interpretation is correct.

21. Elizabeth Schüssler Fiorenza, *Bread Not Stone: The Challenge of Feminist Interpretation* (Boston: Beacon Press, 1984), has shown how so-called objectivity is in fact partisan interpretation. More broadly on the failure of objectivity as a plausible epistemology, see Langdon Gilkey, *Society and the Sacred* (New York: Crossroad, 1981); Michael Harrington, *The Politics at God's Funeral: The Spiritual Crises of Western Civilization* (New York: Holt, Rinehart & Winston, 1983). On the general intellectual crises of "objectivity," see Alvin W. Gouldner, *The Coming Crises of Western Sociology* (New York: Avon Press, 1971).

22. See Jürgen Habermas, *Knowledge and Human Interests* (Boston: Beacon Press, 1968).

23. Kermode, *Genesis of Secrecy*, 127, characterizes hope as the pathology of every interpretation.

24. Kermode, *Forms of Attention*, 77, 93.

25. Kermode, *The Genesis of Secrecy*, 20.

26. Mary Douglas and Aaron Wildavsky, *Risk and Culture* (Berkeley: University of California Press, 1982).

27. Ibid., 83–101.

28. Ibid., 102–25.

29. When the margin decentralizes the old center, we begin to have a new framework for interpretation. On such a shift see Thomas Kuhn, *The Structure of Scientific Revolutions* (Chicago: University of Chicago Press, 1962). Thus "scientific revolutions" are "revolutions in interpretation."

30. Robert R. Wilson, *Prophecy and Society in Ancient Israel* (Philadelphia: Fortress Press, 1980).

31. James A. Sanders's program of "stability and flexibility" contains elements of the same dynamic of social consolidation and social criticism. See his "Hermeneutics," *Interpreter's Dictionary of the Bible, Supp.* (Nashville: Abingdon Press, 1986), 407. He writes, "The two basic modes are the constitutive and the prophetic, according to context." See also, idem, *God Has a Story Too* (Philadelphia: Fortress Press, 1979). His more programmatic essay is "Adaptable for Life: The Nature and Function of Canon," in *Magnalia Dei: The Mighty Acts of God*, ed. Frank Moore et al. (Garden City, N.Y.: Doubleday & Co., 1976), 531–60.

32. The phrase is from W. B. Yeats, "The Second Coming": "Things fall apart; the centre cannot hold. . . ." In a peculiar way, Yeats anticipates the literary-canonical notice of Kermode and the social analysis of Douglas and Wildavsky.

33. Such assaults on accepted institutional authority have been especially visible in the Roman Catholic church concerning Vatican

authority and the work of Leonardo Boff and Charles Curran, among others. But the same kind of assault is present in every church tradition. The visible cases concern a rightest center and leftist margin, but there are examples where the opposite situation pertains.

34. When expressed in absolutist form, insistence on canon may seem to be an act of decontextualization. I intend to argue, however, that to raise the question of canon as it is now raised is itself a reflection of a particular sociohistorical context. On the problem of decontextualization, see James Barr, *Holy Scripture: Canon, Authority, Criticism* (Philadelphia: Westminster Press, 1983), 81, 159, and passim. Barr employs the category of contextualization in his strictures against Childs. On the dispute between Childs and Barr concerning canon, see Frank Kermode, "The Argument against Canons," *The Bible and the Narrative Tradition*, ed. Frank McConnell (New York: Oxford University Press, 1966), 78–96.

35. To set the margin against the center in an ongoing confrontation is very different from a kind of relaxed pluralism which seeks no norm but permits a variety of "private truths." This uncritical, uncaring pluralism that is reduced to individualism is the target of the analysis of Robert Bellah et al., *Habits of the Heart* (Berkeley: University of California Press, 1985). Such a pluralism lacks the toughness of the dispute of center and margin. On such uncritical, uncaring pluralism as the "tradition of modernity," see the trenchant analysis of Alasdair MacIntyre, *Whose Justice? Which Rationality?* (Notre Dame, Ind.: University of Notre Dame Press, 1988), 326–48 and passim.

36. I use the word "breed" with intentional reference to Amos Wilder, "A Hard Death," *Poetry* 107 (1965–66): 168–69, where he writes: "Accept no mitigation/but be instructed at the null point:/the zero/breeds new algebras." The verb bespeaks a kind of newness that is both organic and surprising.

37. Cf. Gerhard von Rad, *The Problem of the Hexateuch and Other Essays* (New York: McGraw-Hill, 1966), 1–78.

38. Johannes Metz has seen the "dangerous" character of the stories. Thomas Ogletree, *Hospitality to the Stranger: Dimensions of Moral Understanding* (Philadelphia: Fortress Press, 1985), 5, poignantly characterizes the dangerous stories at the margin: "In laboring to build up an alternative social world and in resisting taken-for-granted patterns in the existing order, people engage in a good deal of story telling. The dynamic, however, is not that of a host entertaining and being entertained by a stranger. It is that of courageous people daring to share forbidden tales, bringing into view features of experience that have been suppressed if not altogether repressed. The listeners do not find strange or unfamiliar the stories they hear. They identify with them,

seeing in them variants of their own stories. The stories disclose the fact that their private troubles have a social basis. The stories are freighted with intense emotion. They uncover deeply buried pain; they bring relief from fruitless acts of denial; they awaken joy in the discovery of companions who are one with them in suffering and struggle. They provoke rage over the irrationality and arbitrariness of the structures of oppression; they heighten a determination to resist to the uttermost any further humiliation and degradation."

39. Phyllis Trible, *Texts of Terror* (Philadelphia: Fortress Press, 1984). In a less direct way, Samuel Terrien, *Till the Heart Sings* (Philadelphia: Fortress Press, 1985), has also born witness to the texts not usually placed at the center.

40. *Minjung Theology* (Maryknoll, N.Y.: Orbis Books, 1983).

41. See Norman K. Gottwald, "Social Matrix and Canonical Shape," *Theology Today* 42[3] (1985): 307–21; and Bernhard W. Andersen, "Biblical Theology and Sociological Interpretation," ibid., 292–306.

42. On the relation of these two texts, see Michael Fishbane, *Biblical Interpretation in Ancient Israel* (Oxford: Clarendon Press, 1985), 307–12.

43. See Frank Kermode, *The Art of Telling*, chap. 8.

44. The clearest example I know of the shift of reading because of context is told me by my kinswoman, Belle McMaster. She is deeply steeped in the psalms, and especially treasures Ps. 103. She had often read and recited vv. 3–5: ". . . who forgives all your iniquity, who heals all your diseases, who redeems your life from the pit, who crowns you with good as long as you live. . . ." That much was long known and valued by her. But it was worship in a Cuban base community of the poor that caused her to notice that after these wondrous verses, comes v. 6: "The Lord works vindication and justice for all who are oppressed." The context clearly required and permitted a new reading not possible prior to this context.

45. Sanders, "Adaptable for Life," 546–52, shrewdly observes how the canon takes on peculiar power and significance in the exile. He concludes that it is then that the judgmental prophets made " 'canonical' sense." That is, the situation of political, geographical, historical marginality caused these voices of social marginality to have peculiar authority and to become in a theological way, central. The exile is a time when voices of marginality are received in the center.

46. In a variety of current efforts at a hermeneutic, it is the texts of marginality that now receive attention. This is true of Trible's *Texts of Terror*, and, in a different way, James L. Crenshaw, *A Whirlpool of Torment* (Philadelphia: Fortress Press, 1984). It is not without the reality of context that new texts emerge in the center of the interpreting process. While this is true in many ways, the most dramatic and most important

is the decision for "God's preferential option for the poor," as a herme-neutical decision in the Roman Catholic church in Latin America. On this, see Donal Dorr, *Option for the Poor* (Maryknoll, N.Y.: Orbis Books, 1983), esp. 157–76; Gustavo Gutiérrez, *A Theology of Liberation* (Mary-knoll, N.Y.: Orbis Books, 1986), 114–19 and passim; and Christine E. Gudorf, "Liberation Theology's Use of Scripture," *Interpretation* 41 (1987): 5–18. It is the context that has forced a revision of the interpretive canon. This contextual requirement of the canon is evident in the more directly sociological presentations of the Latin Americans. These vari-ous works will not be recognized in their full significance unless they are recognized as an argument and proposal about the canon.

47. I submit that here we are very close to the evangelical *habitus* about which Childs is concerned. The move of the margin against the center is at work in canonical interpretation. Formal canonical ques-tions pose a *substantive* theological question about the character of God. On that basis we may say that the struggle of the margin against the center culminates in a theology of the cross. On this, see Douglas Hall, *Lighten Our Darkness* (Philadelphia: Westminster Press, 1976). This struggle is variously expressed christologically in such affirmations as Mark 8:35; 10:29–31; Phil. 2:6–8; and 2 Cor. 8:9.

48. On the role of the division of power as a way of preventing monopoly at the center, see Norbert Lohfink, *Great Themes from the Old Testament* (Edinburgh: T. & T. Clark, 1982), 55–75. The sociological notion that prophets are constituent for Israel is a counterpart of saying the voices at the margin are crucial for the canon.

49. The most obvious case of marginalization through interpretation is the loss of psalms of lament from the functioning repertoire of the church in its liturgy. This loss is accomplished by their banishment, by selecting out "usable parts," or by encasing them in such music that their abrasiveness is toned down.

50. Thus the tension of center and margin (an idea for interpreta-tion suggested to me by Kermode) is, I submit, a telling way to under-standing canon. I have explicated this theological tension in the tension between structure and pain in "A Shape for Old Testament Theology, I: Structure Legitimation," *Catholic Biblical Quarterly* 47 (1985): 28–46; and "A Shape for Old Testament Theology, II: Embrace of Pain," ibid., 395–415. On this tension generally in Old Testament scholarship, see my "A Convergence in Recent Old Testament Theologies," *Journal for the Study of the Old Testament* 18 (1980): 2–18.

51. The social analysis of Douglas and Wildavsky is surely pertinent to our understanding of the social forces that operate both in the tex-tual shape of the canon and in the shape of canonical interpretation. It is staggering that the church as a text-based community does regularly

assent to the marginal text as central. See, e.g., Conor Cruise O'Brien, "God and Man in Nicaragua," *The Atlantic Monthly* (August 1986): 50–72.

52. Robert Polzin, *Moses and the Deuteronomist* (New York: Seabury Press, 1980), has shown one case in which a countervoice is operative in the text, a voice that protests against and challenges a voice too long established and central.

53. The theme of margin and center has as its theological counterpart God's mercy and God's majesty, on which see Claus Westermann, *The Psalms: Structure, Content, and Message* (Minneapolis: Augsburg Pub. House, 1980), 90 and passim; and Walter Brueggemann, *Israel's Praise: Doxology against Idolatry and Ideology* (Philadelphia: Fortress Press, 1988).

54. Douglas and Wildavsky, *Risk and Culture*, 192.

55. MacIntyre, *Whose Justice? Which Rationality?* esp. 349–403, has explored the difficulty and importance of different traditions being in conversation and understanding each other. The theme of different voices of course evokes reference to Carol Gilligan, *In a Different Voice* (Cambridge: Harvard University Press, 1982). In important ways, Gilligan has called attention to a female voice that has been made marginal while the male voice has become central in our culture, even to having a monopoly. I suspect my understanding of the matter with reference to the canon is more dialectical than Gilligan's, but her study is important for the general argument.

56. The phrase is from Jürgen Habermas, who envisions communications free of domination. A helpful exposition of Habermas's ideal is offered by Rudolf J. Siebert, *The Critical Theory of Religion—The Frankfurt School* (Berlin: de Gruyter, 1985), 9–32. Pertinent to our discussion, Siebert asserts, "Nothing brings Habermas closer to the contemporary critical political theology and the Basic Christian Communities, in which it has its seat in life, than his universal communicative brotherhood-sisterhood ethics and his mystical interest" (p. 250). The base communities yearn to be "ideal speech situations" in which the margin is heard and taken seriously by the center.

57. Paul Van Buren, *Discerning the Way* (New York: Seabury Press, 1980).

58. Van Buren, ibid., 13, used the word "conversation" to translate *derek*. The conversation is "on the way" together.

59. On "how we talk together" see George A. Lindbeck, *The Nature of Doctrine* (Philadelphia: Westminster Press, 1984), esp. chap. 6. On p. 122, Lindbeck also alludes to the problem of locating the "center" of the text.

60. On truth in a world of lies, see Scott M. Peck, *People of the Lie:*

The Hope for Healing Human Evil (New York: Simon & Schuster, 1985). Peck's analysis is helpful, even though it is not as sociologically aware nor as textually focused as I would make the argument.

61. James Muilenburg, *The Way of Israel* (New York: Harper & Brothers, 1961), 128–29.

INTERPRETATION AND OBEDIENCE

7

The Commandments and Liberated, Liberating Bonding

THE PEOPLE OF ISRAEL had just departed from the Egyptian empire. They were certain of only two things. First, they would no longer submit to the brick quotas set by the empire. Second, Yahweh the Holy God was the great new fact and force in their life. Indeed, it was precisely Yahweh who had uttered the liberating decree, "Let my people go" (Exod. 5:1; 7:16; 8:1, 20; 9:1, 13). And they had gone! Pharaoh had not wanted them to because they were cheap labor. But they had gone. Yahweh was so powerful that Pharaoh could not stop the power of Yahweh for liberation. Now they were free.

A NEW BONDING IN COVENANT

In saying, "Let my people go," Yahweh had also said, "that they may serve me" (Exod. 7:16; 8:1, 20; 9:1, 13; 10:3). The exodus was not an offer of unbridled, unqualified, unfocused freedom that had no projection into the future. The exodus was to embrace a new bondage, that is, a new bonding (cf. Lev. 25:42).[1] The oppressive bonds of Egypt are broken. Now the liberating, covenantal bond of Yahweh is offered. Israel makes its way to Mt. Sinai for the new bonding, to be linked in a covenant with Yahweh that displaces Israel's submission to Pharaoh. Everything for Israel is at stake in this exchange of bondage for bonding.

They arrived at Mt. Sinai. The meeting with Yahweh is awe-inspiring, rooted in the awe of God's holiness. It is enveloped in the terror, splendor, danger, and inscrutability of God's theophany (Exod. 19:16–25).[2] God comes powerfully into the midst of Israel. God's massive presence intruded. God's overriding purpose pervades. Israel is caught up in a purpose more powerful than it can comprehend, in a presence more sovereign than it can imagine. The *awe of theophany* moves to the *offer of covenant*. The holy God of liberation commits God's own life to solidarity with Israel. This God is not ashamed from now on to be known as the God of Israel, to be with, care for, and preside over the life of Israel (Heb. 11:16). Yahweh's intention for Israel is not simply a liberating moment but an ongoing life together in covenant.

But on the way from the awe of theophany to the offer of covenant, there are terms, conditions, stipulations. The centrality of law in Israel means that Yahweh has a determined moral intention for this relation. The God who goes with Israel is not merely an available patron but a sovereign who will outgovern the empire. The ten commandments are the decree of the inscrutable God for the shape of the new, bonded relationship. These commands as decrees are to be taken as nonnegotiable terms for this alternative to the empire. They are policies that require interpretation, but they set the character and shape for new life.[3] They specify who God will be in Israel, and they make concrete the institutional life of this odd community whose destiny is in contrast to the empire.

The preacher's task is to set the commandments, the burden of obedience, in the context of the liberating memory. More than that, the preacher's task is to set us, the listening community, in the context of the exodus story, so that it becomes our story. We are the ones who have been offered liberation from the empire. We are the ones invited to a new bonding in covenant. We are the ones who watch in awe for the inscrutable presence and power of Yahweh. We are the ones who have been graced with the terms on which new life is possible. That is why the commandments begin, "I am Yahweh who brought you out of the house of bondage." What an opportunity for the preacher—to invite the congregation to begin acting outside the loyalties and possibilities, policies, and prospects of the empire!

On this beginning point for obedience, Christians need help

1. in seeing that deliverance from imperial power that dehumanizes and crushes is now available for us;[4]
2. in knowing that the alternative to the empire and its brick quotas is not unqualified, autonomous freedom but a new summons to obedience;[5]
3. in trusting that the terms of covenant law are an offer of bonding freedom, which is the only lasting freedom.[6]

The crucial relation between exodus and Sinai, between liberation and bonding, is at the center of the preaching task. Preaching in the American church is caught between two mistaken ideas. The first is the notion that we are rightfully and dutifully children of the empire, so that our proper destiny is to conform politically, submit economically, and obey morally whatever power is in charge.[7] The exodus narrative refutes such a conformist posture, because we are destined for liberation given by God from every such tyranny— political, intellectual, theological (cf. Gal. 5:1).[8]

The second mistaken notion is that having been made free, we are free to do whatever we want and be whomever we choose. The Sinai narrative refutes such a notion by asserting that the God who liberates is also the one who sets the terms for a human future. Preaching on these matters must attend to both mistaken notions, as well as to the central claim that true liberation lies in trust and obedience to the God of the exodus who binds us in a new bonding—outside the deathly reach of the empire. That is why the Lord of Sinai begins in self-identification with the exodus: "I am the God who freed you from slavery."

EXODUS MODES OF NEIGHBORLINESS

The purpose of the decalogue is to confirm in social, sustained, institutionalized, community form what was begun in the events of exodus.[9] The shape of the decalogue sets the perimeters for a new life that is neither oppressively conformist nor unrealistically autonomous. With these texts the preacher may help the congregation to think through an evangelical alternative to oppressive conformity and destructive autonomy, an alternative that is experienced as faithful covenanting.

The decalogue easily divides into two "tablets," the first concerning relation to God, and the second, relation to neighbor. To sustain the new freedom initiated in the exodus, these two relationships must be maintained faithfully, knowingly, and with discipline.[10] If either is distorted, the covenant vision of Sinai is put at risk.

1. New life in covenant requires a faithful, undistorted relationship with God. The clue to this proper relation is to remember that the God of the covenant is the God of the exodus. The God who there acted to liberate is the God who wills continued liberation in the community. The God who is to be honored and obeyed in covenant is none other than the one who had compassion for and solidarity with the slaves and authority and power over the rulers of the empire. The covenant community willed by this God is a community that continues to practice compassion and solidarity and that maintains vigilant criticism against every totalitarian agent and ambition.

Israel's life as a covenant community depends on a clear vision and a sharp memory of who God is. To forget God's radical character is to engage in idolatry, to imagine a God who is not so free, dangerous, powerful, or subversive as is the God of the exodus. Israel is tempted to tone down Yahweh's compassion for and solidarity with the powerless, to make God a bit more compatible with social "realism." Or else Israel seeks to tone down the abrasive power of Yahweh against oppressive powers for the sake of some modest, provisional accommodation to the rulers of this age.

But the liberating, sovereign presence and purpose of Yahweh that are asserted in the commandments are not negotiable and must not be toned down. Idolatry consists of harnessing God for our purposes, regarding Yahweh as a reliable ally in our interests, so that God finally becomes "useful" to us.[11] Viewing God as useful is a temptation of all zealous religion, conservative or liberal. The same temptation is a component of political ideology—in Israel's old royal-temple establishment or in contemporary claims that God is "with us" and endorses our way.

The second and third commandments (Exod. 20:4–6; 20:7) exposit this claim of the sovereign, liberating God who will be obeyed but not used, who will initiate new life for us but will not conform to our arrangements of life. To shun "graven images" means that God's power for life must not be captured in ideology, program, or institution.[12] To avoid "using the name" means that God's power must not be domesticated by us and for us. Thus, these commandments positively assert God's faithful power which takes initiative for new life. The commandments function critically as a warning against our temptation to "enlist" God in our efforts to have life on our own terms. Recovering the powerful freedom and free power of God is an urgent and critical task facing the preacher in our cultural setting which on the right harnesses God to our social inclinations and on the left trivializes God away from God's proper role in our life.

2. New life in covenant requires faithfully honoring and taking seriously covenant neighbors and the proper use of covenant property. New life entails sorting out who are persons to be honored and cared for, and what is property to be properly used. The "second tablet" insists that neither persons nor property are to be abused, that is, enlisted for other than their true purpose. The fifth through tenth commandments are assertions about the kind of caring neighborliness that ensures that a community of covenant will not degenerate into a society of abuse, disrespect, oppression, and, finally, brutality. The commandments are a line drawn against brutality. They insist that people do not *earn* standing in this community but are *entitled* to an honorable place simply because they belong in the community. Again the exodus memory is decisive, for it insists that the first liberated slaves received a new option for life from Yahweh, not because of merit but because Yahweh had freely entitled them to it according to Yahweh's sovereign, compassionate decree. That same sovereign, compassionate decree of entitlement is and must be operative in the community evoked by Yahweh. This link between neighborliness as social policy and the exodus is made explicit by Moses: "Love the sojourner therefore, for you were sojourners in Egypt" (Deut. 10:19).

The entitlement of communal dignity is extended to the elderly who may have lost their usefulness to society: "Honor your father and your mother" (Exod. 20:12).[13] The entitlement extends to the valuing of all members of the community, all of whom are to be given life and let live: "Do not kill" (Exod. 20:13). The entitlement extends to familial relationships, in which binding loyalties are to be honored and taken seriously: "Do not commit adultery" (Exod.

20:14). The entitlement extends particularly to the poor and defenseless who are not to be confiscated into debt slavery: "You shall not steal" (Exod. 20:15).[14] The entitlement extends to the right of all for justice, so that the courts are to stand as a defense and protection against distorted public power and public administration: "Do not bear false witness" (Exod. 20:16). Finally and decisively, old land boundaries of inalienable family land are to be honored and not perverted by commercial business or legal practice: "Do not covet" (Exod. 20:17).[15] This climactic commandment is to protect the weak in their small land holdings against the great power of government or those connected with the levers of government.[16]

The neighbor commandments derive from the radical claim of God's holiness in the first three commandments. God's holiness must not be domesticated. Nor must the dignity and value of the neighbor be violated.

While we may think of other areas of community life that should be brought under the claims of covenant, commandments five through ten are an astonishingly comprehensive statement concerning the dimensions of life to which the covenantal will of the liberating God is pertinent. The promise of the new, liberating bonding is forfeited when people are reduced to commodities, when the fragile social fabric of community is reduced to a set of technical transactions, when entitlements given as free gifts from God are reduced to merit and based on worth or productivity.[17] It is clear that the commandments envision a community that continues to be at work in liberating its members from all practices that cheapen, enslave, or brutalize.

In viewing the two tablets about a faithful, undistorted relation with God and a serious concern for covenant neighbor and covenant property, we may observe the relation between the first and tenth commandments. The first (Exod. 20:3) is about the truth of God's holiness, compassion, and freedom. The tenth (Exod. 20:17) concerns right land relations, in which the weak do not have their proper life-space taken from them. In considering these two commandments together, it is evident that Israel understood the close relation between the holiness of God and the humanity of the community. It is for that reason that the two "great commandments" are held together (cf. Matt. 22:34–40; 1 John 4: 20–21). Negatively, Israel understood that idolatry always leads to exploitative land policy, or coveting. The preaching task is to make clear and understandable the inextricable relation between a distinct discernment of heaven (the character of God) and a distinct discernment of earth (the organization of social power in the community). Distortion in either of these causes distortion in the others, which ends either in death in a disordered community, or oppression in a tyrannical community that has returned to the dehumanizing ways of Pharaoh.

A CALL FOR RADICAL EGALITARIANISM

In my discussion of the two tablets, I did not comment on the fourth commandment concerning sabbath (Exod. 20:8–11). That is because this commandment concerns both tablets and cannot be placed simply with one or the other.[18] Indeed, the sabbath commandment functions as the center and interpretive focus for the entire decalogue and therefore as the center of Israel's ethical reflection. The commandment looks back to the *rest of God*. It dares to affirm that Yahweh (unlike imperial gods) is so well-established, so surely in charge, so greatly respected by creation, so gladly obeyed by all creatures, that God's governance is not anxiety-ridden or frantic. The world is confidently, serenely ordered as God's good creation. That affirmation can lead to a "basic trust" among us about our place in the world.[19]

The commandment also looks forward to the practice of the human community. It asserts that responsive to God's well-believed governance, the human process in the world is not and must not become an endless rat-race of achievement, productivity, and self-sufficiency. Rather the goal and crown of life in the community of covenant is the freedom, space, and delight of sabbath rest.[20] In keeping sabbath rest, the human community replicates and participates in the tranquility God has ordained into the structure of creation. Sabbath as that "sacrament of basic trust" is sociologically radical, for it invites all members of the community to be in well-being and peace, without reference to power or position. Indeed, the commandment envisions an act of radical egalitarianism modeling new social relations, for in that day, "Your servant will be *as you,"* that is, entitled to equal rest.[21] One can hear in this commandment echoes of the powerful egalitarianism of the exodus. In the empire there is no day when slave is like master, but in covenantal sabbath practice there is such a day for "as you," when all social class distinctions and differentiations of power are dramatically criticized, jeopardized, and overcome. In this commandment, Israel acknowledges both *the precious rule of God* which is not harsh or anxious and *the precious possibility of human community* which, in imitation of God's generous governance, oppresses none. Taking this command as the center of the decalogue, I suggest that the entire decalogue proposes a radically different ordering of heaven and earth. It is modeled not after conventional modes of power but after the astonishing transformation of the exodus. The commandments envision a community so ordered that such liberating work goes on as the normal way of ethics.[22]

INTERPRETATION AS AN UNENDING RESPONSIBILITY

I suspect that for the preacher the most difficult yet most important task regarding the commandments is to handle their absoluteness while at the same time doing the required interpretive work necessary to faithfulness.[23] It is clear that for biblical faith, the ten commandments are absolute and nonnegotiable, God's sure decree. It is equally clear in the Bible itself, however, that Israel and the church maintained and practiced amazing *interpretive openness* in order to keep the commandments pertinent to the ongoing ethical burdens of the community in its various and changing circumstances.

Both points are important. The absoluteness and the nonnegotiability must be stressed against a kind of moral softness or indifference that dissolves or trivializes the ethical claims of biblical faith. The nonnegotiability must be insisted upon, even when it strikes some as authoritarian. Conversely, the need for interpretive openness must be stressed against every legalism and moralism that imagines all the questions are settled and so makes the character of command cold and unresponsive to the realities of life. That interpretive openness must be insisted upon, even when it strikes some as relativizing the claims of the covenant.

Nonnegotiability and interpretive openness must be held together in order to avoid both imperial absoluteness and destructive autonomy. I will take the fourth commandment on sabbath to illustrate this point. It is clear that (1) the Bible takes this command with abiding seriousness; and (2) the Bible continues to struggle with and reinterpret the claim and intention of the command. As the Bible itself is engaged in an open interpretive process, so the preacher may seek to engage the congregation in an interpretive process to ask how the liberating will of the covenant God is to be enacted among us.

It is clear that the sabbath commandment is part of an ongoing interpretive tradition in which we can participate. The commandment is neither dismissed as unimportant nor treated as flatly and absolutely obvious. It is and must be interpreted. Among the critical points to be noted in that ongoing work of interpretation are:

1. The version of the fourth commandment in Deut. 5:12–15 already departs from the Sinai version of Exod. 20:8–11 by articulating a new motivation. Now the reason for the command is not that God rested on the seventh day of creation, but that Israel remembers the exodus. Deuteronomy has handled the commandment in a sociologically more radical way by suggesting that sabbath is a sacramental reenactment of exodus which delivers people from the imperial burden. This version focuses on community experience, not the structure of creation.

2. Amos 8:4–8 indicates how the commandment is taken up into radical prophetic analysis. In this passage the sabbath command is said to function as a protection for the poor against sharp economic practice. Sabbath is a cessation from commerce so that the needy have a brief respite from relentless exploitation. The command becomes a ground for criticizing public practices in Israel that may have become as abusive as any in ancient Egypt before the exodus.[24]

3. In exilic and post-exilic thought, the sabbath becomes a crucial mark for the covenanted community that distinguished it from those in the empire who had no memory of the exodus. Isaiah 56:2 identifies sabbath-keeping as a characteristic mark of a blessed person, that is, one who enjoys the benefits of covenant. Then in Isa. 56:3–7, sabbath is made the qualifying mark by which to admit foreigners and eunuchs to Israel's worship. The command becomes

here the not very demanding entrance point through which unqualified people qualify for the covenant. The sabbath is a vehicle for countering extreme legalism that wants to make requirements a good deal more stringent.[25]

4. In his ministry Jesus violates the sabbath for the sake of humaneness. In Mark 3:1–5 he heals on the sabbath, and in Mark 2:27–28 he delivers his magisterial dictum that sabbath exists for the sake of humanity. In Jesus' circumstance, the sabbath had become an oppressive practice of social control. His response is congruent with and derived from the notion of exodus bonding, that is, acting against the commandment for the sake of liberation in the community. The commandment is valid, he seems to affirm, only insofar as it serves its intended witness to the exodus as a mode for continuing life in covenant. Jesus' dangerous ministry is in rescuing people from many "houses of bondage," each of which has been constructed by commandments that have lost their exodus orientation. Commandments that do not serve exodus stand under harsh criticism.

Briefly presenting such a trajectory of interpretation for the fourth commandment permits the congregation to see that while Israel took the commandments with great seriousness, it practiced interpretive openness so that the concern in each case is that the commandment be a vehicle for God's liberating bonding.

The contemporary church must criticize law and commandment which in fact enslave those who have been entitled. Thus the prohibition against killing, when read in the presence of the exodus, sounds different to oppressed peasants in Latin America than to middle-class Americans. The command to honor father or mother is heard differently in a family in which there is child abuse than in one in which children are respected. Serious evangelical faith understands the commandments as guides for God's liberating activity, and recognizes that when they work against that liberating activity, they must be reconsidered, as Jesus did with the sabbath commandment.

The purpose of such biblical preaching and teaching is not simply to exhibit interpretive diversity in the Bible (which in itself is worth doing). It is rather to summon the congregation to join this conversation about the commandments, to see what this command may now "mean" in order that liberated obedience may take place. In recent history, we have had to work against excessive restrictiveness practiced in the name of sabbath in a puritanical society. Now we need to ask instead what the sabbath commandment means in a society that reduces humanness to technical transactions.[26] In a society that reduces people to commodities, the acknowledgment of God's restfulness and the embrace of our own rest may make sabbath a crucial moral opportunity, and an important sacramental protest against the busy profanation of our common life.[27]

It is my suggestion that a similar and more detailed history of interpretation for each commandment could be identified in the Bible, and, beyond the Bible, in the history of the church. For preaching, the purpose of such historical recovery is to nurture the congregation away from moralism and toward serious bonding, away from self-sufficiency and toward serious liberating responsibility.

TRANSFORMATIVE OBEDIENCE

The decalogue is an invitation to evangelical obedience, that is, obedience rooted in the gospel, the practice of which is genuinely good news. Such obedience is good news because it replicates God's own action in the world for us. It is good news because such obedience lets our actions come into agreement with our proper identity as slaves liberated by God, as children welcomed to the household of covenant. It is good news because such obedience makes a community of human bonding possible in a world dead set against serious human bonding.

The first task for the preacher, I suggest, is not explication of particular commandments. It is, rather, showing that the Bible believes that the liberating alternative set into motion in the exodus continues to be a proposal for sustained, ordered social life. Because Yahweh is a different kind of sovereign, Israel is permitted to embrace a very different kind of obedience. This obedience is not the oppressive, despair-inducing obedience of the empire. Nor is it an obedience so rigid and narrow as that of some opponents of Jesus. It is an obedience rather, that is a genuine delight, because it makes humanness possible. No wonder Israel delights in the law (Ps. 119:97). Such obedience is not conforming but transformative (Rom.

12:2). It requires our best intellectual effort because in every new situation the intention of the commandments requires fresh and careful, bold and daring articulation.

The preacher and the congregation can celebrate that we do not have to guess about God's main intention for us. That has been disclosed. But such faith still seeks understanding. Such commands still await specific implementation. Such liberated bonding still awaits the concreteness of covenant community toward brother and sister, toward land and property.

NOTES

This essay appeared originally in *Journal for Preachers* 10 (Lent, 1987): 15–24, and is reprinted by permission.

1. On the implications of the new bonding at Sinai, see Martin Buber, *The Prophetic Faith* (New York: Harper & Row, 1949), chap. 5; and, more fully, idem, *The Kingship of God* (New York: Harper & Row, 1967), esp. chaps. 7 and 8.

2. On this theophany, see Samuel Terrien, *The Elusive Presence* (New York: Harper & Row, 1978), chap. 3.

3. George Mendenhall, *Law and Covenant in Israel and the Ancient Near East* (Pittsburgh: Biblical Colloquium, 1955), esp. 3–6, first saw that the decalogue constitutes "policy" from which other law is derived.

4. I have explored the grip the empire has on our imagination under the rubric of "royal consciousness" in *The Prophetic Imagination* (Philadelphia: Fortress Press, 1978), chap. 2.

5. On the powerful temptation to autonomy and unmitigated freedom as an ideology, see Robert Bellah et al., *Habits of the Heart* (Berkeley: University of California Press, 1985).

6. On the yearning in our society for more serious bonding, see Daniel Yankelovich, *New Rules: Searching for Self-Fulfillment in a World Turned Upside Down* (New York: Random House, 1981). Even William Masters and Virginia Johnson, *The Pleasure Bond: A New Look at Sexuality and Commitment* (New York: Little Brown, 1975), have come to see that real "pleasure" requires some bonding.

7. See Dorothee Soelle, *Beyond Mere Obedience* (Minneapolis: Augsburg Pub. House, 1970).

8. Michael Walzer, *Exodus and Revolution* (New York: Basic Books, 1985), has exposited the revolutionary impetus contained in the exodus narrative.

9. Walter Harrelson, *The Ten Commandments and Human Rights* (Philadelphia: Fortress Press, 1980), has well explored the potential in the decalogue for matters of social policy and the institutional shaping of public life.

10. Douglas Hall, *Imaging God: Dominion as Stewardship* (Grand Rapids: Wm. B. Eerdmans, 1986), has recently suggested a third decisive relation with the nonhuman world. While he is surely correct, that relation lies outside the explicit structure of the decalogue.

11. On the theme of "usefulness" as a distortion of God, see Walter Brueggemann, *Hopeful Imagination* (Philadelphia: Fortress Press, 1986), chap. 4.

12. On the social power of contemporary idolatry, see *The Idols of Death and the God of Life*, ed. Pablo Richard (Maryknoll, N.Y.: Orbis Books, 1983).

13. On the ethics of the elderly in the Bible, see J. Gordon Harris, *Biblical Perspectives on Aging* (Philadelphia: Fortress Press, 1988).

14. Here I accept the persuasive hypothesis of Albrecht Alt, "Das Verbot des Diebstahls im Dekalog," in *Kleine Schriften I* (Munich: C. H. Beck, 1955), 333–40. Alt argues on the basis of the texts such as Deut. 24:7 that the command originally had a direct object, "Do not steal a man," and prohibited kidnapping in which the object was sold into slavery. More generally, see Robert Gnuse, *You Shall Not Steal* (Maryknoll, N.Y.: Orbis Books, 1985), who relates the commandment more directly to economic policy and practice.

15. On the commandment, see Marvin Chaney, "Thou Shalt Not Covet Your Neighbor's House," *Pacific Theological Review* 152 (1982): 3–13.

16. Chaney, ibid., takes Mic. 2:1–5 as an important interpretive comment on the tenth commandment. He follows the suggestive proposal of Albrecht Alt, "Micha 2:1–5," in *Kleine Schriften III* (Munich: C. H. Beck, 1959), 373–81. More generally, on Micah as a critic of rapacious social policy, see Hans Walter Wolff, "Micah the Moreshite—The Prophet and His Background," in *Israelite Wisdom*, ed. John Gammie et al. (Missoula, Mont.: Scholars Press, 1978), 77–84. See my discussion in chap. 11, below.

17. Abraham Heschel, *Who Is Man?* (Stanford, Calif.: Stanford University Press, 1965), has most eloquently articulated this crisis in our understanding of humanness in modernity.

18. On the cruciality of the sabbath commandment in the decalogue, I am indebted to the discerning analysis of Patrick D. Miller, Jr., "The Human Sabbath: A Study in Deuteronomic Theology," *Princeton Seminary Bulletin* 6 (1985): 81–97.

19. I am, of course, appealing to the poignant phrase of Erik Erikson; I intend it, however, not simply in a psychological mode but in a more inclusive way as "at homeness" in the world.

20. Abraham Heschel, who has so wisely exposited our human crisis, has also well and eloquently understood the alternative carried in the sabbath (*The Sabbath: Its Meaning for Modern Man* [New York: Farrar, Straus, & Young, 1951]). For Heschel the sabbath is the source of any alternative to our rampant profanation of human life.

21. See Hans Walter Wolff, *The Anthropology of the Old Testament* (Philadelphia: Fortress Press, 1974), 139–40.

22. Brevard S. Childs, *Old Testament Theology in a Canonical Context* (Philadelphia: Fortress Press, 1985), chap. 7, has presented a suggestive exposition of the decalogue, esp. stressing its theonomous claim.

23. On the need for interpretation to keep a timeless document timely, see David Tracy, *The Analogical Imagination* (New York: Crossroad, 1981), chaps. 3 and 4, esp. p. 102.

24. See Bernhard Lang, "The Social Organization of Peasant Poverty in Biblical Israel," *Journal for the Study of the Old Testament* 24 (1982): 47–63, esp. 58–59.

25. On the intention of Isa. 56 in contrast to a more rigorous alternative, see Elizabeth Achtemeier, *The Community and Message of Isaiah 56—66* (Minneapolis: Augsburg Pub. House, 1982), 32–37.

26. W. Gunter Plaut, "The Sabbath as Protest: Thoughts on Work and Leisure in the Automated Society," in *Tradition and Change in Jewish Experience*, ed. A. Leland Jamison (Syracuse: Dept. of Religion, Syracuse University, 1978), 177, writes: "I therefore view the sabbath as potentially an enormous relief from, and protest against, these basic causes of unrest. Once a week it provides us with an opportunity to address ourselves to the who-ness rather than the what-ness of life, to persons rather than to things, to Creation and our part in it, to society and its needs, to ourselves as individual and yet as social beings."

27. Matitahu Tsevat, "The Basic Meaning of the Biblical Sabbath," in *The Meaning of the Book of Job and Other Biblical Studies* (New York: Ktav, 1980), 49–50, says of the sabbath, "Every seventh day the Israelite renounces his autonomy and affirms God's dominion over him. . . . Keeping the sabbath is acceptance of the sovereignty of God."

PART 3

OBEDIENCE AS AN ACT OF INTERPRETATION

8

The Transformative Agenda of the Pastoral Office

PASTORAL CARE INFORMED BY THE GOSPEL is entrusted with a ministry of transformation:

Do not be conformed to this world but be transformed by the renewal of your mind, that you may prove what is the will of God, what is good and acceptable and perfect. (Rom. 12:2)

Like all evangelical activity, pastoral care is to permit, legitimate, and evoke change toward life in the kingdom and away from life with the "rulers of this age." The promise of pastoral care is that we may be transformed and need not be conformed.

Evangelical pastoral care knows about the "bondage of the will," about fearful conformity to the "rulers of this age," about submission to alien value structures, worldviews, and symbol systems. It knows about our helplessness, hardness of heart, and our paralysis.

It also knows the transformative truth of the gospel, the operation of God's life-giving spirit, the gift of new possibility given from outside us. It knows that human life is not a closed system. Even where life seems closed, God's gifts are inscrutably given. Thus evangelical pastoral care is an act of powerful, resilient hope against the despair of our world which believes no change is possible. But it also hopes against the romanticism of our age which believes change is an easy painless option. Change is not impossible, but it is not easy or painless. Pastoral care is buoyant about the prospect for change and candid about the cost.

Pastoral care in our culture is tempted to equate the transformative promise of the gospel with a practice of Stoicism. Like its classical counterpart, modern Stoicism is committed to coping, adapting, and enduring, because it believes that facing hurt honestly will lead to diminishment, failure, and rejection. A modern model of health and pathology which closely adheres to Stoic perceptions of reality is offered by George Vaillant in his book *Adaptation to Life*,[1] which raises acutely the contrast between Stoic and Christian discernments of care.

The Stoic tradition proceeds without reference to matters of transcendence, holiness, and mystery, and therefore without reference to faith, obedience, and discipleship. Inevitably, the self is treated as an autonomous system that retains control over self and has no compelling conversation partners who are privileged to intrude in ways that decisively matter. Vaillant concludes that healthy people are capable of adaptation, and the less healthy are not. In general, Stoicism values a kind of health that raises no serious value questions beyond the health of the subject.[2]

The presuppositions of modernity do not permit the theological issues in contemporary pastoral care to be raised. There is a growing awareness among us that modernity in and of itself is a pathology.[3] To find norms for health in the constructed world of modernity is rather like calling evil good, darkness light, bitter sweet, and sickness health (cf. Isa. 5:20). In this chapter I will explore resources in biblical faith for a practice of pastoral care that is distinct from and critical of dominant notions of health in our society.

Pastoral care that is biblically based must join issue with the views of health and pathology offered by modernity, and it can do so only on theological grounds.[4] We are at a moment in pastoral care when a fundamental critique of the Stoic values in our culture must be mounted. But more importantly, we are at a time when the counteroffer of evangelical faith must be clearly stated and intentionally practiced. Otherwise we may only endorse and enhance the sickness to which we have grown uncritically accustomed. Pastoral care will have the capacity to join such an issue only as it is intentionally grounded in and authorized by a truth claim that is based outside our cultural values. In what follows I explore an intentionally biblical rootage for pastoral care which offers a powerful alternative to the mode of health offered by our culture.

REDEFINITION THROUGH
BIBLICAL METAPHOR

Pastoral care that is biblically based is essentially a dramatic enterprise. Like all healthy human interaction, it is shaped and mediated through a specific set of metaphors[5] that are covenantal and that allow free and dangerous roles for both parties to the drama.[6] The drama itself, which is an interaction between covenant partners, is the only route to real healing. Pastoral care that understands itself as a part of this drama insists that certain metaphors, based in the traditions of biblical faith, are nonnegotiable for life and health. The interactions of pastoral care are explorations to see how life is discerned, appropriated, lived, and hoped differently when it is discerned, appropriated, lived, and hoped through these metaphors. I mention here three such metaphors of the biblical tradition through which health is mediated to us.

1. Biblical faith is an invitation to become a *child of God*.[7] The metaphor stretches back to exodus (Exod. 4:22; cf. Hos. 11:1; Isa. 1:2) and forward to the lyrics of John 1:12. The world is affirmed as a home to orphans who have now been adopted (Hos. 14:3). The world is offered as freedom to slaves who have now been emancipated (Gal. 4:1–7). The child of God belongs with the family and is destined for a rich inheritance with other members of the family.

2. Biblical faith is an invitation to be *God's friend* (John 15:15).[8] A friend of God is one who knows ahead of time what is to be done, who can speak candidly, critically, and supportively, and who can participate in the work God is to do.

3. Biblical faith is an invitation to be *a servant*, to live a life of following that is costly and healing (Mark 10:43–44; Isa. 42:1–4). Servanthood introduces the category of obedience, for a disciple does obey her teacher. But it also bespeaks risk, for it entails being on the way, joining with a purpose whose destination is left safely in the hands of the one who leads.

These metaphors are invitations to transformation: a child of God who is at home, adopted, emancipated, awaiting inheritance; a friend of God who participates with God in a practice of openness, vulnerability, and candor; a servant of God who is under way in obedience and risk.[9] Each of these foundational metaphors resists the pathological values of our culture and cannot help but yield certain kinds of health. Pastoral care in practice is the exploration and embrace of these metaphors as a countercultural activity of health. Pastoral care involves theological reflection on the adequacy and reliability of such metaphors to see if they will hold and if they can be trusted amidst the realities of our experience. The absence of these metaphors in the values of modernity is noteworthy and appalling. The modern person tends not to be child, but orphan, not friend but stranger, not servant but independent operator.

The conversations that constitute pastoral care are dramatic—not moral, psychological, ontological—in the sense that the metaphors of the tradition provide a language that invites to playful probing of new identities, vocations, and destinies that are given through this language. Much of the conversation itself is participation in this drama which mediates new life. Transformation comes in the awareness that new dramatic possibilities are available—but only by the embrace and practice of these metaphors. None of these metaphors permits or encourages adaptation to the circumstances around us or to the ideologies of alienation and competence which beset us. None of them accepts the Stoic temptation to remain docilely in situations of despair or domination. All of them invite to a restless reception of newness about to be given and press toward a new world over which we do not preside, but in which we live at home, adopted, freed, open, vulnerable, obedient, at risk. A child is always vulnerable. A friend is always at risk. A servant is always called to accountability. The relation discerned through these metaphors permits, indeed, requires a sense of self which is either unrecognized or resisted in our culture.

HEALTH SHAPED BY FAITH

Behind and through these metaphors which invite to an alternative drama, we can identify five claims of biblical faith that offer different characterizations of health and therefore matter decisively to pastoral care. Each offers a decisive alternative to the perceptions of modernity.

God's Reality Is the Source of Health

Health has to do with the reality of God's character. This is not simply an old doctrinal conviction, but a claim of immediate pertinence to our daily life.[10] To begin with this affirmation is to assert that an autonomous self who lives from self and toward self without transcendent reference is not and finally cannot be healthy. God is not an old convention, but the only source of power for life.

Much contemporary personality theory makes the individual person both the unit of meaning and the norm of reference. Karl Barth has seen clearly that "autonomy" not "rationality" is the real issue for modern men and women; what the individual wants, seeks, desires, and fears has become the real problematic.[11] In a popular way, Carl Rogers has carried this to the extreme, and the undirected conversation waits for meaning to be generated and articulated by the individual who is an isolated subject.[12] The problem is not only a theological one that ignores the truth of God, but pastorally it places too much demand on the person who finally must receive and cannot generate identity.

Against such a notion, John Calvin may be taken as a normative voice in evangelical faith (without all the scholastic baggage of much derivative Calvinism).[13] Calvin is clear at the outset that there is no right knowledge about human personhood unless there is right knowledge about God, and, conversely, there is no right knowledge about God without right knowledge of human personhood. The two elements of knowledge are not the same, but they are intimately linked. That is a given of this pastoral tradition. For that reason the pastoral care community is not free to opt for a Stoic anthropology which believes the banishment of God is necessary to health and freedom. Serious pastoral care must engage in serious intellectual reflection on who the true God is and what, if any, difference the reality of God makes.

The unit of healthy meaning, then, is not the autonomous individual. The unit of meaning is at least the individual person bound in a deep and unresolved covenant with this prior One.[14] The pastoral care agenda can neither escape the claims of covenant nor ignore covenant because it has been distorted in authoritative ways, but must instead ask who the real covenant partner is. The question to be asked in determining health is whether the God thought to be present in the conversation or in one's life is a false god or a false covenant partner.[15] Our theological work is to find ways of articulating this other One who initiates a relation and conversation of life and health. The responsibility to identify idols and articulate the true God who gives life should energize and summon those in pastoral care to more serious reflection on the narrative memories of Israel and the church which disclose to us the truth of God. It is precisely in those narrative memories that the God who initiates health-giving transactions is primally available.

It is the *holiness* of God that keeps life open to mystery, keeps our achievements and fears tentative and provisional, and provides contexts for our dysfunction and for our faithful function (Isa. 57:15–16). That holiness prevents life from closing in on us and crushing us with burdens.[16]

It is the *sovereignty* of God that provides a norm for our conduct and our values (Isa. 37:26–29). We finally live not in a relativistic world but in a world where some moral wheels do not need to be reinvented. God's rule provides ground for a critique of those values of modernity that destroy. Without such reference we ourselves (as well as those seeking pastoral care from us) are likely to be excessively fascinated with the values of modernity, destructive though they may be, especially if we can "work" those values to our advantage.

It is the *graciousness* of God that assures us of worth we cannot generate for ourselves and value which we need not in anxiety daily establish for ourselves (Matt. 6:25–34). Evangelical faith confesses that God gives God's self for our life and health. It is nothing other than such transcendent self-giving that makes our life possible. Nothing brings life like an act of costly vulnerability.

Pastoral care is committed to the truth of theological reality, so that the issue of the character of the true God cannot be avoided. It is of course true that bad theology has been destructive for many people, but that is no warrant to abandon the theological dimension of human health. Pastoral care has effectively addressed the issue of authoritarianism in the name of God, but, as Richard Sennett has shown, autonomy is equally problematic because it also has power to destroy.[17] Pastoral care has not addressed the issue of autonomy with equal effectiveness and has at times not perceived it as an equally serious problem. We serve no one by throwing over authoritarianism for the sake of autonomy. Autonomy is neither a live nor a life-giving option, because we are inevitably made and modeled in the image of someone or something. Religious pathology, then, may appear either as authoritarianism which crushes or as autonomy which seduces.

The work of pastoral care is to find ways to articulate and discern the true rule of God—holy, sovereign, gracious—which transforms both categories. In the rule of this God, authoritarianism yields to glad authorization and autonomy yields to an obedient belonging which is perfect freedom. One has a right to expect the pastoral care community to insist upon and practice this peculiar claim entrusted to us, which makes a decisive difference to models of health in our society. Very likely some who seek pastoral care are more ready to receive such a word than we are to speak it.

Pastoral care is entrusted with witness to the true God whose sovereignty does not crush and whose graciousness does not abandon. The true God who is known in holiness, sovereignty, and graciousness is the one who enters life with transformative power. This is the God who liberates the slaves, gathers the exiles, feeds the hungry, and raises the dead. It is precisely the reality of this transformative God that permits pastoral care to practice transformation in the midst of human reality. We are required to ask: What if this gospel of God is true? Have we the right to bracket it out, if we judge it to be the source of life?

The Centrality of Call

A second claim of biblical faith that concerns us in transformative pastoral care is vocation.[18] A pastoral care community which moves from an affirmation of a God who creates and calls dares to discern human life as purposefully related to the hopes and dreams of the holy God. God hopes powerfully for every human person. That hope is the engine and power for living that lets life be worthy and significant as well as buoyant and joyous.

The Stoic tradition teaches that an unexamined life is not worth living. The biblical tradition in parallel fashion affirms that an uncalled life is scarcely possible to live, for its outcome is failed energy and finally fatedness. The transformation of human life comes from identifying the One who calls and finding out the substance of that call in a concrete way.

1. Evangelical faith sets the human vocation as *praise*. The Westminster catechism in its well-known first answer was able to say,

"Man's chief concern is to glorify God and enjoy [God] forever." That sounds medieval, but if we are indeed God's creatures, bound to and made for God, this doxological affirmation follows.[19] The alternatives to this work of praise, which were all anticipated by Ecclesiastes before modern Stoicism—work, leisure, money, power —all end in fated cynicism and vanity. Today, when people accomplish things our culture defends as adequate, the gods of modernity have been served and there is nothing more to do except enjoy the blessings of modernity. Such service misses completely the theological reality, however; the gods of modernity do not expect or evoke praise, for praise is a practice of self-abandonment. The gods of modernity require much, but what they require ends in self-mastery, not self-abandonment. To have life referred to God in glad self-abandonment transforms human life. Then life ends not in self-fulfillment; instead, it is "lost in wonder, love and praise."[20]

2. Evangelical faith sets the human vocation as *obedience*. God's calling is not only to refer life back to God in praise. God's calling is to obedience in the world for the sake of the neighbor. Since the Enlightenment, and particularly since Freud and the advent of modern psychoanalytic theory, obedience has become a deeply problematic category.[21] If we are to escape the trap of modernity which makes the individual the unit of meaning, we must think with reference to a will other than our own. The God who calls, and from whom we receive vocation, identity, and personhood, is not an amorphous mass or a romantic sensitivity, but a moral will.[22] God intends something for creation through human persons and human community. It is not only that the healthy person enjoys communion with God, but that the healthy person seeks to discern the will of God and submit their own will to that overriding purpose. We may understand such submission in quite concrete ways with reference to the commandments (cf. Mark 10:19). Or we may embrace the general sweep of God's purpose in terms of liberation and reconciliation (cf. Mark 10:21). Either way, the person is not only a recipient of God's love but also an agent for a purpose that overrides individual work and in doing so strangely enhances personal worth and joy.

3. Evangelical faith sets the human vocation as *mission*. One's life may be put in the service of God's intention for creation. Excessive

attention to success, well-being, security, and comfort is not a focus for a pastoral understanding of human existence. Such a goal is at best an idol of modernity. Because of the ideology of autonomy and the modern notion that full humanness requires the banishment of God, modern people live uncalled lives and understand themselves in relation to no transcendent mandate, no holy purpose, no aim larger than their own well-being.

The outcome is likely to be either a kind of fanaticism that focuses life energies on a self-determined goal that is finally unworthy and beyond criticism or a frittering away of one's life and, finally, despair. One can indeed manage in either of those ways; in fact, the values of our culture celebrate and legitimate such lives. Pastoral care grounded in biblical faith, however, cannot settle for such a thin understanding of human destiny. It hopes for much more and promises more.

The categories of praise, obedience, and mission sound strange to us. In our culture we do not readily think of health in such terms. These elements nonetheless articulate what our theological tradition has judged to be faithful and responsive to the reality of God. We are at a critical point in the redefinition of pastoral care, wherein we need to think through the tradition entrusted to us, to see if it provides the elements that are essential for well-being. The crisis of categories we face not only concerns how to arrive at well-being but how to determine afresh what we mean by that term.

The Neighbor as Indispensable Other

Whereas Stoic thought is content to have the individual be detached, the biblical tradition has to do with passionate engagement with the neighbor. This dimension of humanness occurs in the earliest memories and mandates of the tradition (Exod. 20:16–17; Lev. 19:4). It is articulated by Jesus as the second great commandment (Mark 10:31). A key question of Jesus' teaching concerns life with the neighbor (Luke 10:29–37).

Today, concern for neighbor surfaces but never becomes a point of critical reference. The awareness of the cruciality of care and love is often limited to those close at hand. It has no transcendent references and does not speak beyond local convenience. The Pauline affirmation (1 Cor. 13:4–7) cannot be confined only to spouses, children, and friends as those who depend on us (cf. Matt. 5:46–47), but applies to a wider circle.

Neighbor love is foundational to both earliest Israel and the early church. John Elliott has suggested that providing a "home for the homeless" is crucial to the earliest Christian ethic.[23] Parker Palmer has identified an entire program of Christian ethics in the formula, "hospitality for the stranger."[24] Thomas Ogletree shows how hospitality is the central substance of a biblical ethic.[25] That is much more radical than the children of modernity would acknowledge.

Is such a practice of hospitality simply religious primitivism or sociological naiveté? Have we outgrown such a mandate, so that competence and self-sufficiency replace the cruciality of the neighbor? Technical control of life that displaces neighbor comes not at a specific evolutionary point. Rather autonomy and self-sufficiency as a mode of living build upon economic development that provides the wealth by which people can substitute controllable machinery for unadministrable partners. Hospitality is the insistence that life must be kept open to those unlike us, not only for their sake but for ours as well. In such a perspective, health does not derive from self-sufficiency, but from openness, interdependence, commitment, and solidarity. Modernity hopes for the banishment of the neighbor in order to live an unbothered life. But pastoral care rooted in the Bible stands as a mighty protest against such a mistaken notion which finally will not yield life.

The neighbor as a health agenda involves not only the mandate to *care* but the foundational need to *receive* what someone else gives unconditionally. The model for such a notion of health is enacted by Elijah in receiving from the widow of Sidon who seems to have nothing to give (1 Kings 17:10–11), and by Jesus who requests from the Samaritan woman at the well (John 4:7). It is indeed blessed to give. But it is also subversive to receive life as gift, and even more blessed to receive from those who seem to have nothing to give or who are so disqualified and contaminated that we would rather not receive.

In a biblical understanding of life, the neighbor is not extra, marginal, or elective. The neighbor is definitional to social reality. The neighbor is indispensable for health, not only to care for but as a giver of gifts which we cannot generate for ourselves.

When Sin and Forgiveness Are
Not Trivialized

A fourth aspect of the biblical tradition related to pastoral care is the honest recognition of the reality of evil and the sense of sin. On the one hand, we are caught in a sin-practicing system of social reality which does evil in our name and on our behalf, and from which we benefit. On the other hand, in concrete ways we too are people who commit acts that leave us in a world of genuine guilt. The Stoic pastoral care model of maturity nullifies the seriousness of sin and evil and therefore makes unnecessary the requirement of repentance and the gift of forgiveness. We never need say we are sorry if there is no sense of the embrace of evil in our midst.

The reality of guilt must be taken with greater seriousness. Robert Lifton has seen that healthy guilt, when properly discerned and resolved, can empower one to new actions.[26] Lifton's analysis of nuclear numbness leads to the conclusion that numbed people who become incapable of guilt are likely to be careless, depressed, or cynical people, incapable of caring in imaginative ways. His point is not to make people feel guilty, but to deal seriously with real guilt in ways that make a positive, liberating, transformative difference.

But the issue of evil, sin, and guilt cuts deeper. Do modern people nurtured in Stoicism have no capacity for criticism of self or the system? Is the capacity for self-transcendence and transcendence of vested interest absent? Can such children of modernity not see that the social system has gone awry, that it serves some at the expense of others, that private virtues are out of sync with public practice and policy? Surely such suspicious awareness (and self-awareness) belongs to maturity. Are there norms from which children of modernity can deduce moral outrage about anything—bombing hospitals or starving and freezing the poor? The extent to which such sensitivities are not present may be a measure of how completely the privileged are domesticated by the system and thus have lost the capacity for humanness. Faithful pastoral care may indeed involve nurture in suspicion about social reality so that we do not fail to notice the massive reality of evil.

In contrast to norms of modernity, biblically based pastoral care promises that forgiveness is possible. The biblical tradition celebrates that there is one who will forgive. There is real opportunity to begin again unburdened. Forgiveness is difficult, however, because it involves being acted upon, being addressed, being given free gift, being intervened for, allowing another to have a voice in one's identity and future. Promise of forgiveness is available, but it cuts deeply against the values that seem operative among the children of modernity. Forgiveness yields a freedom to begin afresh, a freedom we crave and dread (Luke 15:11–32).

The Public Task of Care

Biblically based pastoral care invites membership in a larger society, participation in a *communal possibility*. The individual exists not in isolation but in deep and crucial networks of interdependence in a larger society.

That larger society, however, is not guaranteed or automatic. It is a human work, a task to be accomplished. Such community is frail and fragile. It depends on some people who not only care about their own survival but who also care about the community inordinately and at great cost. That larger society depends on some people who receive their identity through keeping the social system functioning for all the others. Communal interdependence offers an invitation to become public persons engaged in the public pursuit of happiness.

The nurture of public persons is a crucial responsibility for us. We are not likely to have the public persons needed for a humane future unless there is a sense of social reality and a structure of values that celebrate such a way of living. Such a social possibility is, as Robert Bellah has argued, resisted by the reduction of life to therapeutic and managerial modes of interaction.

The nurture of public persons is countered by the nullification of public identity. There is among us a shift in public consciousness; our dominant political rhetoric voices greed—under the rubric of "opportunity"—as a defensible public policy. The more affluent we become, the more we have license to presume upon public life in selfish ways, caring only about defense to protect the disproportion from which we benefit. We have witnessed the emergence of a new political phenomenon: activism driven by the greed of affluent, self-preoccupied, and secure people, who count heavily on the public process for its benefits but have no sensibility for that process when they are called to participate at a cost to themselves.

Public life today is undertaken either to enhance self or to advance a specific social interest. This is an important issue facing the pastoral care community. Our privatized models of health need to be reviewed. We cannot, according to the claim of the gospel, be healthy if we are not engaged in the public process of caring.

Pastoral care informed by biblical faith is committed to perceptions, claims, and possibilities of a very specific kind. Each of these claims is in deep conflict with the dominant values of our culture and the Stoic values of modernity which have shaped some forms of uncritical pastoral care.

What in fact constitutes health and well-being is now a matter of dispute. In doing pastoral care, we may intentionally participate in that disputed conversation. The pastoral care community, grounded in the biblical tradition, has a vision of humaneness that is increasingly and deeply at odds with the dominant notions of humaneness in our culture. The issue facing us is whether the pastoral care community will recover its authority and its nerve to hold firmly a view of humaneness and humanness that runs increasingly counter to dominant models. Or will that community be content simply to echo values which in fact run counter to our own grounding? It will not do to proceed uncritically about daily practice without joining issue in critical, theoretical reflection. While much energy in pastoral care has focused on the processes and modes toward health, it is also crucial to reflect more intentionally on the new substance of health. The processes of health are not unrelated to the substance of health.

The pastoral care movement, in its yearning to be freed from authoritarian religion, in recent time found aid, comfort, support, and freedom in secular theory. That has been an important gain. It was necessary to free the human prospect from the conventional focus of authoritarianism. Now, however, the shoe is on the other foot. Whereas such secular theory functioned for a season in emancipating ways, now that same theory pushed to extremes is seductive and destructive. The secular, Stoic vision of autonomy—uncalled living, individual detachment, moral indifference, and isolation— cannot in fact yield health. Such an ideological commitment ostensibly serves personal liberation but in fact is allied with the worst, most hopeless kinds of uncriticized public conformity. In such a secular theory there is no power for transformation. The outcome is a kind of privatized well-being, devoid of community, unrelated to public reality. In the end such privatized well-being is no well-being at all.

In this context, pastoral care is obligated to reflect critically on its own identity and the normative tradition which gives it substance and raison d'être. Pastoral care rooted in the biblical tradition is inherently subversive, because it clashes with the dominant ideology of modernity. In that clash there is much at stake economically, politically, socially, and morally. The subversive mandate of biblically formed pastoral care goes hand in hand with a practical judgment that certain categories and questions about health can no longer be bracketed out. It insists on the reality of the transformative God, the centrality of call, the cruciality of neighbor, the reality of evil and the possibility of forgiveness, and participation in a larger community, not because they are treasured ideas of a religious tradition, but because they are true. Health defined apart from them is false and is in fact a mode of death.

PASTORAL CARE AND IMAGINATION: A PROPOSAL

Finally I consider imagination in the process of healing and transformation. Being whole is neither simply a process of getting older nor the development of techniques for coping and living. In biblical faith, wholeness depends on having our imagination fed in regular and intentional ways so that we are not reduced to one-dimensional living.[27] Such nurture makes available promises, visions, possibilities, fears, and hurts to which we may then respond in faithful and free ways. But the chance we have for faithful and free response depends on the imagal realities through which life is mediated.

The question we must raise in pastoral care is this: Who or what has fed the imagination of the people with whom we minister? Who has provided the images around which life can be organized in new ways? In raising this question, I refer especially to Craig Dykstra's work on imagination as the guide to wholeness of character,[28] and Stanley Hauerwas's on the power of stories to shape character.[29] Both Dykstra and Hauerwas urge that the formation of character depends on an alternative vision of self in the world. That alternative vision is mediated precisely through narratives, metaphors, and memories of biblical faith.

The exercise of imagination that largely shapes self-perception in our culture exists in pictures of production and consumption, of possession and control. The functioning self in the dominant ideology is in control and well-defended. Such a vision of personal well-being is handmaiden to public policy that is also legitimated in terms of competence control and adequate defense. Stoicism as a mode of personal self-sufficiency nurtures a world of hostility in which no new peacemaking is possible. The practice of faithful, gospel-informed imagination finds a way between a reductionist banishment of imagination in the interest of technical control and the undisciplined fantasy that any liberated notion is of value, no matter that it is not rooted in social reality. Against both the banishment of imagination and unrooted fantasy, we understand imagination as the practice of the biblical memory in ways that transform our presumed world. That concrete, rooted memory feeds, legitimates, and evokes alternative imagination which permits alternative persons in alternative community.

We who hold to biblical faith are heirs to an alternative tradition that operates as a minority opinion in our culture.[30] The biblical tradition is not about control but about vulnerability, not about self-sufficiency but about risky reception of life as gift. The Christian notion of pathology and health was correctly discerned by Nietzsche, even if he viewed it with hostility.[31] He rightly saw that pathology according to the gospel includes autonomy and self-sufficiency, that health is by way of obedience, submission, and vulnerability. The cross is a strange reality to have present in the historical process, in the therapeutic process, in the political process. The cross is not a magic sign but is the modeling of an alternative mode of living. It is our normative claim about God, about us, about our life with God, and about our life with each other. Jesus articulates this odd perspective on life and health:

> For whoever would save his life will lose it; and whoever loses his life for my sake and the gospel's will save it. For what does it profit a man, to gain the whole world and forfeit his life? For what can a woman give in return for her life? (Mark 8:35–37)

This is the gospel at its most terse and most dangerous. But it is not simply a religious teaching. It is, rather, a proposal about greed and economics. It is a proposal about the psychological wars we wage in our families. It is a proposal about public policy, public security, and arms. It is a proposal that our hurt and loss cannot be "mastered," only embraced. It is about the possibility of well-being that this alternative affirmation makes available. This evangelical tradition claims that the embrace of pathos and the practice of community pain is the locus from which God's new life is given. The verses which follow this affirmation (Mark 8:38—9:1) make an enormous eschatological claim. But that claim is not naive or romantic. It reckons with the power of evil and the reality of death. It reckons also with the power of God's goodness that overrides evil, the power of God's life that overcomes the real power of death.

Personal health largely depends on the shapes of imagination through which one perceives self and through which energy and authority are mediated. That imagination may be shaped as control, possession, and self-celebration, or it may be shaped as yielding, gift, and vulnerability.

Not only is the substance of this imagination crucial, but so is where and in what ways it is practiced and made available among us. This alternative imagination is shaped, mediated, and made available primarily through the practice of liturgy in a variety of modes. (By liturgy I mean the management and practice of symbols around which to organize life.) We must therefore ask: in what liturgies have we and our parishioners been participating? The answer seems evident to me. The liturgies that largely shape our common life and our imagination are the liturgies of status quo consumerism—the somber liturgy recited by Dan Rather, the repressed aggression of John Sununu, or the pleasant ideology of Robert Schuller.[32] They are all of a piece. They teach us that the way to keep our life is to keep it at all costs. This is the Stoic proposal. Such liturgies mediate certain modes of imagination that largely determine our notions of health and wholeness and permit and legitimate the anti-humane policies now regnant in our society.

A Proposal: Communal Imagination Made Concrete

Pastoral care is essentially a liturgical enterprise. In the professionalism of pastoral care, the conventional ritual includes fee negotiation and intake interviews which are done with enormous authority. But these practices constitute a liturgical process that is narrow in scope and limited in possibility. It is a liturgy of control that in itself has no transformative power. What would happen if the pastoral care community began to think about a theologically intentional liturgic process that sought to offer an imaginative counter to the Stoic, modernist liturgy? What if the great metaphors of liberation, healing, forgiveness, reconciliation, homecoming, and new birth were regularly enacted in churches and pastoral care centers in ways that countered the defensive and destructive liturgies of production, possession, and consumption? What if a prerequisite for pastoral care were regular participation in an alternative liturgy that enacts and makes available alternative metaphors that feed the imagination in alternative ways? What power if both practitioners and benefactors of pastoral care visibly, intentionally, and publicly participated in this particular liturgic process!

Our responsibility is to practice an *alternative liturgy* that will mediate alternative imagination, which in turn will yield different notions of health and wholeness and which will eventually permit and legitimate different public policies.

Practitioners of pastoral care have remarkable authority in determining the circumstances under which one may participate in and receive pastoral attention. It would be possible to set as a requirement for personal or individual conversation regular, disciplined participation in a liturgical activity of the pastoral care community. That would begin to assert something fresh, subversive, and faithful about health in a biblical perspective. Without regularized involvement in this imaginative memory, this alternative offer of life is not available. The offer entails a specific public cost, a cost too demanding for many today.

The purpose of such a liturgy would be to make available the grand themes of biblical faith, such as the metaphors friend of God, servant of God, child of God, as the stuff out of which new self and new community may emerge. The practical effect of such liturgy is to people the imagination with alternative resources.[33] The theological ground for such a practice is that health does not emerge out of the immobilized parishioner or out of the wits of the pastor, but out of the memory of the tradition that has long mediated life and health to this community.[34] Through such a corporate, intentional practice of a concrete imagination persons could reread their life in fresh and healthful ways, for there would be present in the conversation mediations of health that have central authority in the community of faith under whose auspices pastoral care is done. The liturgic act intrudes a "third voice" into the pastoral conversation— the voice of the gospel.[35]

We do not choose or generate health out of our isolation. The offer of health is never immediate; it is always mediated. We need to pay more attention to the modes of mediation, of which I here stress the stories and memories of the faith community. We receive health (or cringe from it) in terms of the metaphors available to us, even when the metaphors are poverty-stricken and offer only diminished life. But what would happen to the healing process if pastors and parishioners together had life-giving metaphors available that challenged, contradicted, and perhaps displaced the dominant metaphors of anxiety and despair that so govern our common life?

Until we undertake new communal imagination around liturgy that intentionally counters the destructive liturgies of the dominant ideology, pastoral care can only be marginally effective. Without this liturgic act, pastoral conversations continue to operate through metaphors/memories which scarcely mediate life. With its intentional resistance to community, modernity has fallen prey to manipulative communities that mostly whitewash. If that is the "field of play" for healing, there will be not much free play and not much real healing.[36] For healing cannot go beyond the mediating materials.

The direction in which our public discernment of what it means to be human is moving requires pastoral agents to reinvest vigorously and intentionally in the biblical theological tradition. If we are interested in addressing the real crisis in our society—the crisis of distorted humanness—members of our community of pastoral care must give as much serious attention to the biblical tradition as has been given in recent time to the psychological disciplines. That will require a serious, sustained engagement with this tradition, not simply a pro forma opening paragraph which rushes on to other matters. In our culture we are at a pivot point, and our radical vision of humanness, inherited from our tradition, is deeply at risk. Those of us entrusted with this radical vision of humanness grounded in this subversive tradition must now rethink and regroup. This is not merely a parochial concern, because it is not only the religious community for which much is at stake. Our public community is also at this brink of forgetting who we are and what it means to be human.

In *The Accidental Tourist*, Anne Tyler narrates the life of a man who struggles with "adjustment." At mid-point, he is characterized this way:

> "If you really think that," Sarah said, "then you're fooling your-self. You're not holding steady. You're ossified. You're encased. You're like something in a capsule. You're a dried-up kind of a man that nothing really penetrates." . . . and Macon's knees went weak with relief. But he remembered forever after how quickly he had adjusted. He wondered, sometimes, if that first adjustment had somehow stuck. . . . But if people don't adjust, how could they bear to go on? . . . Any other time he would have swung into action—called for the manager, pointed out the restaurant's lack of concern for the handicapped. Today he only stood hanging his head, waiting for someone to help him.[37]

Macon had adjusted until he didn't exist. Macon is promised more than that.

NOTES

This chapter was initially delivered as an address to a meeting of pastoral care supervisors in Washington, D.C., February 25, 1984.

1. George Vaillant, *Adaptation to Life* (Boston: Little, Brown, 1977). This paper was initially prepared as a critical response to Vaillant's work.

2. The socio-theological presuppositions affirmed by Vaillant, ibid., seem very close to those critiqued by Robert Bellah et al., *Habits of the Heart* (Berkeley: University of California Press, 1985).

3. See the analysis of Langdon Gilkey, *Society and the Sacred: Toward a Theology of Culture in Decline* (New York: Crossroad, 1981).

4. See Robert L. Katz, *Pastoral Care and the Jewish Tradition* (Philadelphia: Fortress Press, 1985), for an interesting articulation of Jewish notions of pastoral care. While my presentation is obviously filtered through Christian perspectives, Katz's presentation calls attention to the fact that Jewish tradition proceeds with categories completely removed from those our culture uncritically accepts. For an intentionally theological model of pastoral care rooted in a theological tradition, see Thomas C. Oden, *Care of Souls in the Classic Tradition* (Philadelphia: Fortress Press, 1984). Note also his documentation on the loss of theological intentionality in more recent modes of pastoral care.

5. On the power of metaphor, see Sallie McFague, *Metaphorical Theology* (Philadelphia: Fortress Press, 1982). McFague has been criticized (rightly, in my judgment) for not dealing adequately with the fact that metaphors which have power are embedded in the ongoing narrative life of the community which utilizes and relies on them.

6. On covenantal metaphors in relation to healing, see Walter Brueggemann, "Covenanting as Human Vocation," *Interpretation* 33 (1979): 115–29.

7. On child as alternative to orphan and slave, see Walter Brueggemann, *In Man We Trust* (Richmond: John Knox Press, 1972), chap. 4.

8. On this metaphor, see McFague, *Metaphorical Theology*, 177–92. Cf. Isa. 41:8, on Abraham in the role of God's friend.

9. While I arrived at these three metaphors independently, see the remarkable treatment of them by Karl Barth, *Church Dogmatics* III, 3 (Edinburgh: T. & T. Clark, 1960), 285–86. Barth treats the Christian under "the Universal Lordship of God the Father," under the rubrics of obedience, faith, and prayer. In this summary of these three aspects of life with God, he concludes: "The grace of God to sinful man is that He encounters him as the hearing God; that He calls him not merely to the humility of a servant and the thankfulness of a child but to the intimacy and boldness of a friend in the immediate presence of the throne, His own presence; . . . In obedience the Christian is the servant, in faith he is the child, but in prayer, as the servant and the child, he is the friend of God, called to the side of God and at the side of God, living and ruling and reigning with Him."

10. On the reality of God and the difference that makes, see Samuel Terrien, *Till the Heart Sings* (Philadelphia: Fortress Press, 1985), 222: "As 'Our Father,' God is not the Ancestor, a metaphor of the past, but the Initiator of the new covenant, the Re-Creator whose passion to some transcends the language of both paternity and maternity." See also Diane Tennis, *Is God the Only Reliable Father?* (Philadelphia: Westminster Press, 1985).

11. Philip Reiff, Philip Slater, and Crawford MacPherson have each explored this contemporary phenomenon. See Philip Reiff, *The Triumph of the Therapeutic: Uses of Faith after Freud* (New York: Harper & Row, 1966); Philip Slater, *The Pursuit of Loneliness: American Culture at the Breaking Point* (Boston: Beacon Press, 1970); and Crawford MacPherson, *The Political Theory of Possessive Individualism* (Oxford: Clarendon Press, 1962).

12. See Carl Rogers, *Client-Centered Therapy* (Boston: Houghton Mifflin, 1951). To be sure, Rogers has been terribly caricatured by those who have singularly exploited his notion of "unconditional acceptance." I do not refer to the caricature, however, but to the model of care Rogers intended. Rogers needs to be understood in his own historical context, which no longer prevails.

13. John Calvin, *The Institutes of Christian Religion*, Library of Classics, ed. John T. McNeill (Philadelphia: Westminster Press, 1960), bk 1, chap. 12, 35–39. On the pertinence of Calvin for personality theory in relation to imagination, see Lucy Bregman, "Religious Imagination: Polytheistic Psychology Confronts Calvin," *Soundings* 63 (1980): 36–60.

14. On this interactionist mode of care, the seminal work is that of Martin Buber, *I and Thou* (New York: Charles Scribner's Sons, 1937); and idem, *Meetings* (La Salle, Ill.: Open Court, 1973). See also the derivative but evocative work of Maurice Friedman, *Contemporary Psychology: Revealing and Obscuring the Human* (Pittsburgh: Duquesne University Press, 1984); *The Healing Dialogue in Psychotherapy* (New York: Aronson, 1985); and *To Deny Our Nothingness* (New York: Delacorte Press, 1967).

15. See Brueggemann, "Covenanting as Human Vocation." The notion of covenant concerns the identity and character of the true God as much as true human personhood. The true God is one who is at risk in the pain of the world. See my "A Shape for Old Testament Theology II: Embrace of Pain," *Catholic Biblical Quarterly* 47 (1985): 395–415. It is a stoic God who is thought to be unrelated to the reality and hurt of the covenant partner. The God characteristically rejected in self-oriented psychotherapy is a distortion of the God of biblical faith.

16. I mean here to be making an explicit claim for the authority and cruciality of the Bible. But the claim for that authority and cruciality is not a formal one. It is sufficient to note that the biblical narratives are the primal carriers for the mediation of this health-giving God. More formal notions of biblical authority derive from this distinctive substantive claim. When this claim is lost, the formal claim has little power or relevance. And when that claim is lost, we will likely have to settle either for an impenetrable God who is irrelevant or a reaction which

banishes God. These two alternatives which distort a biblical notion of God are both in evidence in the practice of pastoral care, on the one hand authoritarian and on the other hand romantic. These potential distortions have been well articulated by Trevor Williams, *Form and Vitality in the World and God* (Oxford: Clarendon Press, 1985). When form and vitality are not in working tension, the theological result is either an excessively objectivist or subjectivist religion.

17. Richard Sennett, *Authority* (New York: Alfred A. Knopf, 1980).

18. A helpful statement on this issue is James W. Fowler, *Becoming Adult, Becoming Christian* (New York: Harper & Row, 1984). Fowler explores the centrality of vocation for healthy adult personhood.

19. On the human vocation of praise, see Daniel W. Hardy and David F. Ford, *Praising and Knowing God* (Philadelphia: Westminster Press, 1985), 50 and passim.

20. Daniel Yankelovich, *New Rules* (New York: Random House, 1981), has explored the ways in which the ideology of self-fulfillment has been found wanting and inadequate. Yankelovich's insight does not, however, go so far as to embrace a theonomous reference. Nonetheless, his critique of the ideology fostered by Maslow and others is telling.

21. See Dorothee Soelle, *Beyond Mere Obedience* (Minneapolis: Augsburg Pub. House, 1970). Stanley Milgrom, *Obedience to Authority* (New York: Harper & Row, 1974), has explored the demonic power of conventional obedience.

22. Don S. Browning, *The Moral Context of Pastoral Care* (Philadelphia: Westminster Press, 1976), has helpfully and persistently insisted on a moral dimension to pastoral care.

23. John Elliott, *A Home for the Homeless* (Philadelphia: Fortress Press, 1981). In Elliott's comments on 1 Peter he offers a sociological interpretation of the letter commonly regarded as a baptismal tract.

24. Parker Palmer, *The Company of Strangers: Christians and the Renewal of America's Public Life* (New York: Crossroad, 1981).

25. Thomas W. Ogletree, *Hospitality to the Stranger: Dimensions of Moral Understanding* (Philadelphia: Fortress Press, 1985).

26. Robert Lifton, *The Broken Connection: On Death and the Continuity of Life* (New York: Simon & Schuster, 1980).

27. See esp. Herbert Marcuse, *One-Dimensional Man* (Boston: Beacon Press, 1964).

28. Craig Dykstra, *Vision and Character* (New York: Paulist Press, 1981).

29. Stanley Hauerwas, *A Community of Character* (Notre Dame, Ind.: University of Notre Dame Press, 1981), and, more succinctly, his "Casuistry as a Narrative Art," *Interpretation* 37 (1983): 377–88.

30. This is the functional power of canon. It provides an authoritative base for a community that holds an alternative view of reality in a cultural context that is fundamentally opposed to that deeply held view. The canon then is not simply an accidental body of literature; rather it functions as a nonnegotiable norm. From this perspective, the yearning to submit to literature that stands outside the canon because it is "more attractive" is either irrelevant or dangerous because it risks the surrender of the basis for a distinctive identity and perspective. On the formal function of canon, see the suggestive comments of Frank Kermode, *Forms of Attention* (Chicago: University of Chicago Press, 1985), 74–93; and idem, *The Art of Telling* (Cambridge: Harvard University Press, 1983), chap. 8, on "institutional control of interpretation."

31. See Karl Jaspers, *Nietzsche and Christianity* (Chicago: Henry Regnery, 1961); and John N. Figgies, *The Will to Freedom: or, The Gospel of Nietzsche and the Gospel of Christ* (Port Washington, N.Y.: Kennikat Press, 1969).

32. See John Kavanaugh, *Following Christ in a Consumer Society* (Maryknoll, N.Y.: Orbis Books, 1981).

33. Bruno Bettelheim, *The Uses of Enchantment* (New York: Random House, 1976), has demonstrated from a very different perspective how a "peopled" imagination is essential to therapy and finally to transformation. As Bettelheim explores the loss of fairy tales among children, we may reflect on the parallel loss of viable liturgy among adults in a technological society.

34. Katz, *Pastoral Care and the Jewish Tradition*, has shown how the memory of narrative in the community functions for purposes of liberation and transformation in pastoral conversations.

35. On the "third voice," the presence of someone we did not expect in the midst of the conversation, see Dan. 3:25. It is that surprising presence where least expected that changes the conversation and makes rescue possible. The "third voice" is to be contrasted with the "fourth man," the one for whom there are no voices other than his own. On this latter notion, see Kornelis H. Miskotte, *When the Gods Are Silent* (New York: Harper & Row, 1967), 1–6. In pastoral care, if we do not attend to the "third voice," we shall find ourselves in the situation of the "fourth man."

36. On free play and the power of liberated illusion as essential to transformation, see Paul Pruyser, *The Play of the Imagination* (New York: International Universities Press, 1983).

37. Anne Tyler, *The Accidental Tourist* (New York: Alfred A. Knopf, 1985), 142–44.

9

Monopoly and Marginality in Imagination

INSTITUTIONS AND INDIVIDUALS have an odd and difficult relationship. The bias of our social and theological tradition and surely the modern tendency are in favor of the individual and individual priorities; we are suspicious of or hostile to institutions. Those of us in the theological community have learned, especially from Reinhold Niebuhr, to think carefully and even suspiciously about institutions and their propensity to be "immoral," and we are less effective in identifying positive influences of institutions in communal life.

At the same time it is clear that individuals are massively dependent upon and decisively shaped by institutions, for institutions mediate life's resources and possibilities to us in at least four ways:

1. They mobilize social *power*.
2. They consolidate and enhance human *knowledge*.
3. They mediate *power for life* or, conversely, *power toward death*.
4. They are *engines for imagination*. They generate and provide for us the images, metaphors, paradigms, and categories through which we will experience and understand our life together.

We are more likely to be aware of social power and human knowledge in relation to institution than of the institutional capacity for social imagination. But it is the capacity of institutions for imagination that leads us to think about ideology, propaganda, alternative constructions of reality, and, finally, theodicy. Thus the capacity of an institution to generate imagination is as important for our practice of public life, as it is an unnoticed, unacknowledged, and uncriticized function of an institution.

When one thinks of an institution such as a hospital[1] with its tradition of public ministry and caring, it is useful to think about such institutions as engines for social imagination. It follows that those of us who are agents in such institutions are at the same time beneficiaries, functionaries, and practitioners of that imagination, usually to a much greater extent than we recognize.

MONOPOLY THROUGH MONARCHY–TEMPLE

In his influential book on social theory, Robert Merton uses the phrase, "monopoly of imagination,"[2] a wonderful phrase that suggests that some agent, body, or force in a society has both the sole voice in determining how things are experienced, and the right and legitimacy to supply the lens through which life is properly viewed or experienced. No one is permitted to have an image outside this approved set of imaginations or images.

Three modern social institutions are pertinent examples of this point. In the church, for example, tightly drawn lines of church orthodoxy are powerful and insidious because they are drawn in the name of all that is holy. In every case such closed orthodoxy that posits a single truth seems to carry with it a monopoly of social, economic, and political power. In government, political chauvinism is tempted to pervert patriotism into support of a particular policy; departure from the policy is readily labeled treason. Such an imaginative construction of reality is characteristically in the interest of social, political, and economic control. Finally, the academic and scientific communities establish their own exclusive categories of perception and knowledge. More specifically, the medical, scientific community has tended to monopolize much of our perception and thought about health. That community has tended to determine the range of hopes, symptoms, and needs concerning our well-being.[3]

In any society, including ours with its staggering pluralism, monopoly of imagination by appeal to ideology and by control of the organs of communication is an exceedingly ominous matter. In the Old Testament, the twin institutions of monarchy and temple are the best candidates for such a monopoly.[4] From my comments here on these institutions, we can draw some parallels to our own situation.

Royal Monopoly of Power

Monarchy exists to establish and maintain social monopoly.[5] The state asserts itself as the bearer of all that is true, right, just, and life-giving. The state no doubt manages a monopoly of hardware, but clearly the propaganda program matters most for serious control.

Israel emerged as a challenge to such an imperial monopoly.[6] At its very beginning in the Old Testament, Israel faced the Egyptian empire which had a monopoly of food, land, and power.[7] We know from the religious literature of the empire that the state also sought to absolutize itself by its imaginative liturgical activity.

At the dramatic close of the Old Testament, in the book of Daniel, Israel continues to be faced with such a royal monopoly. In the dramatic narrative, Nebuchadnezzar, the alien king (presumably Antiochus), wants Israel to bow down (Dan. 3:4–6).[8] Nebuchadnezzar does not simply want control of hardware and political power, but yielding of the imagination. He wants command of Israel's heart. The king seeks to reduce Israel's imagination to a single establishment option and insist that the royal system is indeed the solution.

From Pharaoh to Nebuchadnezzar, from Moses to Daniel, Israel is under pressure to let its imagination be monopolized, reduced, and co-opted. When that happens, then oppression, conformity, docility, and exploitation soon follow.

But, of course, monopolistic tendencies of imperial power threaten not only from outside Israel, from Egypt and Babylon. They appear within Israel, as well. Solomon brings into Israel the same monopolistic tendencies so feared elsewhere.[9] His political, economic, and military power is matched by his crass confiscation of Israel's hope. I have argued elsewhere that the claim of 1 Kings 4:25, "Every man continued at peace under his vine and his fig tree," is a usurpation of Israel's imaginative hope by Solomon.[10] That hope, once an important peasant dream, is now embodied in the state. Solomon seeks to claim that the regime now sponsors, mediates, and makes available the best life that Israel is capable of imagining and hoping. There is indeed a monopoly: Solomon wants to claim that well-being for life is not available beyond the confines of his regime.

Priestly Monopoly of Symbols

The other monopolizing institution in ancient Israel was the temple. The reference to Solomon is an appropriate point to make the transition from monarchy to temple, because Solomon's great achievement was to legitimate the temple. The temple located and centralized the presence of God's holiness. Priesthood emerged as the guardian, custodian, and eventually gatekeeper of holiness, which determined who has access.[11] Almost in principle, temples tended in a monopolistic direction, for if the temple was the only true place of holiness and the only right place of sacrament, there could be no valid source of imagination anywhere else.

The monopoly of monarchy and temple of course turned out to be not disinterested. As a result it became the object of prophetic critique (see especially Jeremiah 7; Isa. 1:10–17; cf. also Micah 6:2–8; Hosea 6:6; Amos 4:4–5). The temple monopoly had become a source of exploitation from which the justice questions had been eliminated. We need not appeal to the prophetic criticism to understand the point, but can instead look to the cultic materials themselves, especially the Levitic texts on clean and unclean.[12] As Fernando Belo has noted, laws of purity are fundamentally forms of social control that let some in and keep others out.[13] The management of ritual qualification, of course, serves social monopoly. This power to control access continues to be an important ritual question among us, ranging from the question of the ordination of women to access to health care. Controlling people's access to well-being is an enormous power. In Israel that power was administered through ritual distinction.

Monarchy is of course a sociopolitical institution, but it is clearly a liturgic construct. And even though temple is a liturgic construct, it functions for quite evident sociopolitical ends. Clearly the two institutions are intimately linked. Together they establish and enhance a royal monopoly of power and access. They serve the monopoly, however, only as they dominate imagination. The monopoly cannot be sustained by sheer force. It depends on compelling imaginative symbols. The dominant imagination must be the imagination of the dominant group.[14] Thus the distinction between clean and unclean works socially only as long as the "unclean" accept those definitions of qualification that disqualify them. The power of the throne over slave or cheap labor exists only as long as the imaginative authority of the throne compels the imagination of the dependent class. When the "unclean" are no longer impressed with the monopoly of cleanness or when the poor are no longer persuaded of the rectitude of those who have more, the monopoly of imagination begins to disintegrate and lose its force.

Amos 7:10–17 is a clear moment when the monopoly of throne and temple is threatened, and then maintained.[15] The priest Amaziah banishes Amos, the voice of an alternative imagination, with the ideological judgment: "But never again prophesy at Bethel, for it is the king's sanctuary, and it is a temple of the kingdom" (v. 13). Institutions have a deep propensity for establishing and maintaining monopoly.

TORAH AS MEDIATING AGENT

Institutions need not be committed to monopoly. John Coleman has made a powerful case for mediating subsidiary institutions that function to the presence of the grand institutions, to quite different effects.[16] Among these subsidiary institutions, Coleman includes families, schools, churches, and neighborhoods, which make a place for and give dignity to the nuances and dimensions of life that tend to be dismissed or ignored by the great institutions.[17] These lesser institutions do their humanizing work because they have kept their freedom from and maintained a tension with the dominant ideological force of the state. What is happening to such mediating institutions in our society? My sense is that two worrisome and dangerous changes are occurring. First, these mediating institutions are shriveling in force and importance.[18] Think what happens to neighborhoods and all the institutions around them in our mobile, individualized society. Second, they are confiscated to be voices for the dominant ideology, so that schools become politicized and churches become useful. Centralized institutions are so powerful that alternative institutions tend either to fade away or to join in alliance with them.

In ancient Israel, the dominant mediating institution is the torah. It is not an institution in the same sense as is temple or monarchy, but perhaps that is precisely its source of power and wonder. In the long run, the torah (not the temple or monarchy) is the basis for the miracle of Israel's survival and faithfulness in so many circumstances. The torah is unlike monarchy and temple because it is democratic, porous, and open.[19] It functions to keep life open and available for the community.

The torah is democratic in that it has not been censored or controlled. It includes within it the voice of those who have voice nowhere else. It is porous (especially in its narrative parts) because it makes images and metaphors available without interpretive hedges. It leaves things always yet to be resolved in each new reading and hearing. It is open because it has no great need to impose, coerce, or give closure.[20]

The torah is the material, tradition, and memory through which Israel practices its "sacred discontent." Those who adhere to torah characteristically maintain freedom and critical distance.[21] There is no need to review this in all its complexity, but I comment here on two elements. First is the Abraham-Sarah narrative about the impossibility of an heir and therefore of a future.[22] This narrative tells a story that is against all the closed definitions of the world around. The narrative is a story of cunning, irreverence, and humor. The narrative process of irreverence serves to mock, debunk, and therefore to treasure the laughs and sighs of people who have not yet been crushed into despair.

Second, the exodus narrative is indeed a faith recital from the underside of social process. It is not a narrative that could have been formed, valued, or even imagined in the royal court or in the well-appointed temple. It is rather a part of the "hidden history" that originates with gossiping midwives who dare to believe in the historical process against all the impressive givens of the day.[23]

This contrast of monarchy-temple, on the one hand, and torah, on the other, leads me to suggest that every institution attempts to monopolize imagination in the interest of order, propriety, purity, efficiency, competence, and control, while wanting at the same time to be democratic, porous, and open. In this latter hope, it wants to entertain and heed imagination that is irreverent, mocking, cunning, and, therefore, finally resistant to clean administration. Institutions that are democratic, porous, and open mediate life because they know that life is not given through the dominant imagination but is emergent, surprising, and eruptive in marginal elements of imagination that the priest, king, wise man, scribe, and technician do not control, value, or even notice. Those who administer the forms of power characteristically do not in fact mediate the substance of power, which is more inscrutable and liberated than they can tolerate.[24]

SYMBOLIC WORLDS:
CONSOLIDATION AND SUBVERSION

Thus I juxtapose *monopoly of imagination* and *imagination at the margin*. The first of these is disciplined, intentional, and interested. The second is undisciplined, more casual, and sporadic. Indeed, the latter is sometimes maddening in the face of our control but may also be powerful and restorative.

The nurture, practice, and legitimacy of imagination at the margin is essentially a liturgic activity.[25] I use the term "liturgy" here in the comprehensive sense of *the intentional public nurture and practice of communal images and metaphors*. In this sense, liturgy is resonant with Peter Berger's notion of the "social construction of reality."[26] Berger refers to the construction, maintenance, and transmission of sets of symbols by which a community experiences, "reads," and responds to reality. That is, reality as experienced in any community is not simply a one-dimensional given but is a carefully selected and shaped entity that accents some matters in certain ways and diminishes or nullifies others.[27]

In a general way, institutions construct social reality through tradition and perhaps ideology. But more specifically, they have agents who carry on this task of social construction by making available and insisting upon certain symbols, images, and metaphors through which reality is mediated.

1. Institutions and their agents may construct reality either around a monopoly of imagination or through an appreciation of imagination at the margin that is not congenial to the monopoly.

2. Practitioners of pastoral care are or can be such agents of social construction of reality, for pastoral care in large part is a hermeneutical/interpretive task of mediating images, symbols, and metaphors.[28]

3. Practitioners of pastoral care may be agents and servants of the monopoly of imagination. The monopoly served may be the dominant psychology, the ruling theological orthodoxy, or simply the administrative mode of the institution. Such pastoral care is likely to be conformist and conservative, designed to channel people into solutions already at hand. Such a way obviously does not honor marginal imagination. This version of care may be done by liberals or conservatives, in the name of theology, science, or psychology.[29]

4. Pastoral care practitioners may enact social reality so that it knows, takes seriously, and engages imagination at the margin, which challenges the monopoly. Such a way of pastoral care is subversive and countercultural. The imagination at the margin that concerns us has a public character and evokes and articulates power against oppressive monopolies that are conventionally committed to temple and throne.

TOWARD SOCIAL TRANSFORMATION

This tension between monopoly of imagination and imagination at the margin occurs in the Old Testament's liturgic practice of hymn and lament. It is primarily through hymn and lament that Israel performed the liturgic functions that we now refer to as pastoral care.[30]

Hymn

The hymn tends to serve a monopoly of imagination at three levels.

1. The hymn tends to focus everything on God and away from the dynamics of human interaction. Indeed, theologically and mythopoetically, the hymn is a presentation of the drama of heaven to which humans have only tenuous access, as, for example, in Psalm 29. The hymn therefore characteristically asserts that the decisive action is not among us but is in the action around the

throne among the gods. The hymn suggests that the important interactions are concentrated at the throne of God and those who want in on the action must go to the power center and be "qualified" in order to have access.

2. The hymn tends toward monotheism. The great hymn to Marduk in Babylonian liturgy, for example, lists fifty names for this one god, no doubt taking names that originally belonged to many other gods and assigning them all to Marduk, a remarkable liturgic consolidation that tends toward monopoly. Morton Smith has argued that this practice of hymn can be applied even to a very minor god, so that in the articulation of doxology, even a lesser functionary among the gods can enjoy a lyrical moment of monopoly.[31]

3. The great hymns are characteristically sung in the temple, an institution that articulates not only theological monopoly but also socioeconomic and political monopoly. The context, mood, and management of temple praise enhance the social group or class that most adheres to and dominates the temple. One need only visit village chapels in England and see the pew of the lord of the manor, or old Presbyterian churches in the rural south of this country and observe the slave balcony to recognize the role these institutions played.

The social effect of the hymn is to serve, enhance, and celebrate the monopoly of social power and social goods that is present and legitimated in the community. Hymns make for social stability, if not social reactionism. They articulate that the main experiences have already been experienced and the liturgic enterprise consists in drawing near and engaging the social settlements already established. Quite clearly those social settlements did not wait for the assent of the present company and do not depend on it. They are already given, absolutely. They have a majestic insistence that we should "get with the program" and join the monopoly.[32]

Lament

The lament, in contrast to the hymn, legitimates and articulates imagination at the margin. The lament dares to acknowledge and present reality that is peculiarly "my own" or "our own." It places emphasis upon immediacy and specificity. The language of hymns consists of familiar words that even a novice can read in Hebrew, while the laments have a richer, more varied vocabulary that brings to speech the quite concrete experience of the speaker. These poems are voices of marginality, of persons and communities who, pre-occupied with their own hurt, refuse or are unable to submit to the reigning monopoly. The experience of marginality is reflected in and served by the marginality of vocabulary.[33]

1. While the psalms of lament focus on God in their address and never doubt the capacity to address God, they do not suggest that all of the action is at the throne. Indeed the burden of such speech is exactly the opposite. The lament serves to summon God away from the throne and back into human life which is so hurtful and raw.[34] The lament psalm urges God to abandon the divine monopoly and move to the marginality of human existence where hurt is. These speakers of laments, like anyone with serious hurt, cannot get their minds or tongues off their hurt to think that elsewhere there may be more important reality. They are fully present to the hurt and insist that God should also be fully present there.

2. In a general way, all Israelite speech, including laments, makes the assumption and affirmation of practical monotheism. But such monotheism is of no great interest to the speaker of lament. Rather, as Rainer Albertz has shown, the greater interest of the lament is the personal, intimate relationship with God.[35] The general issue of monotheism is bracketed out because the urgency of this moment is about the speaker. The speaker of lament, unlike the managers of the temple, has no great social or economic interest to justify, and so the justification of monotheism is of no compelling interest. The lament does not engage in flattery but moves to the real issue of hurt and insists that God move there too.

3. The theological move from heaven to earth that is urged in the lament psalms is matched by a sociological move away from the stability of the present order and toward a recognition of the dysfunction of the present system and the passionate insistence that something must be done about that dysfunction. While the social concern is not often explicit, it is certainly latent and powerful. If God be urged to depart the monopoly for the sake of a concrete need, there is a corresponding sense that the social monopoly is also wrong and needs to be broken up for the sake of those at the margin.[36]

The structure and theological function of the lament psalms has been well presented, especially by Claus Westermann.[37] The general thesis I urge is that the liturgic life of the church, that is, its practice of social construction of reality, has been largely conserving and consolidating in its propensity to use hymns, and has missed the action of healing at the margin by neglecting laments. This neglect has not only denied important resources, but by practicing and encouraging a monopoly of imagination through hymns, we have served the interests of the status quo and have been advocates of a *theology of glory*. The recovery of laments in pastoral care is a way to value the imagination of marginality, to serve the interest of social transformation, and to bear witness to a *theology of the cross*.[38] The shift from an accent on hymns to a practice of laments posits that liturgic activity can aid in the breakup of both the monopoly of heaven which diminishes the earth, and the monopoly of monarchy and temple which diminishes those who are at the social margin.

LAMENTS AS
SOCIAL POWER "FROM BELOW"

I suggest five theological themes that are important in the context of lament psalms as a practice of imagination of marginality. The themes fly in the face of much conventional theology and romantic psychology.

1. The lament psalms affirm that God can be impinged upon and mobilized by the cries of the earth. The entire presupposition of the lament psalms, as Claus Westermann has discerned, is that the daring speech of earth, when done with passion and shrillness, can change the affairs of heaven (cf. Exod. 22:21–27). Truth can speak to power. Power will be changed when the truth-pain is spoken from the margin of earthly life.

Such a notion that God is impinged upon is, of course, difficult for scholastic theology with its categories of omniscience and immutability. For if God knows all, then such prayers are rather irrelevant. Such notions of omniscience are more compatible with hymnic theology, which presumes God is all knowing and parallels the notion that the government should be trusted because it has more information and expertise. The speaker of lament is not inclined to trust the

government or to concede that God knows. Indeed, the lament proceeds in the awareness that the one thing God does not know is
how painful and urgent our circumstance of hurt is. These prayers,
as Moshe Greenberg has seen, seek to establish that something is at
stake for God which will mobilize God to act. The lament thus
drives to the heart of every complacent, settled theology. We become
aware of the extent to which our doctrine of God has presumed a
monopoly. Theological monotheism resonates with sociological
monopoly, and that monopoly is now under assault in these poems.

Conversely, lament speech that takes God so seriously (but not
with undue deference) of course moves against romantic psychology with its heavy stress on the self. Indeed much of that psychology
is failed faith, because it assumes that there is no one to address,
and thus understands these kinds of prayers as autosuggestion or
autotherapy. It is odd that conventional theology and romantic psychology, by very different routes, have arrived at the same place—to
insist together that serious conversation with God is either impossible or irrelevant. Conventional theology judges that God is beyond
such talk. Romantic psychology echoes that conclusion because there
is no such attentive God.[39] Imagination at the margin dares to think
and practice otherwise, to engage in serious conversation that summons God from the throne into the fray. Clearly such an imaginative act is exceedingly bold, even reckless. Theologically such nerve
is unorthodox; sociologically such boldness is subversive.

2. The lament psalms affirm that healing is essentially a communal activity and the neighbor is the proximate source of life. Albertz
has seen that God is addressed as intimate friend, companion, kins-
man. Indeed the substance of these psalms is that God is there as a
present friend,[40] precisely when other friends, companions, and
relatives have failed or betrayed.

Erhard Gerstenberger has shown decisively that these laments
are communal acts of rehabilitation.[41] He proposes that they are not
transacted in the temple but in the village, the tribe, the house
church, the base community. Gerstenberger's way of thinking has
challenged a long line of scholarly interpretation which placed the
lament psalms in the temple. Scholarly thinking about the psalms
has been captivated by the monopoly of the temple. But Gerstenberger, not so fascinated with the temple, has argued that these

psalms carry another liturgy conducted by lay elders who do not belong to the priestly establishment and who have a different authority and different capacity for health in the community.

These psalms maintain a form of life and engage in a construction of social reality that is an alternative to the dominant social reality centered in king and priests. The work of healing is done by the community, and the individual need only receive. The very form of the psalm, when enacted, bestows life without the intervention of the great central powers.[42]

Notice how this changes the shaping of life. By insisting that the uncredentialed community is the fulcrum of rehabilitation, one critiques the theological premise that only God as the dominant establishment can be a source of healing. One diminishes the exclusive claims of the priestly establishment and the temple which always claim a monopoly. The community becomes the sine qua non of mediation. God's power is shared in more or less democratic ways.

3. The lament psalms recognize and assert that evil is real and powerful. This does not come through in a reasoned statement about theodicy but is simply a cry out of hurt. Indeed, the affirmation that evil is real is already a hint of marginality. Evil is perceived very differently in the monopoly than it is at the margin. The imagination of the monopoly stresses guilt. It believes trouble comes because of guilt and wants to label as guilty anyone who does not function in the terms and categories of the system. But these lament psalms have little to say about guilt. Serious statements of guilt are largely confined to the so-called seven penitential psalms (Pss. 6; 32; 38; 51; 102; 130; 143), and even they talk about the processing of guilt, not its abiding state. Those who live painfully at the margin do not reduce evil to guilt. They do not imagine that all suffering is due to failure.

Rather, these psalms view evil historically, publicly, and experientially. They regard evil as a powerful social act that can be resisted only by the intervention of Yahweh. Evil is experienced as injustice that makes the marginal into victims.[43] I believe that Mowinckel's fascination with "evildoers" as those who function by magic is fundamentally misguided. Mowinckel's hypothesis has the effect of removing evil from the arena of power relations among members of the community. I submit that the evildoers are the ones who are able to manipulate the social apparatus to their own ends. What may be termed "magic" is in fact the special capacity to make the social system work in particular ways. But such "magic" is open to social analysis and criticism.

An accent on the power of evil that requires the counterintervention of Yahweh is opposed to romantic psychology which fails to think systematically about evil and believes life to be a series of unfettered choices. The psalms know that the choices are skewed and circumscribed by the way social power is arranged. The reality of evil thus does not lead to guilt and repentance but to an insistence that God should intervene.

4. The lament psalms are speeches of hope which believe that new life is possible. Westermann has shown how such psalms are structured to end in praise and resolution. Erhard Gerstenberger has seen that the *Anklage* (as distinct from the *Klage*) is indeed an act of hope.[44] The complainer calls out to God and expects and insists that things be changed by God. This very act of speech is a refusal to accept things as they are. God is the one who is looked to in hope, who can be mobilized to do a new thing. This insight into the theological structure of the psalm is the primary gain made in recent psalm study. Gunkel had seen the formal elements but, I think, not the theological import of the form. Complaint is an act of insistent hope, because when God is reached and genuinely mobilized, evil is not able to withstand.

This hopeful faith stands in stark contrast to conventional establishment theology. Conventional theology casts morality as a closed system in which we only get what is coming to us theologically, economically, politically. Against that, this poetry of possibility dares to assert that there are unadministered forces outside our systems which may intrude with newness and healing. Life is not reduced to an explanation or a contract, because God is able to override our managed schemes.

Clearly this poetry of possibility is also against romantic psychology. Romantic psychology believes that the self is the only agent of newness, that is, the self is an autonomous agent and has no external resources. This belief leads to anxiety, because manifestly we can never do enough for such self-securing. It ends in despair, because we learn that we are not finally sources of newness.

5. The lament psalm dares to affirm and act on the claim that pain brought to speech is the only gate to new life. (This daring insight was given credibility by Freud, although most psychology since Freud has backed away from it.) The very structure of the lament psalm in its move from plea to praise is an experiential, liturgic, dramatic argument that pain brought to speech in the community is the hard path and the narrow gate to new life.[45]

On the one hand, there is no newness, no fresh gift of God's grace as long as there is business as usual. On the other hand, pain in and of itself is as likely to immobilize as not. It is pain brought to speech and made available in the community that is the mediator of new life. We do not understand how this is so, but we stake our life on it. Theologically this is the structure of the move from crucifixion to resurrection (cf. Phil. 2:5–11). In our own time, it is the public cry of pain that has been the engine of energy for every liberation movement—from Latin American peasants to blacks to women. The cry of pain focuses energy and identifies truth at the margin. It asserts that God comes to be present at the margin and there does a new thing.

Clearly the rulers of this age want the pain to be unnoticed or, if noticed, unspoken and unshared or, if spoken and shared, crushed in the docility of guilt and penitence. The dominant order is zealous to cover over the pain. Here in our textual tradition are the models for a refusal to knuckle under in debilitating ways.

GIFTS BEYOND MONOPOLY

While I have enunciated five points, it is clear they are of a piece. The reality of evil, the possibility of newness, the mediation of communal form, the cruciality of pain, and the availability of God, all converge into a single affirmation. They come together to assert that the real life of faith lives, functions, and has power underneath, against, and in spite of all our grand monopolies. The crisis in our society grows because the reality of social pain at the margin is a voice growing in credibility and volume. The powers of the monopoly—religious, political, economic, psychological, moral—are accustomed to keeping the marginal in check. Indeed that is the ground and purpose of monopoly. The evidence around us is that marginality will not be contained any longer by the monopoly.

Our theological tradition has a peculiar congeniality with these shrill voices at the margin because the biblical story is a tradition of marginality that begins in the slave labor camps of Egypt or among Canaanite peasants and culminates in the cross.[46] Our recent magisterial theological tradition has been excessively impressed and shaped by hymns of the monopoly. It has become increasingly clear, however, that such hymns must come later, must be held in abeyance until the abrasive voice of marginality has its say.[47] While pastoral care is uniquely suited for hearing marginality on an interpersonal basis, every such act of marginality also has important public implications. These public implications must be given more attention in our pastoral work.

I have spoken here only of imagination. I have not mentioned action, policy, rules, or doctrine. This is because I am persuaded by Paul Ricoeur that all else follows imagination.[48] The key pathology of our time, which seduces us all, is the reduction of imagination so that we are too numbed, satiated, and co-opted to do serious imaginative work.[49] It could be, as is so often the case, that the only ones left who can imagine are the ones at the margin. They are waiting to be heard, but they have a hard time finding a place and a way for their voices.

The argument can be made that we need both hymns and laments, both monopoly and marginality. We need marginality to keep us honest to the brute reality of our own life. We need monopoly of a theological kind to keep life centered against the chaos. No doubt we need times of gathering around the monopoly. But my sense about our Western cultural situation, with its enormous repression and denial on the one hand, and its frightening monopoly of symbols on the other, is that the tradition of scattering is now most urgent for us.

There is an odd text, Exod. 16:10, in the manna story. It says:

And as Aaron spoke to the whole congregation of the people of Israel, they looked toward the wilderness, and behold, the glory of the Lord appeared in the cloud.

It is precisely in the wilderness, which I have called margin, that the glory shows. That is a primary claim of our tradition. It is a staggering invitation made to us, most of whom are children of the monopoly who know and love the hymns best!

The pastoral office is mandated to attend to all kinds of voices of marginality that make harsh sounds of pain, odd noises of hope, and surprising possibilities of healing. These enactments of pain, hope, and healing fit only awkwardly with the monopoly. But they matter enormously not only to the marginal who sound them, but to those in the monopoly who may be inconveniently addressed.

NOTES

1. This chapter was initially delivered as an address at the anniversary of Lutheran General Hospital, Chicago, April 24, 1985.

2. Robert K. Merton, *Social Theology and Social Structure* (Glencoe, Ill.: Free Press, 1957), 157.

3. The scholarly, scientific form of monopoly occurs by managing a controlling paradigm which exercises a monopoly of imagination in a learned discipline. On the power of such a paradigm, see Thomas S. Kuhn, *The Structure of Scientific Revolutions* (Chicago: University of Chicago Press, 1970). On the power of the controlling paradigm in medical education and practice, see Ivan D. Illich, *Medical Nemesis: The Expropriation of Health* (New York: Pantheon Books, 1976).

4. See John M. Lundquist, "What Is a Temple? A Preliminary Typology," in *The Quest for the Kingdom of God*, ed. H. B. Huffmon, F. A. Spina, and A.R.W. Green (Winona Lake, Ind.: Eisenbrauns, 1983), 205–19.

5. George Mendenhall, *The Tenth Generation* (Baltimore: Johns Hopkins University Press, 1973), 69–104, has shown how the royal monopoly was necessary to curbing vengeance as a private practice.

6. This case has been best argued by Norman K. Gottwald, *The Tribes of Yahweh* (Maryknoll, N.Y.: Orbis Books, 1979).

7. This refers especially to the situation of the exodus, but notice, already in Gen. 12:10–20, Egypt had a monopoly of food.

8. On the theological significance of the Daniel narrative for political theology, see John Goldengay, "The Stories in Daniel: A Narrative Politics," *Journal for the Study of the Old Testament* 37 (1987): 99–116.

9. George Mendenhall, "The Monarchy," *Interpretation* 29 (1975): 155–70, has termed the Solomonic monarchy the "paganization" and the "Canaanization" of Israel.

10. On this symbolic usurpation, see Walter Brueggemann, "Vine and Fig Tree: A Case Study in Imagination and Criticism," *Catholic Biblical Quarterly* 43 (1981): 188–204. The hope in a premonarchal form is expressed in Mic. 4:1–4, but now it is contained in the royal system.

11. See Paul Hanson, *The Dawn of Apocalyptic* (Philadelphia: Fortress Press, 1975), esp. chap. 3, on the social power of the priesthood. On the history of the tension in Israel's priesthood, see Frank M. Cross, *Canaanite Myth and Hebrew Epic* (Cambridge: Harvard University Press, 1973), chap. 8.

12. On the issue of clean and unclean, see the articulations of the priestly function in Ezek. 22:26–31 and 44:23–32; Hag. 2:10–19; and Marla J. Selvidge, "Mark 5:25–34 and Leviticus 15:19–20, a Reaction to Restrictive Purity Regulations," *Journal of Biblical Literature* 103 (1984): 619–23.

13. Fernando Belo, *A Materialist Reading of the Gospel of Mark* (Maryknoll, N.Y.: Orbis Books, 1981), part 2.

14. I mean, of course, to paraphrase Marx's statement, "The ruling ideas of each age have ever been the ideas of its ruling class." Cf. David McLellan, *The Thought of Karl Marx* (London: Macmillan, 1971), 46.

15. On the critical issues related to this text, see Peter R. Ackroyd, "A Judgment Narrative between Kings and Chronicles? An Approach to Amos 7:9–17," in *Canon and Authority*, ed. George W. Coats and Burke O. Long (Philadelphia: Fortress Press, 1977), 71–87.

16. John A. Coleman, *An American Strategic Theology* (New York: Paulist Press, 1982), chap. 11. See Edward L. Long, Jr., *A Survey of Recent Christian Ethics* (New York: Oxford University Press, 1982), 57 and his references to the work of James Luther Adams, Peter Berger, and Richard L. Neuhaus.

17. On the mediating function of the *Kleinkult*, see Rainer Albertz, *Persönliche Frömmigkeit und offizielle Religion*, Calwer Theologische Monographien 9 (Stuttgart: Calwer, 1978), 81 and passim. The *Kleinkult* performed important social functions to which the *Grosskult* of the temple had no access.

18. Robert Bellah has frequently observed the diminishment of human life when such mediating institutions fail. See his brief analysis of the function of the family in "Walk Away . . . Don't Look Back: Rampant Individualism," *Concern* 27 (1985): 17–19.

19. On the critical literary and social function of the torah, see Herbert Schneidau, *Sacred Discontent* (Berkeley: University of California Press, 1976).

20. Susan A. Handelman, *The Slayers of Moses* (Albany: State University of New York Press, 1982), has seen how the very different character of this literature requires very different modes of interpretation

and criticism. This point has not been well understood and for that reason, according to Handelman, we have a long history of doubtful criticism.

21. On the practice of critical freedom and critical distance from dominant values because of this textual tradition, see Richard L. Rubenstein, *The Age of Triage* (Boston: Beacon Press, 1983), 229–40.

22. On this text and motif, see Walter Brueggemann, " 'Impossibility' and Epistemology in the Faith Tradition of Abraham and Sarah (Gen. 18:1–15)," *Zeitschrift fur die alttestamentliche Wissenschaft* 94 (1982): 615–34.

23. In such a context, gossip has the creative, salvific effect of creating an alternative, subversive world against dominant truth claims. It is not unimportant that "gossip" is etymologically related to "gospel." Such talk tells good news which is officially hidden. Cf. Jud. 5:10–11 for a powerful example. On "hidden history" as an alternative to the dominant history, see Howard Zinn, *A People's History of the United States* (San Francisco: Harper & Row, 1981).

24. The Elijah narratives are a clear example of the ways in which the royal apparatus controls the forms of power but lacks power, i.e., cannot produce rain. The narrative shrewdly asserts that it is the uncredentialed Elijah who in fact has power. See my analysis of this subversive claim in the text, "The Prophet as Destabilizing Presence," in *The Pastor as Prophet*, ed. Earl E. Shelp and Ronald H. Sunderland (New York: Pilgrim Press, 1985), 49–77.

25. This is in contrast to the dominant imagination that does not depend on an intentional liturgy because it is sustained by the routinized dramas of power. Imagination at the margin has no such routinized dramas and so must be nurtured in intentional liturgy.

26. See Peter L. Berger and Thomas Luckmann, *The Social Construction of Reality* (Garden City, N.Y.: Doubleday & Company, 1966).

27. On the constructive character of social and personal reality, see Robert Kegan, *The Evolving Self: Problem and Process in Human Development* (Cambridge: Harvard University Press, 1982). Kegan helpfully suggests that fixed points of reality are "negotiated truces" which may last for longer or shorter periods of time.

28. On the cruciality of the hermeneutical-interpretive task, see Charles V. Gerkin, *The Living Human Document* (Nashville: Abingdon Press, 1984), 19 and passim; idem, *Widening the Horizons: Pastoral Responses to a Fragmented Society* (Philadelphia: Westminster Press, 1986); and, more generally, Sallie McFague, *Metaphorical Theology* (Philadelphia: Fortress Press, 1982), 22 and passim.

29. My impression is that military chaplains almost inevitably must utilize their liturgic office to enhance the monopoly of imagination. The

same pressures are on every liturgic officer, but not in ways that are so formal, visible, and compelling.

30. See my general statement in *The Message of the Psalms* (Minneapolis: Augsburg Pub. House, 1984).

31. Morton Smith, "The Common Theology of the Ancient Near East," *Journal of Biblical Literature* 71 (1952): 135–47.

32. Harvey H. Guthrie, Jr., *Theology as Thanksgiving* (New York: Seabury Press, 1981), 18–30, nicely contrasts the social function and context of hymns and songs of thanksgiving.

33. Paul Ricoeur, "Biblical Hermeneutics," *Semeia* 4 (1975): 108, 122, and passim, links "limit expressions" and "limit experiences." Marginality of social location may be a limit of a quite concrete time and evokes limit expressions. Ricoeur does not raise such social issues.

34. Moshe Greenberg, *Biblical Prose Prayer* (Berkeley: University of California Press, 1983), 11–14.

35. See Albertz, *Persönliche Frömmigkeit*, 77–96.

36. On the voice of religion at the social margin, see Robert R. Wilson, *Prophecy and Society in Ancient Israel* (Philadelphia: Fortress Press, 1980), and his attention to the periphery. I suggest a connection between Wilson's social periphery and Ricoeur's linguistic limit. The social periphery and the linguistic limit meet in the lament psalms.

37. Claus Westermann, *Praise and Lament in the Psalms* (Atlanta: John Knox Press, 1981). See also idem, *The Psalms: Structure, Content, and Message* (Minneapolis: Augsburg Pub. House, 1980). See also Patrick D. Miller, Jr., "The Trouble and Woe (Interpreting the Biblical Laments)," *Interpretation* 37 (1983): 32–45; Roland E. Murphy, "The Faith of the Psalmist," *Interpretation* 34 (1980): 229–39; and Walter Brueggemann, "From Hurt to Joy, from Death to Life," *Interpretation* 28 (1974): 3–19.

38. On the use of the laments in pastoral care, see Donald Capps, *Biblical Approaches to Pastoral Care* (Philadelphia: Westminster Press, 1981), chap. 2.

39. On the sequence of scholastic irrelevance and romantic impossibility, see Daniel Yankelovich, *New Rules* (New York: Random House, 1981). Yankelovich shows that romantic psychology was a reaction to a tight system of retribution, but that there is now a growing sense of the inadequacy of such romanticism.

40. McFague, *Metaphorical Theology*, 177–92, has explored the metaphor of "friend" for God-language.

41. Erhard Gerstenberger, *Der Bittende Mensch* (Neukirchen-Vluyn: Neukirchener, 1980). See Patrick D. Miller, Jr., "Current Issues in Psalms Studies," *Word and World* 5 (1985): 134–35.

42. On the rescuing power of the form, see Walter Brueggemann, "The Formfulness of Grief," *Interpretation* 31 (1977): 263–75.

43. José Miranda, *Marx and the Bible* (Maryknoll, N.Y.: Orbis Books, 1974), chap. 4. See also J. Severino Croatto, *Exodus, A Hermeneutics of Freedom* (Maryknoll, N.Y.: Orbis Books, 1983).

44. Erhard Gerstenberger, "Der Klagende Mensch," in *Probleme biblischer Theologie*, ed. Hans Walter Wolff (Munich: Chr. Kaiser, 1971), 64–72. See his distinction between *Klage* and *Anklage* in "Jeremiah's Complaints," *Journal of Biblical Literature* 82 (1963): 405 n. 50.

45. See the recent discussions of A. Kleinman, *The Illness Narratives* (New York: Basic Books, 1988); and Howard Brody, *Stories of Sickness* (New Haven: Yale University Press, 1987).

46. John Elliott, *A Home for the Homeless* (Philadelphia: Fortress Press, 1981), has shown, concerning 1 Peter, how a theology of the cross becomes social practice in a way consistent with the initial slave and peasant experiences of ancient Israel.

47. See my argument of this matter in *Israel's Praise: Doxology against Idolatry and Ideology* (Philadelphia: Fortress Press, 1988).

48. Paul Ricoeur, "Listening to the Parables of Jesus," in *The Philosophy of Paul Ricoeur*, ed. Charles E. Reagan and David Stewart (Boston: Beacon Press, 1978), 245: "And it is in the heart of our imagination that we let the Event happen, before we may convert our heart and tighten our will."

49. This point has been variously articulated by Robert Jay Lifton. See esp. *The Broken Connection* (New York: Simon & Schuster, 1980).

10

God's Faithful Plan: A Context for Caring Citizenship

It is ENORMOUSLY LIBERATING to recognize that peace and justice are fundamentally in conflict with dominant American values. It is, of course, very difficult for us to come to such awareness, given our convictions about American history and the notion of America as a "Christian nation." But this recognition will provide fresh space and vitality for our spirits.[1] Once freed of the mistaken ideological notion of a "Christian America," we can discern our true situation and find sustenance for living in that situation.

A COSMIC COMMITMENT TO PEACE

When I think in biblical categories about holding to passions that society rejects, I am drawn to the texts on exile. Much of the Old Testament is generated in the sixth century B.C.E., when Israel's leadership and most of its tradition, energy, and hope were carried off into exile in Babylon.[2] In Babylon, a hostile empire, the people of Israel learned to be believers in the midst of exile, if they were to be believers at all.[3] Israel in exile could not live its life and faith as it had prior to exile. The situation of exile required a different form of faith, a different rhetoric, a different discipline, a different set of public, institutional practices. Israel's primary concerns in exile were to (1) maintain *identity* in an empire that wanted to destroy that identity; (2) maintain *freedom for imagination* in an empire that wanted to domesticate imagination; and (3) maintain *capacity for hope* in an empire that wanted to preempt hope and thus reduce Israel to despair that would end in conformity.

The administrative goals of the Babylonian empire and the faithful passions of Israel were in conflict. The empire not only wanted to conscript young soldiers and tax personal property but, like all imperial powers, also wanted to capture Israel's imagination, hope, courage, and possibility. For as long as Israel maintained imagination, hope, courage, and possibility, the empire would be unstable, restless, in jeopardy, and provisional. Exiles must maintain their distinct identity as outsiders and must not permit the domestication of the spirit. A number of Old Testament texts evidence the exiles' struggle to resist the domestication of their spirit and the loss of their distinct identity.

Israelite exiles had to practice their faith in a hostile environment. I cite that reality in order to illuminate our own situation. People who care about peace and justice in American society are essentially exiles who must practice their faith in a hostile environment.[4] Israel in exile no longer had the luxury of living its faith in a context of values and institutions that were congenial and hospitable to that faith. In like manner, it is self-deceptive for peacemaking people in our society to imagine that we live amidst values and institutions that are congenial and hospitable to our dreams. In other times and circumstances, Israel could practice its faith less radically, less subversively, and with less risk. It was very different to practice faith under the stable regime of Solomon with the temple as a legitimator, but the temple as legitimator is now gone. By the measure of Babylon, the faith Israel holds is illegitimate.

So for us, there were earlier days when the claims of Christian faith were more central to our culture and more hospitably received. Now we must hold and practice our faith in an empire that is deeply hostile to our faith traditions and to our most precious social vision. If this is a correct perception of our situation, we are given clues to the kinds of biblical texts that may be most important for our sustenance. If we are indeed in exile in an alien culture, then we would do well to live in the presence of the great exilic texts that our mothers and fathers formed in their exile. If we learn to trust these texts, we will have important resources to rely on. It is not so fatiguing to live in exile. What is fatiguing is to live in exile yet imagine one is not in exile. An honest recognition of our status as dreamers of peace in a culture bent on war will give us considerable freedom.

The texts pertinent to us in our exile are the great poetic texts of alternative imagination that are found especially in Jeremiah 29—33 and Isaiah 40—55.[5] These texts are the voices of poets, of pastors, who kept reminding Israel of its identity, its vocation, its proper posture in any circumstance. The poets spoke not so much about Israelite action as about the grounding of Israelite life in the fidelity of Yahweh, which endures and would sustain in every circumstance. Such theological grounding is not susceptible to imperial assault. These poets spoke not about activism but about the power and purpose of God who was and is committed to well-being, security, dignity, justice, and peace, even in the face of a demonic and ruthless empire that rejected such covenantal values.

Thus, for example, Jeremiah could hear God say to the exiles:

For I will restore health to you,
      and your wounds I will heal, says the Lord,
because they have called you an outcast:
"It is Zion, for whom no one cares!"
                              (Jer. 30:17)

Or Jeremiah could assert that as God caused judgment and exile, so God will now preside over well-being and homecoming:

And it shall come to pass that as I have watched over them to pluck up and break down, to overthrow, destroy, and bring evil, so I will watch over them to build and to plant, says the Lord. (Jer. 31:28)

Or 2 Isaiah could break out in lyrical expectations:

He does not faint or grow weary,
      his understanding is unsearchable.
He gives power to the faint,
      and to him who has no might he increases strength.
Even youths shall faint and be weary,
      and young men shall fall exhausted;
But they who wait for the Lord
      shall renew their strength,
they shall mount up with wings like eagles,
      they shall run and not be weary,
      they shall walk and not faint.
                              (Isa. 40:28–31)

Yahweh's power and fidelity are not conditioned by or accountable to Babylonian realities. Yahweh acts in Yahweh's own freedom according to Yahweh's own intentionality. The power of the poetry is that exiled Israel is the immediate and intended beneficiary of this announced reality. The situation of exile can do nothing to rob the exiles of this fresh gift of energy and faith.

These poets who address exiles provide a model for us. They dare to affirm that faith is not simply a burden to which Israel is summoned but a stance Yahweh takes toward the exiles. We may affirm from these texts that peacemaking is not only a vocation to which we are summoned but a cosmic commitment structured into reality that originates in the very heart of God. Exiles then and now need to know not simply about their burdens, responsibilities, and vocation but about the commitments made "from the other side" by God. These lyrical poets speak of such commitments. These commitments are deeper than our performances; they outlast our resolve and withstand the assaults of the empire. My suggestion is that our fatigue in the face of the peace vocation must be set in the context of God's deep and enduring commitment to peace that stands in the face of our failure and in the face of the determined, hostile empire. God has made a resolve on which we can rest our very lives. It is a resolve that frees us for acting. Because peace is rooted in the very heart of God, the posture, pretense, and ideology of the empire cannot finally stop the movement toward peace. This conviction stands as our ultimate safeguard against cynicism, conformity, and despair.

THE CRUCIALITY OF LITURGY
AMONG EXILES

The question is, How can this cosmic commitment rooted in the very heart of God be real and available to us in ways that make a difference, that deliver us from despair? When we can answer this question confidently, we will have before us the resources to overcome despair and to remain open to God's hope for our future. The answer I would like to explore is this: *Exiles are sustained in their alternative passion with power and freedom by the regular practice of intentional, alternative liturgy.* First, it is important that we have an understanding of liturgy that is adequate for our situation.

1. Liturgy is the regular communal processing of our life and our experience through an alternative set of metaphors, symbols, narratives, memories, and hopes that the community takes to be normative, reliable, and nonnegotiable. When the processing of life is mediated through memories of exodus and exile, through crucifixion and resurrection, we experience and discern our life differently.[6] What fatigued peacemaking exiles most need is to have life mediated in fresh ways, in ways alternative to Peter Jennings, Paul Harvey, and James Baker. These "conventional mediators" give us life that is flat, one-dimensional, safe, symmetrical, settled. Such mediations function as a narcotic and screen us from real hurt and real hope. We become drugged by such ideology, and finally our spirit dies.

How different the world seems when our "day-to-dayness" is given us through the stories of God's power and Pharaoh's drowning (Exod. 11:30–31), Daniel bold before Nebuchadnezzar (Dan. 3:1–30), Jesus before Pilate (John 18:33—19:16), and Paul before Agrippa (Acts 26:1–32). Each such account stuns the empire and gives freedom, hope, and courage to the listening community. The biblical tradition of public transformation mediates to us a powerful subversion in which we are invited to participate. It enacts for us again the possibility that there is a source of power and legitimacy that lies outside imperial administration.

2. Liturgy rescues us for a moment from imperial language and images. This alternative liturgy affirms life coming to us as a gift, not life generated by us, because after a while we are spent and dry, and we cannot generate anymore. This liturgy is a season in which we do not have to think about strategy, resources, effectiveness, safety, or adequacy. This liturgy is a time when we do not have to ask if we are adequately radical or theologically correct. We do not have to ask about us, because the liturgy in the first instant is not about us, but about the other One who is oddly available in this moment.

This liturgy is a moment when we do not have to be ethically pure, morally strident, or politically insistent. It is a time when the deep, powerful passions of God are enacted before us; that enactment connects our life to a buoyant, unambiguous purpose beyond our capability. To yield to the liturgic alternative and to participate in this bold counterdramatization of life is, I submit, the only alternative to fatigue. For if peace and justice are not deep resolves of

God out beyond us, we will surely be defeated by the empire, which is enormously resilient. Peace is indeed a possibility that depends mightily upon us. But the news of this liturgic tradition is that peace is a purpose and promise of God deeper, more powerful, and more resolved than our power and resolve.

3. The substance of liturgy among the exiles is first an articulation of fear, hurt, doubt, anger. The empire rightly takes this to be subversive. In biblical language, exiles gather to practice lament, to bring to public expression all that hurts, diminishes, dehumanizes, brutalizes, and immobilizes.[7] Such lament is in fact a foundational, symbolic, dramatic break with the imperial ideology that claims that the system is the unquestioned solution. The lament embodies an important critique of the dominant system. Israel dares to express its hurt, and in so doing it asserts that the empire was not keeping its promises.

In its situation of exile, ancient Israel generated a variety of models for complaint, protest, and lament. Through this process Israel was theologically and dramatically in touch with its true situation. It did not pretend that the empire was an acceptable home or that the situation of displacement was natural or bearable. It said a bold, pathos-filled No to the circumstance of alienation. Chief among these exilic articulations is the book of Lamentations which expresses the core experience of displaced Israel.[8] The poetry begins in the dramatic voice of beloved Jerusalem now abandoned:

> How lonely sits the city
>   that was full of people!
> How like a widow has she become,
>   she that was great among the nations!
> She that was a princess among the cities
>   has become a vassal.
>   (Lam. 1:1)

Out of that initial acknowledgment comes the repeated refrain:

> She has none to comfort her (Lam. 1:2)
>
> She has no comforter. (Lam 1:9)
>
> For a comforter is far from me,
> one to revive my courage. (Lam. 1:16)

Zion stretches out her hands,
but there is none to comfort her. (Lam. 1:17)

Israel in exile finds powerful words to express its sense that God or any other kind of solace is absent and beyond reach.

In other liturgic poetry, Israel gathers to specify what it was like to have the world taken from it, to be abandoned and bereft. Israel describes for God in great detail the sights and sounds of the temple being destroyed:

At the upper entrance they hacked
the wooden trellis with axes.
And then all its carved wood
they broke down with hatchets and hammers.
They set thy sanctuary on fire;
to the ground they desecrated the dwelling place of thy name.
(Ps. 74:5–7)

Israel puzzled about why God does not care, and why God did not act against the blasphemy and barbarism committed against the beloved temple.

Ancient Israel convened around Psalm 137 to express its rage, indignation, and deep, undeniable hunger for vengeance:

Remember O Lord, against the Edomites
the day of Jerusalem,
How they said, "Rase it, rase it!
Down to its foundations!"
O daughter of Babylon, you devastator!
Happy shall he be who requites you
with what you have done to us!
Happy shall he be who takes your little ones
and dashes them against the rock!
(Ps. 137:7–9)

To our protected ears and restrained mouths, this hardly seems like peacemaking. My point, however, is that in the freedom and drama of the liturgy, this people could bring all its hurt and loss to honest speech. Such speech is not the end of the matter but the crucial beginning. It is necessary that exiles speak in raw, dangerous, honest ways that settled people never find necessary or permissible. Those who are "at home" with the empire never have the need to speak such hurt, for they still trust that the empire can manage the hurt. Exiles, in their very experience, however, know this is not so. The empire in its ideology is not capable of touching human reality, can neither manage the hurt nor justify the loss. Israel in exile fashioned patterns of speech that expressed its impatience with the historical process and at times, its impatience with God who had made promises but not kept them. The standard form of lament and complaint is decisive for Israel in its liberated liturgy.

In speaking their hurt in a stylized way, the exiles understood that their untamed hurt must be honored, taken seriously, and expressed to God. In its speeches of complaint, Israel committed acts of rhetorical terrorism against God. The empire surely will not comfort. Jerusalem is now burned and cannot comfort. Even God now seems absent and cannot comfort. It is no wonder that Israel in its liturgy of exile could echo, "None to comfort, none to comfort, none to comfort." The exiles in their candor are left only with their tears and their anguish, utterly bereft.

4. The miracle of this liturgical candor, as the exiles seem to understand intuitively, is that despair is not the last word. Thus, there is a second central move to the liturgy: liturgy among exiles is also a reception of hope, joy, and rescue given by the Holy One who comes decisively and transformatively into the exilic situation of hurt and loss. The exiles learned and trusted that their dangerous candor about lament and complaint invited transformation and evoked the rescuing power of God in the midst of their abandonment.[9]

The liturgy may linger in the grief and alienation a long time, but it does not finally rest there because the exiles are people of evangelical faith. They know that the absolutizing truth claims of the empire are not finally true and cannot finally prevail. The liturgy finally can turn its attention away from the empire and toward the healing truth that the empire cannot affirm, nullify, or outlast. The liturgy enables exiled Israel both "to wait and to hasten," "to hasten and to wait." The wait is in the midst of terrible hurt. But then there is hastening to the One who strangely, faithfully enters the exile and so transforms it.

Into the liturgy enacted by the exiles comes the intruding fresh voice and fresh power of Yahweh. It is this unexpected God who cuts through the hurt and alienation with words and acts of healing. The liturgy is a way in which an utterly fresh start is made available to the exiles, free from their despair and the diminishments of the empire. This God, so the liturgy witnesses, has the freedom and will to permit a real newness.

The newness that ends all the old despair is announced:

Remember not the former things,
　　nor consider the things of old.
Behold, I am doing a new thing;
　　now it springs forth, do you not perceive it?[10]
　　　　　　　　　　　(Isa. 43:18-19)

The newness is rooted in the faithful love of God toward Israel, even in exile:

I have loved you with an everlasting love;
　　therefore I have continued my faithfulness to you.
Again I will build you, and you shall be built.
　　　　　　　　　　　(Jer. 31:3-4)

God speaks an assurance that changes the world for the exiles:

Fear not, for I have redeemed you;
　　I have called you by name, you are mine.
　　　　　　　　　　　(Isa. 43:1)[11]

Notice that this is a peculiarly liturgic enactment. It is not public action in the public world that the Babylonians can see. It is rather the processing of exilic experience through the memories, stories, and metaphors of the old tradition, the memories of exodus, deliverance, and covenant.[12] The liturgic processing in the world of poets invites the exiles to perceive their situation in a fresh and very different way, without reference to Babylonian power and intimidation.

The substance of the liturgy is to assert that Israel does not belong to Babylon and must not submit its future to Babylon, because there are another power and another loyalty that override Babylon. At the center of this alternative rendering of reality is the liturgy of Yahweh's enthronement which asserts and celebrates the victory and rule of Yahweh, the God of freedom, justice, and mercy.

This poetic liturgy takes up the old memory and asserts it with fresh relevance and pertinence. It asserts that the old, liberating God of Israel is now freshly evident as the real governor of history. The exiles have only to notice, accept, and embrace that new, visible sovereignty:

> Lift up your voice with strength,
>   O Jerusalem, herald of good tidings,
> lift it up, fear not;
>   say to the cities of Judah,
>   "Behold your God."
>
>   (Isa. 40:9)

> How beautiful upon the mountains
>   are the feet of him who brings good tidings,
>   who publishes peace, who brings good tidings of good,
>   who publishes salvation,
>   who says to Zion, "Your God reigns."[13]
>
>   (Isa. 52:7)

Tell anyone who wants to know, the God of justice has delegitimated all powers of injustice! Say to those who resist hearing, the giver of *shalom* has nullified all the perpetrators of death! Say among the trees and fields and beasts, creation prevails and chaos is tamed and driven out. Say to Pharaoh, to Nebuchadnezzar, to Pilate, to Herod, to the Kremlin, to the Pentagon, to racist regimes, to land grabbers and peasant exploiters, say here and everywhere: believe, trust, sing, dance, proclaim, "Yahweh is king." Freedom, mercy, justice, and peace are decreed by Yahweh and cannot be defeated.

This radical alternative claim is as old as Moses, who sang with Miriam and the women at the edge of the waters of freedom.

> I will sing to the Lord, for he has triumphed gloriously. . . . The Lord will reign for ever and ever. (Exod. 15:1, 18)

It is a dangerous claim as sure as the mouth of Jesus:

> The time is fulfilled, and the kingdom of God is at hand; repent, and believe in the gospel. (Mark 1:15)

> The blind receive their sight, the lame walk, lepers are cleansed, and the deaf hear, the dead are raised up, the poor have good news preached to them. (Luke 7:22)

This lyrical invitation is as buoyant as the hope of the church:

> The kingdom of the world has become the kingdom of our Lord
> and of his Christ, and he shall reign for ever and ever. (Rev. 11:15)

The coming of God's rule (wrought first of all liturgically) cancels the grief, overrides the hurt, nullifies the resistance. The exiles have been honest in their painful assertion, "There is none to comfort" (Lam. 1:2). In the evangelical turn of the liturgy, however, there is this other voice, the voice of the gospel which comes to say, "Comfort, comfort my people" (Isa. 40:1).

The liturgical drama among the exiles moves from "none to comfort" to "comfort, comfort." These words are, to be sure, only a liturgic enactment. All around the world of the liturgy, the old power of the empire still persists, the old pathologies are intransigent, the old brutalities continue. The voices of imperial "realism" doubt the liturgy and hold to visible, conventional forms of power. Nonetheless the trusting, embracing exiles hold desperately and passionately to the claim of the liturgy in the face of heavy-handed imperial claims. Israel may be in exile in a hostile empire; they are, however, still the children of an alternative liturgy, and they will not yield the world of their liturgy, even in the face of the empire.

So it is with those who work for justice and peace in our world. They are people situated in a hostile setting. They are also, however, children of a different liturgy, perceiving the world through a different set of memories and hopes. They will not abandon that different world to the fears, threats, and failures of the empire.

There are a number of texts from this alternative liturgic enterprise located in the exile. In their powerful, dramatic words, we may discern the assurances we need today to maintain courage, stamina, and freedom for our particular vocation as exiles.

ISAIAH 40: LITURGY OF
DARING TRANSFORMATION

Isaiah 40 is one of our most poignant assurances to exile. The poet of Isaiah 40 knew the cynical resilience of the empire. He was well acquainted with the normative, authorized, imperial liturgy that kept the empire credible, that worked to sustain its economy, legitimate its dominant order, and control its policies. The poet of Isaiah 40, however, was equipped with more than knowledge of the realities of imperial politics. That knowledge by itself would have resulted only in despair, conformity, abdication, and resignation among the exiles.

The poet of Isaiah 40 was also equipped with bold imagination rooted in faith, which enabled him to say daringly and subversively:

> Have you not known? Have you not heard?
>   Has it not been told you from the beginning?
>   Have you not understood from the foundations of the earth?
> It is he who sits above the circle of the earth,
>   and its inhabitants are like grasshoppers;
> who stretches out the heavens like a curtain;
>   and spreads them like a tent to dwell in;
> who brings princes to nought,
>   and makes the rulers of the earth as nothing.
>   (Isa. 40:21–23)

This poem has wondrous movement. It begins in cosmic claims about the God who orders the heavens, but by its conclusion, the poem has become a political scenario: the God who made the heavens can indeed nullify princes and make the rulers of the earth as nothing. The poet knows that if the exiles credit imperial authority excessively, they will be robbed of identity, cowed, deprived of the freedom to act. And the empire in its despairing conformity will be yet another degree absolutized. The poem speaks exactly against the absolutizing of the empire to show that the empire, in the face of the real governance of Yahweh, is provisional and fragile and should not be unduly embraced, either in fear or in trust.

This incredible poetry therefore has both liturgic and political intentions. Its purpose is to set the powerful claims and the shrill voice of the empire in proper perspective, so that they are not taken too seriously. The poem is an invitation for a liturgic, imaginative act of civil disobedience that affirms that the rulers of the empire in fact do not warrant obedience or fear, and should not be given trust or allegiance.

Israel, in its exilic vocation, is caught, even as we are, between *imperial reality*, which is harsh, flat, uncompromising, and ultimately brutalizing, and *the counterclaim of the liturgy of Yahweh*, which invites exiles to candid complaint and liberated praise, to hurt shared and enthronement acknowledged. This liturgy for exiles evokes transformation that the empire fears and resists. In that moment of liturgic fantasy, Israel is invited to choose between *ideological reality* and *liberated imagination*. Those who choose ideological reality will withdraw from the protesting liturgy and, sooner or later, will die in obedient despair, having succumbed to imperial ideology.

Those who risk the imaginative transformation of the liturgy are permitted another destiny which the empire does not understand and cannot credit. Those who share in the counterworld of this liturgy are promised that this peculiar God

> gives power to the faint,
>   and to him who has no might, he increases strength.
> Even youths shall faint and be weary,
>   and young men shall fall exhausted;
> but they who wait for the Lord shall renew their strength,
>   they shall mount up with wings like eagles,
> they shall run and not be weary,
>   they shall walk and not faint.
>
> (Isa. 40:29–31)

Those who "wait upon the Lord" are those who trust the alternative liturgy and its subversive presentation of reality, and who are prepared to act on that presentation.

Serious energy for justice- and peacemaking never comes from the normative, authorized liturgy of the empire. It comes from an alternative liturgy, evoked by bearing witness to a very different God, addressed to people tilted toward marginality, mediated through the raw reality of social pain and incongruity. It is the children of that daring liturgy who dream of peace and who act on their dream. It is that liturgy which mocks imperial claims and subverts them (cf. Isa. 46—47). It is the children of this liturgy who have the freedom and courage to embrace and trust this other vision, to internalize, objectify, act, risk, believe, and hope relentlessly against the empire that resists peace in the name of legitimacy, order, and absoluteness.

GOD'S PLAN FOR PEACE

Those who work for justice and peace will not be able to persist if they derive their energy from the "real world," for the real world is intransigent, unresponsive, and unforgiving. Peacemaking requires a kind of freedom that comes from the imaginative disengagement from the visible power arrangements around us and the imaginative embrace of another scenario of the world rooted in another voice, based in another memory, authorized toward another humanity. In the context of the political economy of the United States, I submit that such imaginative disengagement and the embrace of another scenario must be done through a liturgy that subverts and sustains, that is honest about our hurt as the empire cannot be honest, that is convinced of another governance as the empire dare not be. The only long-term sustenance for subversive ethical imagination rests not in policy statements and ethical determination but in the liturgical affirmation that "Yahweh governs," "Yahweh has just become king." Such an affirmation frees us beyond our resolve and willpower to think, act, and hope with different energy and passion. The great justice movements in our dangerous world have derived precisely from such liturgies, which do not take life from the hand of the empire.[14]

Those who work for justice, therefore, must trust in this One who has just displaced the empire and who rules in its peace. This holy God whom the empire mocks (cf. 2 Kings 19:4, 22–23) is resolved for peace and justice. The resolve of God's own heart is the only reality that will sustain exiles in their work for peace. We are driven to despair and cynicism if we imagine that the prospect for success is no more durable than our occasional gains. The good news on which we rely is that God has a resolve for peace that endures in the midst of our gains and in the face of our failures. Reliance on this resolve gives us energy to continue to care and to risk.

I consider now three great texts that reflect God's own resolve on which we can rely. In these texts that resolve is captured in the word "plan." God has a plan that is distinct from ours and to which God is relentlessly committed.[15] That "plan" becomes crucial to exiles when they are ready to capitulate to the empire.

ISAIAH 55: SPACE OUTSIDE
THE EMPIRE

Isaiah 55 is placed at the end of the long exilic poem commonly called Second Isaiah. It begins with an invitation to exiles to rely on the nourishment of Yahweh and to desist from the satiation of the empire:

> Ho, every one who thirsts,
>   come to the waters;
> and he who has no money,
>   come, buy and eat!
> Come, buy wine and milk
>   without money and without price.
> Why do you spend your money for that which is not bread
>   and your labor for that which does not satisfy?
> Hearken diligently to me, and eat what is good
>   and delight yourselves in fatness.
> Incline your ear, and come to me;
>   hear, that your soul may live,
> and I will make with you an everlasting covenant.
>
> (vv. 1–3)

The exiles are urged to pay careful attention to their appetites and to the source of their food and their satisfactions. They are warned not to become enslaved to the bread and satisfactions of the empire.

The poet then issues a call to disengage from the empire and from trust in Babylonian shapes of reality:

> See the Lord while he may be found,
>   call upon him while he is near;
> let the wicked forsake their way,
>   and the unrighteous their thoughts;
> let them return to the Lord, that he may have mercy on them,
>   and to our God, for he will abundantly pardon.
>
> (vv. 6–7)

It is striking that this bold, daring summons has become for us a conventional, routinized "call to worship." That such a summons has become routinized hints at how our liturgy has lost its danger and has become acclimated to the empire. It is possible, however, to recover the summons and rehear the danger of this liturgical alternative.

The good news of these verses is that God is available in exile, that the true God is still at work in the empire where all seemed lost. Yahweh is not to be sought in a futile domination of the Babylonian gods of brutality and exploitation. The call to forsake the "wicked way" is a specific indictment of the embrace of imperial gods and the acceptance of their rule and their definition of reality (v. 7). The "unrighteousness" that is to be rejected is not narrow moralism but the mistaken and destructive notion that the empire is true and should be honored or obeyed.

What we have taken to be a call to worship is in fact an invitation to depart emotionally, ethically, and spiritually from the empire. The basis for the invitation is that the God of the covenant is ready to be merciful while the gods of the empire are relentlessly lacking in mercy (v. 7). The turn from the harshness of the empire to Yahweh's gracious rule is a turn to a genuinely human prospect rooted in covenantal openness. That human prospect cannot be had by adhering to imperial loyalties and definitions of reality, for the empire has no vision of humanness, embraces no covenantal possibility, and allows for none of the openness or mercy necessary to human life.

In vv. 6–7, the poet draws a sharp contrast between the hopes of Yahweh and the demands of the empire. Then in vv. 8–9, a powerful theological conclusion, the poet articulates the ground on which the contrast is made:

> My thoughts (*ḥšb*) are not your thoughts (*ḥšb*),
>   neither are your ways my ways. . . .
> For as the heavens are higher than the earth,
>   so are my ways higher than your ways
>   and my thoughts than your thoughts.

The poet gives the exiles an affirmation to lean upon in confidence. The resolve of God, the plan, the thought of Yahweh is not to be equated with the plan of either the empire or those who submit to the empire. Our accommodating religion carelessly imagines that God is only "us" writ large, so that God's plan is only our desires pushed upstairs. This poem resists such imperial reductionism and asserts that this God has another will to work in the world.

The God of Israel has a tough, resilient intention about the shape of human history that is other than our intent and other than imperial programs. Exiles need not always invent the next move. Exiles need not be inordinately fascinated with the resolve of the empire. Exiles from time to time must ask about the resolve of God's own life, which outruns our posturing. Peace, justice, mercy, and forgiveness are God's own resolve, which finally will not be defied and cannot be defeated or nullified by the empire:

> As the rain and the snow come down from heaven,
>   and return not thither but water the earth,
> . . . .
> so shall my word be that goes forth from my mouth,
>   it shall not return to me empty,
> but it shall accomplish that which I purpose,
>   and prosper in the thing for which I sent it.
>
> (vv. 10–11)

God's word, decree, and resolve are very sure. God will do what God says. Nothing can deter God, not the grief of Israel who imagines there is "no comforter" (Lam. 1:2) nor the cynical autonomy of the empire (cf. Isa. 47:7–10).

Finally, the poet ends with a wondrous affirmation of God's plan: there will be a homecoming. Alienation and displacement will end. Exile will be no more. The destiny of the exiles is that they shall come home and be accepted:

> You shall go out in joy,
>   and be led forth in peace;
> the mountains and the hills before you
>   shall break forth into singing,
>   and all the trees of the field shall clap their hands.
> Instead of the thorn shall come up the cypress;
>   instead of the brier shall come up myrtle.
>
> (vv. 12–13)

God is resolved to do nothing less than transform all of creation, end the old, tired curses of brier and thistles (cf. Genesis 3), remove the broken quality of life, heal the fractures, bridge the gulfs, and restore joy, peace, and well-being. God has intended peace. The exiles embrace that intent, for all the hostilities of the empire cannot resist it.

Do not miss what a wonderful evangelical offer this is. The poet dares to speak of God's grand intent for all the nations. The specific

intent of the poet, however, is to permit exiles to trust in the promises of Yahweh, to resist imperial seductions, and so to act with
freedom and courage. Efforts toward peace and well-being occur
not in a vacuum, but spin off and derive precisely from God's own
powerful commitments in the face of the empire.

JEREMIAH 29: PEACE AS
TASK AND GIFT

Jeremiah 29 offers important assurance to the exiles. The prophet
writes a pastoral letter to the exiles in Babylon that sounds a note of
political realism. He advises them to settle down in the empire, for
Israel will be in Babylonian exile for a long time and should entertain no illusions about going home soon. Indeed, it is God's will that
they should be in exile. In the midst of this sobriety, however, Jeremiah speaks a word of remarkable counsel: "Seek the welfare of the
city where I have sent you into exile, and pray to Yahweh on its
behalf, for in its welfare you will find your welfare" (v. 7). This is
an extraordinary affirmation. Israel will have no "separate peace."
Israel cannot withdraw from its place in the empire. Rather it must
live there, committed to the well-being and the transformation of
the empire.

Two things are striking about this prophetic advice. First, the
Israelites are invited to care about the city, Babylon, the empire, the
place where they did not want to be. Jeremiah has understood that
exiled Jews have no obedient alternative but to be in the empire.
They are not permitted a sectarian withdrawal into a private world
of well-being, because only a healthy human empire will permit
Jews to have health. Peacemaking can never be a separate peace or
a private peace, but must be a peace comprehensive of the human
world, all its power relations, and all its economic arrangements.
This is indeed a daring invitation, for it charges this little company
of Jews to address the shape of the empire and to believe that the
whole empire can and must be transformed toward wholeness.

Second, the pivotal word in the text is *shalom*, which we regularly translate "peace." The RSV rendered the word as "welfare"
before "welfare" became such an unpopular word. It is of course a
proper rendering of the term, for the peace to which Israel is sum-

moned is precisely human wholeness in human community. Verses 4–9 thus give an assurance to exiles that they must be in exile actively caring about the empire.

Verses 10–14 is the oracle which more directly concerns us. Yahweh announces to the exiles that their ultimate destiny is not to be exiles in a hostile empire. The Israelites are not fated to live forever in the face of the hostile reality of the empire. God promises that there will be another, better home:

> I will visit you, and I will fulfil to you my promise and bring you back to this place [to your home]. (v. 10)

God is at work even in the empire to bring the exiles home. God has promised homecoming and watches over that promise.

The next verse articulates one of the great decrees of the Bible:

> I know the plans (*ḥšb*) I have for you. (v. 11)

The word "plans" is the same as "thoughts" in Isa. 55:8—I know the plans, thoughts, dreams I have for the exiles. God has an overriding purpose for God's trusting people, even if that purpose is not yet visible in the political process. Of course, the empire also has a plan for the exiles: that they should be forever displaced, homeless, at risk, restless, administrated. Yahweh's plan is precisely counter to the empire's. The empire is not the one who dreams the ultimate dream of the exiles and so the exiles must take care not to trust the empire or commit themselves excessively to its dream or promises. God asserts, "I know the plans I have for you, plans for welfare and not for evil, to give you a future and a hope" (v. 11).

Again the word *shalom* is translated as "welfare." Peace is asserted as God's intended future for Israel. In v. 8 Israel is commanded to do *shalom*, the proper work of Israel in exile. Now in v. 11, Israel is assured that God will do *shalom* for the exiles in the face of the empire. Israel's work of peace is done within a context of Yahweh's own powerful resolve to do *shalom* all around Israel (v. 11). Yahweh is resolved to bring into existence a healthy functioning human community, "to give you a future and a hope." God will not let imperial displacement be the destiny of God's beloved people.

It is a critical purpose of the hostile Babylonian empire (and indeed of all empires) to rob people of hope, to deny dreams of human possibility, to close off the future so that the present will be uncritically and abidingly valued. Yahweh's exiles know better. They are given hope for a possibility beyond the present, a hope that is not even on the horizon of the Babylonian military-industrial complex or within its understanding.

The oracle then explicates the promised homecoming (vv. 12–14). God will hear the prayers of exiles who pray. God is not beyond the reach of the faithful in the empire. All that is required to find God is to seek "with all your heart," that is, with a single loyalty, with a centered hope (v. 13). God will be found and will "restore fortunes," will end the pressure of the empire and give a good homecoming (v. 14). Exiles will come to this place where they ought to be and will say, "Free at last, free at last, . . . at home at last, at home at last."

What an extraordinary promise, set directly in the mouth of God! Verses 5–9 affirm realistically that the exiles must not escape the empire, be blind to its power, or fail to take it seriously. They must be in its midst in real, effective, and caring ways, not passively but transformatively. But, say vv. 10–11, do not take the context of empire with ultimate seriousness. Do not let it claim and domesticate you, because it is quite provisional, and it would be foolish to make a long-term commitment to such a passing arrangement.

Of course the empire did not seem a passing arrangement to any who simply looked at it. It is only a passing arrangement in the powerful, poetic imagination of Israel. Israel is to seek peace in and for the empire. God, at the same time, intends welfare and peace well beyond the empire. Israel is thus urged to be in the empire, but not to be finally in it (John 17:15–16). The exiles are to trust the plan of God, which is more powerful than any present circumstance or any imperial plan. If exiles trust Yahweh's counterplan, they will not succumb and they will not despair.

PSALM 33:
AN OVERRIDING PLAN

In both Isaiah 55 and Jeremiah 29, the exiles reflect on God's determined plan, for only God's plan can counter the hostile empire.

That focus on God's plan leads me to a third magisterial text, Psalm 33. This psalm is a disciplined, faithful reflection on what it is like to live in a world in which Yahweh rules, even though visible evidence and circumstance might lead us to think the God of liberation and justice does not rule.

The psalm begins with a summons to praise God with stringed instruments, to enter the liturgy with abandon (vv. 1–3). Praise, when given freely and passionately, is in itself a break with the numbed conformity of the empire. It is an act that gets Israel beyond the managed perimeters of human ingenuity and control. The praise urged in this psalm is a "new song" (v. 3), which is written for the sake of this new theological reality. Israel at worship observes that the "old, old story" of memory becomes a "new song" of possibility. Israel in its praise is singing out beyond the permit of every empire. In its doxology, Israel is daring in offering a reality not governed by the empire. Praise is an act of subversion and becomes the taproot of civil disobedience.

The psalm concerns Yahweh's governing word (vv. 4–9). This is a rule of One who governs simply by the words, by issuing a decree. There is no coercion, no force in Yahweh's rule; creation is eager to obey. This God says to the stars, "shine," and they rush to shine. This God commands heaven and earth, and all creation gladly complies. That word which governs is marked by faithfulness (*'amûnah*), righteousness (*ṣedeqah*), justice (*mišpaṭ*), and steadfast love (*ḥesed*). The entire vocabulary of Israel's faith is offered in vv. 4–5, where the poet uses the most freighted words Israel knows in order to assert the most formidable reality. God's speech intends and evokes a world of healthy covenantal transactions in which there is no trace of brutality or oppression. The social reality of righteousness, justice, faithfulness, and steadfast love is precisely what is missing in the empire, which is organized against serious covenant. Yahweh's resolve is that the anticovenantal power of the empire is to be displaced by genuinely covenantal life.

This sovereign word from Yahweh frames the world. This saving word summons the nations and sets them in a possible world of freedom and obedience, caring and compassion. The world is forever marked by Yahweh's decree of fidelity which means that these characteristics of covenantal life are not negotiable or optional but are structured into creation. Yahweh's word of utter fidelity shapes the world, and the creation must keep groaning until it practices the decree of fidelity (cf. Rom. 8:19–23). This is God's word. It will surely prevail and the empire cannot stop it (cf. Isa. 40:6–8; 55:10–11). We are invited to see that the world, even the world of Babylon, is not autonomous. It is a world that finally answers to the good will of Yahweh (cf. Isaiah 47). The exiles are those who know that coming, assured reality well ahead of the kings and rulers who always learn late.

The psalm moves from this comprehensive sweep of creation to the political process of nations and peoples (vv. 10–17). The nations have wills and intentions, plans and programs of their own. Nations are not puppets of Yahweh, but make their own way amidst the realities of power. Sometimes they do the purpose of Yahweh, wittingly or unwittingly. Sometimes, indeed often, the nations do not obey Yahweh. Sometimes they pursue policies that deeply offend Yahweh and evoke Yahweh to anger (cf. Ps. 2:1–6).

Psalm 33, which begins in celebration of God's good purposes, is not romantic. It knows that the great nations, even the empires, are locked in conflict with Yahweh. The exiles are set exactly between God's resolve for justice and righteousness and an empire of injustice and unrighteousness. Inhabitants of an empire are always tempted to believe that might makes right, that the empire is autonomous, that the military-industrial complex can shamelessly do whatever it wants. When one believes that, one inevitably ends in despair.

Israel at its best, however, holds to the poem and does not believe the imperial ideology. The psalm discerns a very different shape to public power:

> The Lord brings the counsel of the nations to nought;
> The Lord frustrates the plans (*ḥšb*) of the peoples,
> The counsel of the Lord stands for ever,
> The plans (*ḥšb*) of Yahweh's heart are to all generations.
>   (vv. 10–11)

The poetic lines juxtapose the counsel of the nations and the counsel of Yahweh and set them in opposition. Then the psalm juxtaposes the plans of the peoples and the thoughts (plans) of Yahweh's heart. "Plans" and "thoughts" both translate *ḥšb*, the word we saw in Isaiah 55 ("my thoughts are not your thoughts") and Jeremiah 29 ("I know the plans I have for you"). The exiles hold to Yahweh's plan, which seems so feeble in the empire, but which is trustworthy and will prevail.

Psalm 33 asserts that (1) Yahweh has Yahweh's own plan that is not an echo of ours; (2) Yahweh's plan is in contrast to the nations' plan; and (3) Yahweh's plan will triumph because it is ordained in the very structure of creation. Peacemaking in the empire means implementing God's good plan. First, though, it means trusting in and relying on God's plan, believing that there is a plan counter to the empire's, which lies outside my responsibility. God's plan is finally not a burden for us to execute but an assurance for us to lean upon.[16]

The nations' "plan," to which Yahweh is opposed, is characterized by economic monopoly, political domination, and military might. Even if such a pursuit of monopoly is not demonic in its conceptualization, it inevitably has incredible human costs, crushing those who are inconvenient or without use. It is easy to believe that this demonic pursuit of control will have its way.

In the face of such power, the Bible places a poem. The first step in rereading social reality and discerning the radical alternative proposed in Psalm 33 is to realize that God's way is not equivalent to our way but, rather, lives in deep tension with it. The second step is seeing that God's resolve for human community is not the soft, romantic dream of naive people, but is shaped in God's very heart and articulated by thoughtful people who have looked the empire in the eye and have suffered but have not succumbed. The third step is seeing that a plan rooted in God's heart may meet harsh resistance and deep delay. But it will prevail.

In v. 12, a verdict is announced:

Blessed is the nation whose God is Yahweh.

The people who practice Yahweh's plan of justice, righteousness, faithfulness, and steadfast love are indeed fortunate, because only that way of life can finally prosper. While the verdict seems to refer to Israel, in fact it allows for the inclusion of any nation which will practice Yahweh's plan. Any nation that is genuinely covenantal will prosper.

The final part of the psalm, vv. 13–22, derives crucial theological reflections out of this hard-nosed political analysis. I note three points.

1. The world operates under God's sovereign eye:

> v. 13 The Lord *looks down* from heaven,
>   he *sees* all the sons of men,
> v. 14 From where he sits enthroned, *he looks*,
> v. 15 he *observes* all the deeds of creation,
> v. 18 behold, God's *good eye* is on faithful people.

The nations do not operate in secret (cf. Isa. 47:10). This Yahweh is indeed the one "from whom no secrets are hid." The psalm makes an enormous claim against the propensity of the great nations for secrecy. Think what it would mean for them to have "no secrets." No public secrets of the "intelligence community," no secret testing of weapons, no covert overthrow of other governments, no deal-cutting on the economy, no intimidation, no blackmail. Communities that practice covenantal life can afford to conduct affairs under the scrutiny of God and under the scrutiny of public observation.

The empire did not know that Yahweh looked and did not believe that Yahweh watched. In Isaiah 47:10, the Babylonian empire thought, "No one sees me." Empires think they are autonomous and not accountable. But there is a moral structure to human history that is uncompromising and will have its say. God rules by watching—not only in censure and judgment, but in healing ways over those who trust and hope (cf. Deut. 11:12). God watches in order to guard and protect the faithful from death and to preserve them in danger. If there were no watchful care from God, the powerful would always win and the weak always die. All of that is changed, however, precisely because God watches in sovereign ways.

2. In vv. 16–17 the psalm arrives at a remarkable political conclusion that has implications for peacemaking and for military pretension:

> A king is not saved by his great army;
>   a warrior is not delivered by his great strength,
> The war horse is a vain hope for victory,
>   and by its great might it cannot save.

Raw power finally does not determine political and human processes.[17] It is this reality that makes peacemaking possible and
credible. The world will not be possessed by technology or ruthless
self-interest. Such attempts at power are endlessly undermined and
checked by the inscrutable rule of Yahweh which permits surprises
and transformation in the political process beyond our control and
expectations.

This political, military conclusion to the psalm is derived from
the very character of the world as God's creation. Covenantal factors—the resilience of God, the surprise of humanity, the ache of
hurt, the power of hope, the miracle of transformation—will not be
denied. They are present and operative even if the military disre-
gards them. That is why the posturing of the German Central Staff,
the massing of Russian troops, and the strategies of war machines
and ideological tramplers of human fragility cannot prevail. Yahweh's world is a world of endlessly surprising human possibility, not
crushed or precluded by ugly and barbaric technology.

Psalm 33 then is a "new song," singing of new human possibility.
The new song asserts that kings will have to participate in the
human, political process and cannot reduce policy to mere arms.
The rule of Yahweh guarantees that the political process is an endlessly open, human process. Political power requires sensitivity to
human factors. Brute strength cannot finally have its way. The psalm
is an assault on the excessive fascination with policies of force.
Affirmations in the psalm which value Yahweh's word (vv. 4–9),
Yahweh's eye (vv. 13–18), and Yahweh's rule (vv. 10–12) are not
presented as revelations from heaven. Rather they are cast as
observations gathered from human experience. Psalm 33 echoes the
sapiential conclusion of Prov. 21:30–31:

> No wisdom, no understanding, no counsel
>   can avail against the Lord.
> The horse is made ready for the day of battle,
>   but the victory belongs to the Lord.

There is something inscrutable that governs, rooted in God and
shaped like faithfulness. The psalm does not ask people to believe in
a religious fantasy. Rather it invites people to step outside the mis-

taken rationality of power politics to observe that the actual course of human history is of another kind. This is not revelation from heaven but wisdom out of human memory, a wisdom about how to operate and prosper. Only "fools" believe their own ideology and champion a rationality at odds with covenantal reality.

3. Psalm 33 ends in a celebration of those who attend to the covenantal-human-Yahwistic dimensions of public reality (vv. 18–22). Yahweh sees not only the grand foolishness of kings and horses, but also the daily attentiveness of the faithful. Yahweh celebrates that fidelity. Thus the psalm ends on a powerful word of hope:

> The eye of the Lord is on those who fear him,
>   on *those who hope* in his steadfast love
> . . . .
>   he is our help and shield.
> Yea, our heart is glad in him,
>   because we trust in his holy name.
> Let your steadfast love, O Lord, be upon us,
>   even as *we hope in thee*. (italics added)

Hope/gladness/trust/hope! The gladness at the end derives from the new song at the beginning.

Psalm 33 sorts out the ways in which people are in the world. There are faithful ones who hope, who live in a world governed by Yahweh; and there are those who engage in the seductions of the empire, who do not hope, trust, or rejoice, but only seek to control and be controlled. In our day-to-day living we are largely ambivalent about this issue. Even when we know better, we are tempted to think that power will prevail. Clearly, to place trust and confidence in raw, unprincipled power, however, is hopeless and leads nowhere. Hope is in a new song that acknowledges the true shape of the world in terms of justice, faithfulness, righteousness, steadfast love— and peace. Human life is ultimately a covenantal operation. To deny that covenantal reality is to choose death. In inscrutable ways the covenantal realities of life push us beyond our preoccupation with security to praise the God who governs. When Israel finished singing its new song, it was still left with the concrete issues of governance. Israel knew—whenever it sang this song—that the "plans of the peoples" must submit to the "counsel of the Lord." In the end, the nations have no serious alternative to covenantal life.

CONCLUSION: A HOPE BEYOND
OUR THIN RESOLVE

Peace has always constituted a decisive, daring, subversive alternative to the modalities of the empire that oppose covenantal peace. Peace is an alternative that requires wise strategy, daring action, and ethical passion. By themselves, however, our strategies, actions, and passions are not adequate in the face of imperial reality. We are much too thin in our resolve to make peace only our work. That by itself can end only in despair.

The claims of biblical faith provide foundations and give us staying power. Biblical faith dares to assert that a resolve for peace is lodged in God's very heart, and therefore it is a resolve of cosmic power and durability. This does not lessen the urgency of our actions, but it provides a context for them that guards against our despair and cynicism.

Thus, in the face of our temptation to despair, we can affirm:

1. *God has a plan (ḥšb)*, an intention, a resolve for peace that persists even where that resolve is not welcomed. That plan is articulated especially to exiles and assures them that God's plan is quite distinct from all other plans. Exiles are invited to embrace that overriding plan as an alternative to the empire (Isa. 55:6–9). That plan is for *shalom*, for well-being. For that reason exiles are assured that God is faithful and will cause a homecoming (Jer. 29:10–14). That plan is rooted in God's word, guarded by God's eye, and brings joy and blessing to the nations who trust in God and in God's plan, who know that there is more to the public process than horses and chariots (Psalm 33).

2. *Those who care about peace in our time have the startling identity of exiles*, predictably and deeply at odds with their social context. Those who trust God's plan for peace can count on being alienated, rejected outsiders, resented for their subversion.

3. That startling identity is sustainable by accepting *the healing invitation to participate in, be shaped by, and yield to the odd liturgy that bestows God's presence, power, and purpose.* In this liturgy, our life is daily reenacted, redescribed, and reexperienced by the freedom to speak our fear, hurt, doubt, and anger, and by the reception of hope, joy, and rescue with the coming of the transformative God.

Exile is sustainable—but only by this liturgy. In that imaginative daring act of liturgy, our hurts and hopes are brought into the transforming sphere of God's plan for peace. Without that transaction, we end in bitterness. With it, Israel and all faithful, obedient exiles are on their way, rejoicing, trusting the plan, knowing their identity, and submitting to healing. The empire will never understand. In the end, however, it will yield.

NOTES

This chapter was initially delivered as an address to a "Peace and Justice" meeting in Cleveland, Ohio, October 23, 1986.

1. That peace and justice are unwelcome amidst the dominant values of our culture is evidenced by the resistance evoked by the recent letter of American Roman Catholic Bishops concerning peace. I regard their two letters as acts of extreme importance in delineating sharply the claims of biblical faith and dominant American values.

2. For a general survey of the theological intention of the exilic literature, see Ralph W. Klein, *Israel in Exile: A Theological Interpretation* (Philadelphia: Fortress Press, 1979); and Peter R. Ackroyd, *Exile and Restoration: A Study of Hebrew Thought of the Sixth Century B.C.* (Philadelphia: Westminster Press, 1968).

3. It is, of course, the case that not all Jews experienced the exile. Jacob Neusner, *Understanding Seeking Faith* (Atlanta: Scholars Press, 1986), 115–49, has shown how exile and restoration became a powerful, even decisive, paradigm for Jewish faith for all Jews, not only the ones who experienced exile.

4. On the contemporary significance of the paradigm of exile, see William Stringfellow, *An Ethic for Christians and Other Aliens in a Strange Land* (Waco, Tex.: Word Books, 1973).

5. See Walter Brueggemann, *Hopeful Imagination* (Philadelphia: Fortress Press, 1986). In that discussion I have included Ezekiel with Jeremiah and Isaiah 40—55. My argument here could readily be extended by reference to Ezekiel.

6. On exodus and exile as dominant paradigms for faith rooted in the Old Testament, see Bas Van Iersel and Anton Weiler, eds., *Exodus— A Lasting Paradigm*, Concilium 189 (Edinburgh: T. & T. Clark, 1987); and Neusner, *Understanding Seeking Faith*, 115–49. On the derivative, powerful function of the exodus memory, see Michael Walzer, *Exodus and Revolution* (New York: Basic Books, 1985). On a contemporary practice

of liturgy that creates an alternative world of liberation, see Rosemary Radford Ruether, *Women-Church: Theology and Practice of Feminist Liturgical Communities* (San Francisco: Harper & Row, 1986). Ruether's attention to practice provides evidence of actual rites which change worlds. Such practices necessarily depend on both old, rooted memories (traditions) and contemporary experience. The juxtaposition of the two requires important interpretive moves.

7. The basic study on the lament form is Claus Westermann, *Praise and Lament in the Psalms* (Atlanta: John Knox Press, 1981). See also Walter Brueggemann, "From Hurt to Joy, From Death to Life," *Interpretation* 28 (1974): 3–19; idem, "The Formfulness of Grief," *Interpretation* 31 (1977): 263–75; and Patrick D. Miller, Jr., "Trouble and Woe," *Interpretation* 37 (1983): 32–45.

8. See Norman K. Gottwald, *Studies in the Book of Lamentations*, Studies in Biblical Theology (London: SCM Press, 1954). Gottwald well discerns the power of the poetry to evoke a reversal, and then a reversal of the reversal.

9. Westermann, *Praise and Lament in the Psalms*, has articulated the characteristic way in which "plea" turns to "praise." That turn is, of course, a theological matter, but in the life of Israel it is also a rhetorical, liturgic matter.

10. This sense of "new thing" follows the suggestion of Brevard S. Childs, *Introduction to the Old Testament as Scripture* (Philadelphia: Fortress Press, 1979), 325–38; and Ronald E. Clements, "The Unity of the Book of Isaiah," *Interpretation* 36 (1982): 117–29.

11. Edgar W. Conrad, *Fear Not Warrior*, Brown Judaic Studies 75 (Chico, Calif.: Scholars Press, 1985), has made an important new analysis of this form with particular reference to the uses in 2 Isaiah.

12. On the use of the old traditions in the exilic poetry of 2 Isaiah, see Bernhard W. Anderson, "Exodus Typology in Second Isaiah," in *Israel's Prophetic Heritage*, ed. Bernhard W. Anderson and Walter Harrelson (London: SCM Press, 1962), 177–95; and idem, "Exodus and Covenant in Second Isaiah and Prophetic Tradition," in *Magnalia Dei, The Mighty Acts of God*, ed. Frank Moore Cross, Werner E. Lemke, and Patrick D. Miller, Jr. (Garden City, N.Y.: Doubleday & Co., 1976), 339–60.

13. I have given extensive attention to this formula in the worship of Israel in *Israel's Praise: Doxology against Idolatry and Ideology* (Philadelphia: Fortress Press, 1988), chap. 2.

14. Among such movements explicitly rooted in liturgy are the U.S. civil rights movement as articulated by Martin Luther King, Jr., the South African human rights campaign led by Desmond Tutu, and the Polish Solidarity movement which has important rootage in the Catho-

lic church. It must also be recognized that biblical religion does indeed on occasion play a demonic role in some social movements, as in the crises in Northern Ireland and Lebanon.

15. Bertil Albrektson, *History and the Gods* (Lund, Sweden: C.W.K. Gleerup, 1967), 68–97, has strongly argued that the notion of "plan of God" is alien to the Old Testament. His is a cogent argument, but I submit that the terms of the discussion have considerably shifted since he made that argument.

16. On God's plan as a source of assurance, see the first question and answer of the *Heidelberg Catechism*. The question is What is your only source of comfort in life and in death? The answer is reflective of a "plan" that gives powerful assurance: "That I belong in body and soul, in life and in death—not to myself but to my faithful Savior, Jesus Christ, who at the cost of his own blood has fully paid for all my sins and has completely freed me of the dominion of the devil; that he protects me so well that without the will of my Father in heaven not a hair can fall from my head, indeed that everything must fit his purpose for my salvation. . . ."

17. On the deabsolutizing of military power, see Walter Brueggemann, *Revelation and Violence; A Study in Contextualization* (Milwaukee: Marquette University Press, 1986), 53 and passim.

11

Land: Fertility and Justice

HUMAN CONNECTEDNESS TO THE LAND is suggested in biblical language by a play on words. *'Adam*, or humankind, has a partner and mate, *'Adamah*, or land.[1] Humankind and land are thus linked in a covenantal relationship analogous to the covenantal relationship between man and woman.[2] A sound theology requires honoring the covenantal relationship. The operating land ethic in our society denies that relationship at enormous cost, not only to land but to our common humanity.

I begin with a most suggestive statement from Wendell Berry, poetic lover of the land, who cherishes the precious land in the face of its abuse by agribusiness:

> I do not know how exact a case might be made, but it seems to me that there is an historical parallel, in white American history, between the treatment of the land and the treatment of women. The frontier, for instance, was notoriously exploitative of both, and I believe for largely the same reasons. Many of the early farmers seem to have worn out farms and wives with equal regardlessness, interested in both mainly for what they would produce, crops and dollars, labor and sons; they clambered upon their fields and upon their wives, struggling for an economic foothold, the having and holding that cannot come until both fields and wives are properly cherished. And today there seems to me a distinct connection between our nomadism (our "social mobility") and the nearly universal disintegration of marriages and families.[3]

On the land theme, he comments:

> The rural community—that is, the land and the people—is being
> degraded in complementary fashion by the specialists' tendency
> to regard the land as a factory and the people as spare parts. Or,
> to put it another way, the rural community is being degraded by
> the fashionable premise that the exclusive function of the farmer
> is production and that his major discipline is economics.[4]

The relation between women and land, between sexuality and
economics, is my theme in this chapter. I suggest that sexuality
(which includes fertility and production) and economics (which
includes the question of justice) cannot be separated. They are the
two great spheres of our life, the ones about which we most trouble,
over which we most quarrel, and toward which we most hope.
When sexuality is connected to fertility and economics is connected
to justice, we are close to the core of all biblical ethics, for the Bible
insists that fertility is impossible without justice. That is, economics
cannot be separated from sexuality, nor sexuality from economics.
We treat the land the way we treat women, "we" being dominant
males who have historically been owners of both.

My articulation of the parallel between issues of land and sexuality is cast in masculine terms and I regret that. I leave the argument
in masculine terms because that is the biblical casting of the problem, and because I believe the contemporary problem is still largely
one of male machismo. A serious relationship with a woman must
avoid two temptations. One is the temptation to *promiscuity*, so that
the woman is used and discarded for the sake of another, and is
thus reduced to a commodity.[5] The relation is held casually, and there
is no abiding or serious relationship, only a momentary convenience.
The other is the temptation to *domination*, to hold with such an
intense commitment that the woman is owned, controlled, without
rights, and in a different way is reduced to a commodity. So also
with the land. It may be regarded promiscuously, as though it had
no significance, and can be bought, sold, traded, used, and discarded as a convenient commodity. Or the land may be held so
closely and so tightly, dominated as though it had no rights, until
the life is squeezed out of it. In either case, the land is treated as if it
exists for the one who possesses it.

The mystery of an adequate relationship is to hold so loyally as to preclude promiscuity, but to hold so freely as to respect another's rights as partner. It is the same with the land. The mystery of faithfulness is to hold the land loyally so as not to reduce it to a commodity, but to hold so freely as to honor its rights as partner and not possession.

In our society we have terribly distorted relations between men and women, between 'adam and 'adamah, distortions which combine promiscuity and domination, precluding in both cases loyal, freely held covenantal commitments. Likely we shall not correct one of these deathly distortions unless we correct both of them. We shall not have a new land ethic until we have a new sexual ethic, free of both promiscuity and domination. Applied to the land, we shall not have fertility until we have justice toward the land and toward those who depend on the land for life, which means all brothers and sisters.

SEXUALITY AND ECONOMICS

The linking of sexuality and economics, fertility and justice, is evident at many places in the Bible.

1. Ezekiel 18:6–8 provides a succinct catalogue of what constitutes moral responsibility, a catalogue on the practice of righteousness that leads to life. Righteousness here consists of only three elements. The first is to shun idolatry. The God questions must be truly discerned so that absolute loyalty is not assigned to any other. Luke Johnson has grasped the economic implications of idolatry, recognizing that oppression regularly derives from idolatry.[6]

Second is the requirement of right sexuality, so that there is no defilement. The righteous man "does not defile his neighbor's wife or approach a woman in time of her impurity" (v. 6b). The third element concerns economics. The righteous man "does not oppress anyone, but restores to the debtor his pledge, commits no robbery, gives his bread to the hungry and covers the naked with a garment, does not lend at interest or take any increase" (vv. 7–8a).

I find it telling that this ethical summary of Ezekiel 18 derives from idolatry the two decisive ethical questions of sexuality and economics. The first of these is as clear as any conservative could desire, and the second as inclusive as any liberal may wish. It would be health-giving in the church if we agreed that every statement on sexuality must be accompanied by one on economics and vice versa. The two are the arenas in which idolatry usually becomes visible. In the language of Wendell Berry, the first concerns how women are treated, the second concerns the treatment of land.

2. Ezekiel 16:46–50 contains a remarkable statement related to our theme. The Sodom story of Genesis 18—19 is commonly regarded as a statement about violence in sexual relations. But the Ezekiel text handles this narrative memory with remarkable freedom and imagination. Ezekiel 16 is a long recital of Israel's history, not as a recital of God's mighty deeds but as a recital of sin, betrayal, and distortion on Israel's part. It is predictable that the Sodom story might occur in such a recital, but its use by Ezekiel is most surprising. Israel's distortion is handled in this way:

> This was the guilt of your sister Sodom: she and her daughters had pride, surfeit of food, and prosperous ease, but did not aid the poor and needy. They were haughty, and did abominable things before me; therefore I removed them, when I saw it. (Ezek. 16:49–50).

The narrative on sexuality has been recast here as an indictment of economic distortions. The prophet is no doubt inventive. But he is also discerning, for he has seen that sexuality and economic justice are of a piece. The treatment of women and of land are parallel.

3. The themes of sexuality and economics require us to pay attention to the insights and interrelatedness of Freud and Marx. Freud understood that concerning the mystery of sexuality we have an endless capacity for distortion and deception. Marx understood that economic self-interest is readily passed off as reality. Both were in the end speaking of the same social reality. They understood that modern civilization is grounded in extraordinary self-deception that distorts both sexuality and economics and ends in deep alienation from self, neighbor, and land.[7]

I suggest that in terms of modern categories of criticism, the interface of Marx and Freud will be necessary, urgent, and decisive for understanding and resolving the large public problem of sexuality and economics, productivity and justice. Separating the categories generally is an attempt to deal with part of an issue, when in fact one part cannot be separated from the other. It means we imagine we can have productivity without justice. As long as we entertain that deception, we will not understand how or why Ezekiel transformed the Genesis narrative of sexual violence into a statement about economic abuse. And if we cannot understand that, we shall not have a land policy that avoids both promiscuity and domination.

Against this background, I now explore three biblical themes that occur at the interface between sexuality and economics and that ask about the relation of productivity and justice: inheritance, coveting, and defilement.

LAND AS INHERITANCE

Israel's theory of land, as portrayed in the conquest traditions and in the torah provisions, is that the land is assigned to the entire community as a trust from Yahweh. Within the community, clans and "houses" hold certain land as entities in the community. This land is regularly designated not as possession but as "inheritance." That is, the connection between the social unit and the land is inalienable and endures in perpetuity. It need not concern us whether this notion of land was implemented in detail or if it is an imaginative social contract that existed only in theory. What matters is that this is the land theory that is appropriate to this community which regarded the land as a gift of God.[8]

Israel's theory of land deeply rooted in the liberation traditions clashed with alternative theories and practices in which the land was regarded as a tradeable commodity, not as a gift, trust, or inheritance. This alternative land theory[9] (which comes to powerful expression in the tale of Naboth's vineyard in 1 Kings 21) meant that in the real world no one's land was safe or secure, but that land became an arena for commercialism and for all the social problems that emerge when the strong are aligned against the weak. That social relationship of conflict resulted, as in the tradition of Amos, in some having monopolies and others being systematically reduced to poverty, dependence, and despair.[10] Israel's fundamental dream is about land.[11] Israel is a social and theological experiment in alternative land management. The God of Israel is a God who gives land, and Israel is a people who holds land in alternative ways. The core tradition is intended to promote an alternative to the imperial system of land known in both the Egyptian empire and the Canaanite city-states.[12]

Prohibitions against Moving Boundaries

Israel's theory of land as inheritance is practical; it is designed to resist monopoly and its resulting social displacement. In the torah maintaining land boundaries is a fundamental anchor of social policy. Thus:

> In the inheritance which you will hold in the land that the Lord your God gives you to possess, you shall not remove your neighbor's landmark, which the men of old have set. (Deut. 19:14)

The language of inheritance[13] is important, but even more important is the theological grounding of social practice and social guarantees in Yahweh's will and gift. Social arrangements are legitimated in theological terms.

In wisdom instruction, the concern and prohibition is the same:

> Remove not the ancient landmark
>   which your fathers have set.
> Do you see a man skillful in his work?
>   He will stand before kings;
>   he will not stand before obscure men.
>   (Prov. 22:28–29)

> Do not remove an ancient landmark
>   nor enter the fields of the fatherless;
> for their Redeemer is strong;
>   he will plead their cause against you.
>   (Prov. 23:10–11)

In the first of these two sayings, it is not clear that v. 29 is to be read with v. 28, but they are placed together in the text. Read that way, the connection between the verses is interesting, because v. 29 observes that technical skills are always in the service of the powerful.[14] Applied to v. 28 and with reference to boundary stones, this suggests that moving boundary stones is not recognized as theft or as random social practice anyone may undertake. Rather it is a sharp legal or economic act by which the shrewd can deprive the simple of their patrimony. The practice involves social know-how, which is a monopoly of the wise, who are characteristically on the side of the haves.[15] Their work is systemic and legal, even though socially destructive. Common people (v. 9, "obscure" people) are helpless in the face of such concentrated, determined technical knowledge.[16]

In Prov. 23:10–11, the third prohibition, the problem of social equality is more obvious; the text warns against taking land from orphans, that is, from socially marginal people who have neither the connections, means, nor know-how to protect their own interests. Indeed, this is why the prophets regularly inveigh against the leaders who "pervert justice" (Amos 5:7; 6:12; Isa. 5:7). When the socially powerful pervert justice through legal channels, the have-nots who are socially disadvantaged have no recourse. Proverbs 23:11 is somewhat enigmatic, but the "powerful guardian" (NEB), or avenger, may indeed be a reference to God who will not tolerate such violation of land rights, especially if done to the marginal and even if done in socially and legally approved ways. It is striking that on as mundane a matter as land boundaries in the literature of Proverbs, such a role is assigned to God.[17]

The most dramatic example of such usurpation is the self-indictment placed in the mouth of the arrogant Assyrian, Sennacherib:

> By the strength of my hand I have done it,
> and by my wisdom, for I have understanding;
> I have removed the boundaries of peoples,
> and have plundered their treasures.
> (Isa. 10:13; cf. Deut. 32:8)

Sennacherib is condemned for the international violation of fixed property boundaries. It is probable that the prohibitions in Deuteronomy and Proverbs concern local transactions, but the problematic is the same. Now, in the face of the "great power," whole nations are cast in the role of the marginal. Seizure of another's land is an act of exploitative greed and violates God's intent for social order, whether done locally or internationally. The prohibitions intend to protect the weak against the strong. The development of large land holdings by the rich and powerful is condemned as a betrayal of Israel's most elemental social dream.

These three prohibitions against moving boundaries contain three interesting notes. Deuteronomy 19:14 mentions patrimony (naḥalâ, NEB), which bespeaks a certain theory of land and property. Proverbs 22:28–29 offers a contrast between the king and common people, indicating that these innocent-sounding prohibitions are quite discerning statements of social criticism. And Prov. 23:10–11 refers specifically to orphans. Together, the three articulate a theory of land division that assumes inheritance and the right to hold land simply because one is entitled as a member of the community (as in the case of an orphan without social power). This view of the land is explicitly contrasted with "royal service" (Prov. 22:28), that is, service in the interest of another theory of land which ignores such entitlements and believes that if power is concentrated and formidable enough to simply claim legitimacy, moving land markers is only a legal transaction to secure land for the strong against the weak. This theory operates in the narrative of Naboth's vineyard; Jezebel is unhindered by Israel's egalitarian dream.

The three prohibitions are stated in absolute terms. F. C. Fensham has studied curse provisions related to moving land markers in other cultures. The recurrence of this concern suggests that the matter is foundational for society. The fact that they are stated as curses indicates that these societies attached to the prohibition the harshest, weightiest religious sanctions available. Society cannot survive when some seize land to which others are entitled simply by being a part of the community, even if the seizure is legally sanctioned.

Enclosure

This biblical prohibition on moving land markers can be related to the modern practice of enclosure, which is the legal capacity of powerful parties to claim exclusive right to land to the exclusion of others so that the land can then be legally enclosed. Kari Polanyi has studied the dramatic emergence of economic theory related to theories of land.[18] Until the eighteenth century, the economy was not held to be autonomous in its operations but was an aspect of social policy. Economic transactions were regarded as a part of a larger social network in which all parts were related to each other and must in some sense take each other into account. But the emergence of the autonomous market meant that each party in society was free to do any economic act with respect to neighbors. "Enclosure" is a formidable act that imagines the land and one's possession of it to be unattached to and unconcerned with other social relations. The right of enclosure meant that some could legally keep others, typically the weak and the poor, off the land. The policy of enclosure was a radical social change that divorced land policy from social interconnectedness and had the effect of further denigrating some to the benefit of others.[19]

Richard Rubenstein judges the policy of land enclosure to be in effect an example of triage, the intentional elimination of those who are judged to be superfluous, marginal, and not of sufficient value to sustain.[20] Rubenstein then traces the practice of triage into the modern world to more dramatic and obvious matters of social policy and practice, but it is crucial to his argument that land enclosure, which excludes some from the land, is in effect triage. Rubenstein's passionate conclusion agrees with my judgment that the Bible in its central social vision opposes policies of land enclosure precisely because they have implicit in them the seeds of triage.

The linkage between enclosure, which denies land to some, and triage is based on the conviction that one cannot live without land or, in an urban society, the social, economic equivalent of land. It behooves us to recognize that free-market theory that seeks to separate economic transactions from social relations is destructive of the poor, who, the equivalent of women and land, are used and thrown away. The church must make the case out of its text that such land practice and economic theory—which blatantly serve certain vested interests—are not value-free "laws" but are the practice of visibly destructive values. Land markers cannot be moved because they enact and assert social relations that include inalienable, guaranteed rights of the weak in the face of the strong, of the poor in the face of the economically powerful.

In Prov. 22:22–23 the inalienable right of the poor to have land is presented by a warning that is pertinent to our argument:

> Do not rob the poor, because he is poor,
>   or crush the afflicted at the gate,
> for the Lord will plead their cause
>   and despoil of life those who despoil them.

It is clear that "robbery" here is not breaking and entering but is a legal transaction "at the gate."[21] The response of Yahweh to such victimization is that Yahweh will "go to court" on behalf of the poor. This same warning is evident in Prov. 23:11:

> for their Redeemer is strong,
> he will plead their cause.

Yahweh is allied with the poor and will engage in legal defense. It remains in our interpretation to see what this means for contemporary social practice, but the Israelite commitment against rapacious confiscation seems clear enough. Israel well understood the costs of such policy and practice.

COVETING: THE STRONG AGAINST THE WEAK

The second biblical motif central to my theme is the familiar tenth commandment, "You shall not covet" (Exod. 20:17; Deut. 5:21).[22] That commandment has been largely trivialized into a psychological matter of jealousy and envy. Marvin Chaney, however, most persuasively argues that the commandment does not refer to such matters which may vex the "introspective conscience of the West" but is to be understood in terms of public policy and social practice.[23] Chaney concludes that the commandment especially concerns land policy: "Do not covet your neighbor's field." In terms of my governing parallel between land and women, it is worth noting that the second most important matter is "You shall not covet your neighbor's wife." It is wife and land that are crucial to the ordering of the community. Moreover, it is plausible to suggest that this tenth commandment corresponds in a special way to the first commandment, "You shall have no other gods." Yahweh, unlike other gods in the Near East, is holy, and therefore beyond location, and acts in freedom.[24] The counterpart to that radical character of God who may not be reduced in idolatrous ways is the dignity and worth of the neighbor. The respect for neighbor comes to its climactic expression in the maintenance of and respect for land and house. Insofar as the tenth commandment is related to the first, we have a structure not unlike Ezek. 18:6–9, which moves from idolatry into matters of sexuality and economics.

Chaney concludes that this prohibition on coveting concerns land management and land ownership. The rapacious land policies of the monarchy (e.g., 1 Kings 21) permitted and legitimated confiscation of a most greedy and destructive kind.[25] The Israelite vision of social organization articulated by this commandment is to prevent such confiscation which takes from the defenseless poor who have no economic or legal means to protect themselves against the economically powerful.

Perhaps the two most important exegetical comments on this commandment are in prophetic oracles from Micah and Isaiah. These two prophets most consistently critique the royal apparatus in Jerusalem which is to be understood, among other things, as an embodiment of land surplus if not monopoly.[26]

Micah 2:1–5

Micah 2:1–5 begins as a sapiential statement simply observing the predictable consequences of land seizure. But in vv. 3–5 the poetry takes a more severe prophetic tone with a double "therefore," laying out the consequences of such land seizure. Verses 1–2 concern scheming and calculation, that is, sharp, exploitative business dealing. The "woe" (v. 1) asserts that those who grab land from others will surely come to death.[27] That in itself is a remarkable statement. Then the "therefore" statements of threat correspond to the violations.[28] Those who devised evil now have Yahweh devise evil against them. Now there is a reaping of what has been sown.

Finally, according to Israelite faith, Yahweh must be reckoned with and answered to for the way land is managed. There is no escape from this accountability. Those who have land that is not rightly theirs, even if legally secured, will come to destruction. Others will come and divide their fields. In context, the poetry presumably refers to the Assyrians. The Bible insists that undisciplined and unneighborly land practice finally leads to a reckoning. The extreme cases among us include the Somozan land in Nicaragua which, sooner or later, will be divided, the aggressive acquisitiveness of the Marcos regime in the Philippines which has come to a sorry end, and the greedy regimes of Eastern Europe which could not nullify or resist dreams of human well-being.[29] But we would do well to think through the social dynamics closer to home. The Bible articulates a remarkable theory of how the historical process works because it is governed by Yahweh. In our postmodern culture, we must see if these same realities must still be heeded.

The result, as noted in v. 5, says simply,

> Therefore you will have none to cast the line by lot in the assembly of Yahweh.

Albrecht Alt has argued that this poetic statement anticipates a time when the adherents of Yahweh, the ones blessed by Yahweh (perhaps the meek), will meet in public assembly to redistribute the land.[30] That assembly, in the name of the liberating, covenanting God, will be a meeting of peasants entitled to their patrimony.[31] The land grabbers will not be present when the boundary lines are redrawn. Indeed, they will not be admitted to the meeting and so will end up landless. This may sound like an extreme social vision, but it is the vision that is being acted out in revolutionary ways in many parts of our world. It is a vision of a complete inversion, in which coveting as social policy comes to its sorry end. In a quite concrete way, the first will become last and the last will finally be first. That terse formula is, among other things, a theory of land distribution (cf. Mark 10:31, in context).

Isaiah 5:8–10

Isaiah 5:8–10 closely parallels the Micah passage. This text also begins with "woe":[32]

> Woe to those who join house to house,
>   who add field to field,
> until there is no more room,
>   and you are made to dwell alone
>   in the midst of the land.

The assault is against buying up large tracts of land, thereby displacing peasants who have lived on the land. Verse 9 departs from the "woe" form (as did Micah 2:3–4) in order to announce Yahweh's immediate engagement on the side of the dispossessed. This great concentration of wealth will come to a sorry end because it cannot be sustained against the intent of Yahweh who opposes monopoly and is inclined toward egalitarianism. Thus the large houses will be abandoned.

Finally, in v. 10, is a consequence that is of interest for our juxtaposition of justice and fertility: ten acres will yield only a little. Land that is handled unjustly will finally not be productive ("bath" and "ephah" are measures of grain.) Because the Bible does not speak in terms of secondary causation, it does not comment on or explain the reasoning which leads to this conclusion. We are not told why or in what way injustice works against productivity. It is sufficient to know that where there is injustice there will, sooner or later, be infertility. The connection between justice and fertility is invisible and never well explicated. But it must be noted that for ancient Israel, just social relations are foundational and prerequisite for productive land.

Hosea 4:1–3

This last point is dramatically stated in Hosea 4:1–3. Every part of this brief poetic unit concerns land. It begins with a summons to court concerning the inhabitants of the land (v. 1a); then it indicts the community for violating torah, because there is no knowledge of God in the land (vv. 1b–2). It concludes with an announcement that the land will suffer drought until the responsible structures and systems of life are destroyed. It is astonishing that the poet dares to say that failure to keep torah leads to life-destroying drought. Failure to practice justice makes fertility impossible.

2 Samuel 12:1–4

In the well-known narrative of 2 Samuel 11, David covets Bathsheba, wife of Uriah, and takes possession of her. He covets and seizes, regarding this woman as something to use and abuse. The connection to my theme here is in the prophetic parable of Nathan in 2 Sam. 12:1–4, which gives a close reading of David's "conquest." It is about a rich man and a poor man. The parable is pliable and can, as Nathan intends, be linked to sexual conquest. But it can as easily refer to land and those who have little and those who have much. The operational verb is "take" (*laqaḥ*) (cf. 2 Sam. 11:4, and Nathan's indictment in 12:9). In 1 Kings 21:19, the verbs are different (*raṣaḥ, yarash*), but the questions concerning land are the same. Thus the parable mediates between land and sexuality, between field (Naboth) and wife (David). Both forms of coveting will finally destroy.[33]

DEFILEMENT AND RITUAL CONTAMINATION

The theme of the *defilement of land* is more radical and more difficult to handle. The difficulty lies in the fact that ritual defilement is a notion quite alien to us. Now we are in the sphere of shame and contamination that is much more elemental than guilt and morality.[34] Such defilement renders its object impure, unavailable for religious use. The holy God of Israel will not and cannot stay in a place that is defiled.

The text which is my point of reference is Deut. 24:1–4. The law there concerns marital relations; the situation is one in which a man divorces a wife. She goes to a second husband, but that marriage also ends. Then she wants to return to the first husband and resume that relation. The point of the legal prohibition is that the first husband, even if he wants to, may not take the woman back again. (Note in v. 4, again we have the word "take," *laqaḥ*). Such a return is prohibited because she is "defiled" (*timē'*). That is, she was intended for this singular "use" of the first husband. Having been put to other use (by the second husband) she is no longer suitable for the first, proper relation. This prohibition may strike us as primitive and severely sexist, for matters are clearly not symmetrical for the man and the woman in this ancient rendition. On its own terms, however, the "misuse" of the woman by the wrong sexual partner constitutes a serious defilement. The prohibition refers to improper use that renders proper use impossible. Improper use is being engaged for something other than intended use. The image will need to be taken in its sexist, asymmetrical casting in order to grasp the intent of its theological, metaphorical use.

The Deuteronomic theological commentary on this prohibition in v. 4b makes an important move in interpretation:

for that is an abomination before the Lord, and you shall not
bring guilt upon the land which the Lord your God gives you for
an inheritance.

First the commentary labels the second relationship an abomination, which means a distortion that endangers the entire community.[35] We may say such marital maneuvering may threaten social
solidarity and order, but the usage attributes an almost material
notion of abomination, as though a substance of destruction is
thereby introduced into the community.

The other theological comment interests us most directly: such
an act will bring guilt on the land of inheritance. The distorted
marital relation causes distortion of the land. Moreover, the land is
nahalah, that is, land which is a trust made according to the promise of Yahweh. Distorted marriage relation leads to distorted land.
The ritual language of contamination makes the land less than productive—under curse, a place where God will not grant fertility.

It is a matter of great interest that this text is utilized by Jeremiah in 3:1–5.[36] Jeremiah lives at a moment when Judah is to be
exiled and lose its land. He is preoccupied with the matter of land
and land loss, and presents an argument about how land is lost,
using the law of Deut. 24:1–4 as a metaphor.[37] In this usage, Yahweh is the first husband who has been violated by the wife, Judah.
Judah has been rejected by Yahweh in infidelity, and so she goes to
a second husband, presumably of Assyrian alliance and Canaanite
religion. But those connections do not work, and Judah wishes to
return to Yahweh to reestablish the covenant relation with God. The
torah precludes that resumption of relation, however, even if Yahweh
had chosen or wished to do so.

Two points interest us here. First, Yahweh is willing to violate the
torah prohibition for the sake of the relation. Against the torah,
Yahweh yearns for a restoration. Against the torah, Yahweh urges
Israel to repent and come home (Jer. 3:12, 14; 4:1–2). Notice that in
Jer. 4:3–4 agricultural images are used as the criteria of return, as in
Hosea 10:12.

Second, Jeremiah uses the language of defilement, as in the old
teaching of Deuteronomy:

Would not that land be greatly polluted? (Jer. 3:1; cf. 2:7, 23)

You have polluted the land with your vile harlotry. (Jer. 3:2)

The language of defilement is used to portray distorted covenant. That language concerns the relation with Yahweh. But at the same time, it is used to characterize the situation of the land and its social organization. The land has now been treated so that it is not productive. And this in turn is because Yahweh refuses to stay in such a place or to grant blessings of fertility in such a context.

The language of ritual contamination is an important one for speaking about modern land abuse.[38] I suggest four dimensions of the problem in terms of a holy God and holy ground:

1. The language of defilement and contamination seems to be operative in much of the current conversation about sexuality, particularly homosexuality. This has escalated with the panic about AIDS. The fear of and the enormous passion against homosexuality appear to be caused by a sense of uncleanness that endangers the entire community and "pollutes the land." The reaction indicates that something more profound and elemental than guilt or moral outrage is at work. The response is of the depth to show that this social phenomenon is perceived as endangering the entire community.

2. There is no doubt that chemicals in the land (particularly pesticides and fertilizer) contaminate the land, threaten the water table, and eventually will endanger the productivity of the soil.

3. It is striking that we refer to nuclear fallout as "pollution" and contamination, and that we speak of "dirty bombs" which so defile the earth as to make life impossible except in its lowest forms.

4. Taken together, the technology of contamination may create a moral situation in which the possibility of life is jeopardized. That in fact is what concerns the priestly tradition in the Old Testament.[39] An ethic of "use, abuse, discard" is evident in every area of life. In terms of land and sexuality, matters of wrong use (injustice) threaten fertility and productivity. In our secular mode, we would not speak of it as such, but such a practice eventually will make the earth a place where God cannot and will not abide. At the least, we might say that the "power for life" may be withdrawn. And where that happens, productivity ends. It is clear that a land ethic of use, abuse, and discarding practices pollution and fickleness. It creates a fundamental cleavage between a Creator who wills life and a creation that squanders and finally rejects life.

These three themes together, (1) moving boundaries, which we translate into the practice of enclosure; (2) coveting, which we understand as rapacious land policy; and (3) defilement, which we understand as pollution of the ecosystem of life, are ways in which the Bible speaks about land management. They concern, respectively, geographic, economic, and ritual dimensions of life. Together they articulate policies that end in death. Death is caused where boundary markers abuse the poor so God's vengeance is evoked. Death is caused where coveting becomes policy and the poor are displaced and despoiled. Death is caused where defilement is practiced and the power for life is withdrawn as a result. The conversation in ancient Israel—which we must continue—is whether the way we relate to the land is a way of death. The staggering discernment is that when death comes as a result of these practices, it comes not only to the weak and poor, who are victims of such policies and values, but eventually it reaches even the powerful and affluent, who are not immune to death when it comes to the community (cf., e.g., Exod. 11:4–6).

LIFE-GIVING LAND MANAGEMENT

Finally, the Bible affirms that land can be managed in ways that give life. It need not be handled toward death. Finally, the Bible is not a warning or a threat but an invitation to another way. It is, however, an invitation that requires a break with the death systems that encompass us. Three themes may be paired with those discussed so far in this chapter. Actually, each functions as a corrective.

Inalienable Patrimony

Against moving boundaries and enclosure systems, the Bible celebrates the old land theory of inalienable patrimony. In Jer. 32:1–15, which is commonly regarded as having a historical basis, the prophet is summoned directly by God to purchase the land. The occasion of the summons is the Babylonian invasion and the collapse of the economic system. But the summons from Yahweh is based on the conviction that the old inheritance rights finally will prevail. Even the great empire is not free to move boundaries and claim land against those old tribal claims. The language of the mandate is careful: exercise the "right of redemption by purchase" (*mišpaṭ hagge'ûlāh leqnôth*, v. 7) and the "right of possession and redemption" (*mišpaṭ hayerûššah, . . . hagge'ûllah qenah*, v. 8). The transaction is done in precise legal terms, and great care is taken to secure clear title. Even the mandate from Yahweh is expressed in those terms.[40] The theological climax of the narrative is the oracle in v. 15:

> Houses and fields and vineyards shall again be bought [*qnh*] in this land.

The economy will be reestablished after the current debacle, and the old rights will prevail. (The argument parallels that in Micah 2:5. In both cases, the old tribal basis of land will endure after the current imperial rapaciousness.) Those who violate those old rights in the interest of land speculation and land seizure will not prevail. The text seems to assume an economic retribalization against the more recent concentration of wealth in the hands of a few, either foreign or Israel's own elite.

Land Redistribution

Against coveting, or rapacious land policy, Israel celebrates land redistribution, which breaks up monopolies and gives land back to those who properly should have it. In Joshua 13—19, care is taken that tribal groups receive their proper entitlements. Joshua 7—8 knowingly observes that this practice of patrimonial land is threatened by Aachan's sin, which holds goods apart from the community. But the narrative of Aachan's sin is only a candid footnote to the main textual tradition of land division. According to the stylized claims of the tradition, the land is held by Israel in alternative ways.[41]

This tradition from the Joshua text was obliterated by royal patterns that violated such covenantal guarantees. The Davidic house ignored and destroyed old tribal land arrangements. Micah 2:1–5 anticipated a new land division. Now Ezekiel 47—48 speaks after the long generations of the monarchal system, after the failure of that system in 587 B.C.E., and after the exile without land. In the later anticipation of Ezek. 47:13—48:29, the land memory of Joshua 13—19 becomes a prototype for the land apportionment to come. The report of this anticipation in Ezekiel is obviously much too stylized and artificial to be regarded in terms of actual policy or action, but the text does show that Israel believes present land arrangements will not be secure in the future. In the coming time, the land will be reapportioned according to the old, enduring promises, which speak authoritatively against current practice.

The land will indeed be redistributed. This relates to the practice of the Jubilee year, which consists of returning land to its rightful owner (Leviticus 25). The land is not managed according to conventional economic transactions. There may be such transactions, but they occur in the contexts of promise and inheritance, which finally override such transactions. It is also worth noting that that powerful tradition of land redistribution can be understood as the center of Luke's presentation of Jesus.[42] Jesus was a threat to vested interests in his time because he proposed to give land and dignity back to those who had lost it.

I judge such matters to be important among us, because today's revolutions against colonial power are, in fact, efforts to redistribute land according to tribal conventions that have been gravely distorted in the interest of concentrated surplus. It will not do to dismiss as "terrorists" or "communists" those who insist on implementing the old promissory land management in the face of present settlements based on seizure.

Fertility Restored

Against defilement and abomination, the Bible anticipates a time when the land is free of such contamination so that production can be full and the blessings of life abundantly available. Two prophetic texts may be cited, Hosea 2:21–23 and Isa. 6:5. Hosea 2:21–23 is an answer to Hosea 5:3 and 6:10, in which Israel's covenantal violations have polluted the land:

> For now, O Ephraim, you have played the harlot.
> Israel is defiled. (5:3)

> In the house of Israel I have seen a horrible thing;
> Ephraim's harlotry is there, Israel is defiled. (6:10)

In each case, land defilement is expressed in the metaphors of fickleness and harlotry.

In the great poem of Hosea 2:21–23, the land will function again, after it has ceased to function.[43] In a lyrical portrayal of new creation, the poet says:

> In that day, says the Lord,
> I will answer the heavens,
> and they shall answer the earth;
> and the earth shall answer the grain, the wine, and the oil,
> and they shall answer Jezreel,
> and I will sow him for myself in the land.
>
> (Hos. 2:21–23a)

The restored land will be a conversation of productivity in which all parts will gladly respond to each other and the land will bear an abundance of grain, wine, and oil. But that will happen only where the defilements and harlotries are overcome by a season of exile-landlessness. After exile this faithful God will say,

> And I will have pity on Not pitied,
> and I will say to Not my people, "You are my people";
> and he shall say, "Thou art my God."
>
> (v. 23)

Isaiah 62:4–5 is an answer to Isa. 6:5, in which the prophet says, "I am defiled and I live among defiled people." The book of Isaiah asserts that judgment comes against such massive defilement. But then in Isa. 62:4–5, after the judgment, exile, and loss of land, the lyrics again assert the coming fullness of productivity:

> You shall no more be termed Forsaken,
> and your land shall no more be termed Desolate;
> but you shall be called My delight is in her,
> and your land Married;
> For the Lord delights in you,
> and your land shall be married.
> For as a young man marries a virgin,
> so shall your sons marry you,
> and as the bridegroom rejoices over the bride,
> so shall your God rejoice over you.

It is amazing that in v. 4, land is referred to three times:
> Your land shall no more be termed desolate,
> Your land married,
> Your land married.

The term "married" is *be'ûlah*, which is derived from *Ba'al* and means fructified, or made productive. The statements about land are surrounded in vv. 4a and 5 with marriage images: you will no more be termed divorced, abandoned; in v. 5 the metaphor twice concerns human marriage and then offers the joy of a wedding.

In each of these cases the power of death is overcome. The laws of patrimony prevail against moving boundaries (Jer. 32:1–15). Land redistribution overcomes coveting and its resulting inequality (Ezek. 47:13—48:29). Productivity recurs in a land marked by defilement (Hos. 2:21–23). The land will again be home. This does not happen by divine fiat, but only by historical activity that is risky and costly.

I suggest that this analysis provides a grid of three pairs of themes:

enclosure	inalienable patrimony (Jer. 32:1–15)
coveting	redistribution (Ezek. 47:13—48:29)
defilement	fertility restored (Hos. 2:21–23; Isa. 62:4–5)

These are ways of life and death.

What we must recognize is that enclosure, coveting, and contamination have become acceptable policy among us. Now we are at a crisis point. The text reintroduces to us the nonnegotiable conditions of life in the land. We hold a view of land that we know has pertinence to public conversation. We are at a place in our society when we must re-ask foundational questions about use, abuse, and discarding. The alternative mediated in these texts is to "tend and care," to caress and cherish (Gen. 2:15). But such work requires a break with an ethic of monopoly and surplus value. It is a costly repentance. So the prophet Jeremiah can say:

> If you return, O Israel, says the Lord,
>   to me you should return.
> If you remove your abominations from my presence,
>   and do not waver,
> and if you swear, "As the Lord lives,"
>   in truth, in justice, and in uprightness,
> then nations shall bless themselves in him,
>   and in him shall they glory.

For thus says the Lord to the men of Judah and to the inhabitants of Jerusalem:

Break up your fallow ground,
   and sow not among the thorns.
Circumcise yourselves to the Lord,
   remove the foreskin of your hearts,
   O men of Judah and inhabitants of Jerusalem;
lest my wrath go forth like fire,
   and burn with none to quench it,
   because of the evil of your doings.
(Jer. 4:1–4)

There is in this poem a massive condition of "if-then," and it is presented as an agricultural metaphor. The poet invites Judah to a repentant life in the land in order to avoid the fire. The human, covenantal issues do not admit of technical solution. Land management must be restored to its place in the fabric of social relations. Productivity requires attention to justice. Fertility causes us to rethink economics. Sexuality raises questions of righteousness. Without righteousness and justice in land management, there may come a destroyer who will "make your land a waste" (Jer. 4:7).

The destruction need not be so. But it can happen and is, indeed, happening before our very eyes.

NOTES

This essay appeared originally in *Theology of the Land*, ed. Bernard F. Evans and Gregory D. Cusack (Collegeville, Minn.: Liturgical Press, 1987), 41–68, and is reprinted by permission.

1. Phyllis Trible, *God and the Rhetoric of Sexuality* (Philadelphia: Fortress Press, 1978), 78, shrewdly names "adam" as "the earth creature" in order to underscore the relation to earth. Moreover, Trible rightly sees that 'adamah has priority over adam in the creation narrative.

2. The relation of covenant and creation is not without problem in current Old Testament theology. Nonetheless, Karl Barth, *Church Dogmatics* III, 1 (Edinburgh: T. & T. Clark, 1958), has wisely seen that the two themes are integrally related to each other. The juxtaposition of the two are necessary to see that humankind has a covenantal relation with creation.

3. Wendell Berry, *Recollected Essays 1965–80* (San Francisco: North Point Press, 1981), 215.

4. Ibid., 191.

5. Abraham Heschel, *Who Is Man?* (Stanford: Stanford University Press, 1965), has characterized human life when there is a loss of transcendence. Everyone then is a tool to be used, and is reduced to usefulness. Phyllis Trible, *Texts of Terror* (Philadelphia: Fortress Press, 1984), has explicated in a most discerning way biblical texts in which women are subjected to promiscuity and domination.

6. Luke T. Johnson, *Sharing Possessions* (Philadelphia: Fortress Press, 1981), 84–95 and passim, has a remarkable analysis of the interrelation between idolatry, possessiveness, and oppression.

7. Erich Fromm, *Escape from Freedom* (New York: Farrar & Rinehart, 1941); and idem, *The Anatomy of Human Destructiveness* (New York: Holt, Rinehart, & Winston, 1973), has most discerningly reflected on the interrelatedness of the themes of Marx and Freud. For a suggestion on the common rootage of their concern, see John M. Cuddihy, *The Ordeal of Civility* (New York: Basic Books, 1974).

8. Norman K. Gottwald, *The Tribes of Yahweh* (Maryknoll, N.Y.: Orbis Books, 1979), has most sharply articulated the socio-economic foundations and implications of this alternative notion of land. Clearly there is nothing romantic in such a view of land, but it has profound and serious social implications that can only be regarded as subversive.

9. See Robert B. Coote, *Amos among the Prophets* (Philadelphia: Fortress Press, 1981), 24–25.

10. On the intentional "management" of such poverty, see Bernard Lang, "The Social Organization of Peasant Poverty in Biblical Israel," *Journal for the Study of the Old Testament* 24 (1982): 47–63.

11. See my exposition of the theme in *The Land* (Philadelphia: Fortress Press, 1977).

12. On the "core tradition," see Walter Harrelson, "Life, Faith, and the Emergence of Tradition," in *Tradition and Theology in the Old Testament*, ed. Douglas A. Knight (Philadelphia: Fortress Press, 1977), 11–30; and Norman K. Gottwald, *The Hebrew Bible: A Socio-Literary Introduction* (Philadelphia: Fortress Press, 1985), 144.

13. See particularly the NEB translation of this passage. The term here rendered "inheritance" is there rendered "patrimony," a term more telling for a theory of land possession.

14. The text contrasts kings with "hidden" people (*ḥsk*). The RSV renders as "obscure," the NEB as "common." In this context, the contrast suggests people who have no public visibility, no social power, and so no chance for "the pursuit of happiness."

15. On the interplay of technical wisdom and established political interest, see Glendon E. Bryce, *A Legacy of Wisdom* (Lewisburg, Pa.: Bucknell University Press, 1979), chaps. 6–7; and George E. Mendenhall, "The Shady Side of Wisdom: The Date and Purpose of Genesis 3,"

in *A Light unto My Path*, ed. Howard N. Bream, Ralph D. Heim, and Carey A. Moore (Philadelphia: Fortress Press, 1974), 319–34. On the social operation of such power, see D. N. Premnath, "Latifundialization and Isaiah 5:8–10," *Journal for the Study of the Old Testament* 40 (1988): 49–60.

16. F. C. Fensham, "Common Trends in Curses of the Near Eastern Treaties and *Kudurru*-Inscriptions Compared with Maledictions of Amos and Isaiah," *Zeitschrift für die alttestamentliche Wissenschaft* 75 (1963): 155–75, has summarized the data on curses related to the movement of boundaries. The use of curse formulas suggests that such religious sanction is the only force available to those who have no social power.

17. It is instructive that the RSV capitalizes "Redeemer," thus interpreting unambiguously with reference to God. That the text speaks so of God may suggest a connection to Job 19:25 and the appeal there to a redeemer. Both texts, in very different contexts, raise the question of theodicy.

18. Kari Polanyi, *The Great Transformation* (Boston: Beacon Press, 1944), presents the Tudor rulers of England as defenders of the poor against the practice of enclosure, but in the end, enclosure prevailed. He cites a key decision made at Speenhamland, Eng., which was pivotal in repositioning the poor in the network of social relation (p. 78). This particular case indicates that the issue of theodicy is not a general speculative issue but relates to quite concrete questions of social policy and practice.

19. One may regard Deut. 24:19–22 as an Israelite articulation against the practice of enclosure. The land must be left open for those not "in possession."

20. Richard Rubenstein, *The Age of Triage* (Boston: Beacon Press, 1983).

21. On the "gate" as a social institution, see Ludwig Koehler, *Hebrew Man* (Nashville: Abingdon Press, 1957), 127–50. References to "the gate" show that the act against the poor is systematic and institutional.

22. On this commandment, see the fine introduction by Walter Harrelson, *The Ten Commandments and Human Rights* (Philadelphia: Fortress Press, 1980), 148–54.

23. Marvin L. Chaney, "You Shall Not Covet Your Neighbor's House," *Pacific Theological Review* 15 (Winter 1982): 3–13. The formula on "introspective conscience" is from Krister Stendahl, "The Apostle Paul and the Introspective Conscience of the West," *Harvard Theological Review* 56 (1963): 199–215.

24. Cyrus Gordon, "A Note on the Tenth Commandment," *Journal of Bible and Religion* 31 (1963): 208–9, has suggested that the tenth commandment is derived from the character of Yahweh, because Yahweh is

unlike the other gods of Canaan who covet. Such a theological contrast with other gods helps link the commandment to the fundamental claims of Yahwism.

25. On the dimension of monarchy, note that Gottwald, *The Hebrew Bible*, 293, refers to the monarchy as "Israel's counterrevolutionary establishment." Clearly Gottwald intends that "counterrevolutionary" apply to socio-economic matters such as land policy. In parallel fashion, George E. Mendenhall, "The Monarchy," *Interpretation* 29 (1975): 155–70, refers to the monarchy as the "paganization" and "Canaanization" of Israel. This also applies to questions of egalitarianism in economic relations.

26. See Mendenhall, "The Shady Side of Wisdom," on the monopoly of knowledge that supports a monopoly of technology which soon leads to a monopoly of wealth.

27. See Klaus Koch, "Is There a Doctrine of Retribution in the Old Testament?" in *Theodicy in the Old Testament*, ed. James L. Crenshaw (Philadelphia: Fortress Press, 1983), 57–87, on the certitude with which consequences follow deeds. The "woe" form does not assert an active agent in punishment, but only that such outcomes inexorably follow such actions. Thus land grabbing does not depend on the action of God for retribution but yields its own destructive consequences. One cannot grab land, so the poem argues, with impunity.

28. On this correspondence, see Patrick D. Miller, Jr., *Sin and Judgment in the Prophets* (Chico, Calif.: Scholars Press, 1982), 29–31.

29. On the inevitability of this social movement, see Walter LaFeber, *Inevitable Revolutions* (New York: W. W. Norton, 1983).

30. Albrecht Alt, "Micha 2, 1–5 Ges Andasmos in Judah," in *Kleine Schriften zur Geschichte des Volkes Israel* 3 (Munich: C. H. Beck, 1959), 373–81.

31. On the sociology of Micah, see the suggestive statement by Hans Walter Wolff, "Micah the Moreshite—The Prophet and His Background," in *Israelite Wisdom*, ed. John G. Gammie (Missoula, Mont.: Scholars Press, 1978), 77–84.

32. On this passage and the "woe" form, see William Whedbee, *Isaiah and Wisdom* (Nashville: Abingdon Press, 1971), 93–98.

33. Gottwald, *The Hebrew Bible*, 210, offers an exposition of the commandment which relates it to land policy.

34. On the elemental character of shame, which is more foundational than guilt, see Erik Erikson, *Identity and the Life Cycle* (New York: International Universities Press, 1959), 65–82; and Paul Ricoeur, *The Symbolism of Evil* (New York: Harper, 1967).

35. On the meaning of "abomination" in Deuteronomy, see Jean L'Hour, "Les Interdits to'eba dans le Deutéronome," *Revue biblique* 71 (1964): 481–503.

36. For one proposal concerning the relation of these texts, see T. R. Hobbs, "Jeremiah 3:1–5 and Deuteronomy 24:1–4," *Zeitschrift für die alttestamentliche Wissenschaft* 86 (1974): 23–29.

37. On the motif of land in the tradition of Jeremiah, see Walter Brueggemann, "Israel's Sense of Place in Jeremiah," in *Rhetorical Criticism*, ed. Jared J. Jackson and Martin Kessler (Pittsburgh: Pickwick Press, 1974), 149–65; and John Bracke, "The Coherence and Theology of Jeremiah 30—31," Ph.D. diss., Union Theological Seminary, Richmond, Va., 1983), esp. chap. 3.

38. On land and its contamination as a religio-cultural problem, see Mary Douglas, *Purity and Danger* (London: Routledge & Kegan Paul, 1966).

39. See Fernando Belo, *A Materialistic Reading of the Gospel of Mark* (Maryknoll, N.Y.: Orbis Books, 1981), for a consideration of the sociology of purity.

40. On the relation of this passage to the issue of theodicy as a social problem, see Walter Brueggemann, "Theodicy in a Social Dimension," *Journal for the Study of the Old Testament* 33 (1985): 3–25.

41. It is telling that in the book of Joshua, it is Rahab the harlot who is instrumental in the well-being of Israel and the downfall of Jericho. Jericho is clearly a walled city that embodies the "Canaanite" monopoly against which Israel is mobilized. It is therefore to be expected that such a marginal person should be on the side of those who assault the monopoly. A great deal will be discerned in such narratives when we read with sociological sensitivity. Gottwald, *The Hebrew Bible*, 258–59, in speaking of the social location of Rahab says the narrative "never ceases to emphasize how much of the 'outside,' both communally and territorially, is 'inside' Israel."

42. See Sharon Ringe, *Jesus, Liberation, and the Biblical Jubilee* (Philadelphia: Fortress Press, 1985).

43. On the structural reversal in this poem, see David J. A. Cline, "Hosea 2: Structure and Interpretation," *Studia Biblica 1978*, JSOTSup 2 (Sheffield, Eng.: University of Sheffield, 1979), 83–103.

12

The Land and Our Urban Appetites

THE CRISES OF LAND USE and land management crowd in upon us. It now affects many people who have seemed immune to modern social displacement. Christians have to think afresh about the land because we are directly included in the crisis and because our faith requires us to think again when such pain is among us. As we think again, we are required to think again about our baptism, about our confession of the gospel, and about our resolve to be in the world in obedience. Our baptismal rethinking bids us not to think as the world thinks, but to imagine what it is like to be available in risky ways for the power of the gospel (cf. Rom. 12:12).

Israel confessed, "The land belongs to Yahweh" (Ps. 24:1). We usually say, more blandly, "The earth is the Lord's." But we must not settle for a bland translation. We deal with *Yahweh* who is the God of the exodus, the worker of liberation, the one who possesses the whole world and our piece of turf. Moreover, we are not speaking of some undifferentiated "earth," but *land* that is occupied, under cultivation, taxed, and about which we quarrel concerning control and ownership. To say *"belongs to,"* moreover, is not a polite nod to religion. We are speaking of Yahweh's entitlement, economic right, control, and governance. We tend to have a romantic notion of land. We speak in religious phrases that are so large they do not seem to touch any daily reality. The Bible is not so evasive about the issue of land and announces that the very land we envision as our own belongs to the God who has not turned it over to any other management, even ours.

The phrase "The land belongs to Yahweh" is of course a doxology. It means to celebrate and to praise God. But it is also a confession loaded with sociological realism. The land has its rightful owner, the same agent who freed the slaves. At the outset we are required to think of land management as an enduring exodus commitment. Land is to be managed in the interest of freedom and justice.

These words about land in Israel's doxology are polemical. Saying that the land belongs to Yahweh, the God of liberation, asserts that the land does not belong to Baal, the seductive giver of fertility, or to Marduk, the god of the empire, or to Dagon, the Philistine god whose name translates simply as "wheat." Israel is a people summoned by God to live in the world in dispute. The dispute concerning God's people is primarily and consistently about the land.

As Americans we are deeply enmeshed in the dispute over land, for our economy and foreign policy largely concern the cynical management of other peoples' land. As Christians we are endlessly haunted by the dispute. Perhaps in ancient Israel the most important question was, Who owns the land? I dare think it is among our most crucial issues as well. How we think about the issue of land ownership decides much else. We decide to whom it belongs in doxology. In the process we also sing a polemic. We assert to whom the land does not belong. There are no more urgent faith questions among us than who owns the land—and who does not.

Israel's *polemical doxology* is aimed at those who thought they owned the land. Throughout Israel's early history, whenever Israel concerned itself with the land, that land was already owned by someone who was hostile to Israel and its dreams. When Abraham came to his land, there were Canaanites there (Gen. 12:6). In Egypt the official imperial ideology asserted that the land belonged to Pharaoh (Gen. 47:20; cf. Ezek. 29:3). In Joshua's time, the land belonged to the Canaanite city-kings, who proceeded on the assumption that they owned the land. These alleged owners all pose the same theological problem, present the same sociological distortion, are committed to political practices that cheat about the possibility of humaneness and humanness.

The people who claimed ownership of the land and chanted to each other in their liturgies that they owned the land—all lived in the city (Exod. 1:11; Num. 13:19–20, 28; Deut. 1:28; Josh. 12:7–24).

This urban power elite always imagined it owned the land, and acted on that presupposition. The social reality of the city is perennially at the center of the land crisis—in ancient Israel and today in the midst of the farm and environmental crises—because the city is not just a place. It is also a way of perceiving and constructing social reality.[1] I suggest that Israel's polemical doxology, "The land belongs to Yahweh," can only be understood if we understand, first, the city and, second, that the doxology is aimed against urban pretensions. Note well, this is not a general comment about urban life, but a recognition that an urban ethos brings with it social stratification and manufactured needs that distort human relations and the relationship to the land.

ALTERNATIVE SOCIAL COMMUNITY

I begin by considering the significance of the city in the Old Testament, and how it has impinged upon Israel's notion of land. Israel's sense about land and promised land did not begin with the city. But Israel soon had to deal with the crucial and central reality of the city. Norman Gottwald has boldly inverted the conventional social typology we use with the Bible, arguing that the Bible begins not with nomadic tribes but with a massive and ambitious state, the Egyptian empire.[2] For our purpose, the construction of the empire is presented in the polemical statement of Genesis 47, which asserts that "Joseph bought all the land of Egypt for Pharaoh" (v. 20), that is, the state and its economic dominance gained a monopoly.[3] The biblical account, constructed and narrated to evoke resentment in Israel,[4] tells of helpless peasants (among them Jacob's family) who give their money (v. 14), their cattle (vv. 16–17), their land, and finally their bodies (v. 19) to Pharaoh in order to get food in the midst of famine. Pharaoh has a monopoly on food because he owns the means of production. Pharaoh understands, as government officials do today, that food is a weapon, and Pharaoh is prepared to use that economic weapon to maintain and expand the imperial monopoly of land and wealth.[5]

That imperial monopoly dominates the beginnings of Israel's memory. It is characterized, as are all urban monopolies, by control of technology (pyramids, irrigation systems), ideology (imperial religion which made Pharaoh god),[6] a division of labor, a power elite, a leisure class, surplus goods, and a supply of cheap labor that made the economic process work effectively. That cheap labor may be variously described. The workers may be called "slaves," as the exodus narrative does. They became slaves not by whips and brutality, however, but by the slow erosion of their economic independence through tax and land policies that enforced the monopoly which claimed all the land. Slavery, "the house of bondage," is an achievement of the imperial economy (Exod. 20:1). Prior to the circumstances of slavery, "peasants" lived close to the land and directly from the land without excessive economic entanglements.

The situation of the peasant, however, is in crisis when the urban power establishment no longer operates with respectful give-and-take, but proceeds with the policies of usurpation, confiscation, and taxation, and begins to seize surplus produce in order to sustain the bureaucracy—priests, scribes, and wisdom teachers—that exists to justify the monopoly. As his surplus is seized by the power elite, the peasant's existence becomes more and more marginal until he is completely indebted to and dependent upon the state. These increasingly marginal people do not participate in the growing urban wealth but are the indispensable economic support for it. The monopoly in the city thrives on the productivity of peasants.

These marginal people are referred to as *ḥabirû* throughout the ancient Near East,[7] the dispossessed people who lead desperate lives always at the edge of the economy.

According to Gottwald, social pain, resentment, and indignation led some of the peasants to gather the courage and energy to disengage from the urban monopoly. Gottwald's sociological analysis of this disengagement does not make clear Yahweh's role. Gottwald is inclined to present Yahweh as a "function" of the social movement of unrest, though he does not deny that the revaluation is also a "function" of Yahwism.[8]

As the Bible tells it, however, it is the powerful invitation, decree, and authorization of Yahweh that initiated the peasant disengagement from the imperial monopoly. The long plague narrative in Exodus 6—11 is the wondrous, painful drama of negotiation and political consolidation. In the end, the company of peasants withdraws allegiance from the urban monopoly and explores an alternative way of common life.[9] Clearly Yahweh's overriding power and relentless fidelity to Israel are decisive in Israel's presentation of the departure. The empire cannot withstand the power of Yahweh, the God of liberation.

The crucial sociological notion here is "withdrawal," departing from the empire.[10] The peasants in the end withdraw from the empire. That "withdrawal" is finally geographical for, according to the story, the peasants leave Egypt. But before they can leave physically, they must emotionally, symbolically, psychologically, and intellectually break with Pharaoh's monopoly and decide they will no longer consent to the monopoly of imagination, honor the monopoly of ideology, depend on the monopoly of technology, or live by the monopoly of values.

This psychological, intellectual, and ethical disengagement is rooted in and sustained by a liturgically constructed alternative which eventually becomes the Passover liturgy. This liturgy, the story of Yahweh and Yahweh's alternative world, invites the peasants to imagine another organization of social reality apart from the monopoly. It is the liturgic alternative that is told the children "when they ask the time to come."[11] Gottwald's analysis is sociological, so he does not linger over the liturgical practice, but he does speak of the "cultic substructure."[12]

Israel departed because its social circumstance was unbearably saturated with pain and despair. But it also acted, and could only act, because of the power, presence, and permission of Yahweh who summoned them out.

When they finally acted in such faith and courage, the departed peasants-become-slaves had much work to do. They had to envision and erect a workable alternative to the social relations of the empire. Israel had to construct a social arrangement not beset by creditors and debtors, elites and slaves. It had to fashion a daring new social possibility. The new social possibility is this bold alternative community we call Israel, an egalitarian community committed to well-being with neighbors, a healing justice in social transactions.

A COVENANTAL ALTERNATIVE

The emergence of Israel in the ancient world thus entails both a decisive break with the empire and a long-term construction of a social alternative. The decisive break is a moment of religious-political emancipation and transformation which we may variously call conversion, repentance, salvation, changing loyalties, and the embrace of new gods (cf. Judg. 5:8).

Having made that decisive break, Israel had done the dangerous work but now faced the tedious work. We are told quite candidly that the Israelites waffled and quarrelled. Some wanted to go back to the satiation of bondage (Exod. 16:3; Num. 14:3). The main story of Israel's faith, however, carries Israel to Sinai. Martin Buber has seen that at Sinai, Israel committed a bold political act in which it pledged itself in binding, bonding ways to Yahweh, thereby rejecting the overlordship of Pharaoh and, by implication, the claims of every urban monopoly which used powerless, marginal people but did not value them.[13]

At Sinai, Israel swore allegiance to a new covenanting God, Yahweh. In swearing that allegiance, Israel also embraced a new notion of land management. As Israel understood its life to be now bonded to Yahweh, it also understood its land to be now governed by Yahweh, who rejected the exploitative way of the urban monopoly. Indeed Moses understood that this new God brings along new land practices. Israel asserted that its land would no longer be in the service of the urban monopoly, but would be used, ordered, and managed in obedience of this new covenant Lord. In speaking this way, Israel no doubt spoke of its marginal land held by individual peasants, but also dreamed about the whole land being reordered according to a new covenanted loyalty.[14]

In the context of this covenanted decision at Sinai Israel is able to say, "The land belongs to Yahweh." It does not belong to Pharaoh or any other part of the urban monopoly. The two themes of new God and new land management are brought together in the mouth of Yahweh in Leviticus 25, which concerns a new vision of the land:

> The land shall not be sold in perpetuity, for the land belongs to me; for you are strangers and sojourners with me. (v. 23)

> For they are my servants, whom I brought forth out of the land of Egypt; they shall not be sold as slaves. (v. 42)

Leviticus 25:23 asserts that the *land belongs to Yahweh*, the real ruler, and therefore can no longer be treated as though it is ultimately possessed by and appropriated for the empire. Verse 42 claims that *Israel belongs to Yahweh* and must no longer participate in the fears and hopes of Pharaoh. Together these two verses assert that neither Israel's land nor Israel's persons must again submit to or participate in the urban monopoly of Pharaoh, for that elitist monopoly will abuse both land and people, and will finally enslave.

There is thus a convergence between radically new faith and radically critical sociology. While in our society these two factors are not usually related, in Israel everything depended on discerning this convergence. The radical covenantal decree of Yahweh remains irrelevant religion without sociological awareness. Radical sociology without this radical religious passion is merely painful insight without courage, passion, or energy. The Moses-Joshua narratives are about both a belief-ful embrace of *a new God* outside the imperial pantheon and a daring practice of *a new sociology* outside the oppressive monopoly.

It is on the basis of that convergence of faith and sociological awareness that Israel set about the hard work of constructing a new social alternative committed to justice and righteousness. This is the work of Sinai. Israel's model for the new mode of life in the land with Yahweh is covenantal,[15] which means respectful reciprocity and mutuality. On the basis of its decision about Yahweh and covenant, Israel understood that the land is to be shared, because it belongs to Yahweh, not to Pharaoh, and finally to no one of us. Israel's great proposal to and dream for the world is that land management be done covenantally, with attentiveness to the needs and hopes of the entire community, including those devalued, marginalized, and rendered hopeless by the empire.

The concrete implementation of this enterprise is one of the primary themes of the torah. Torah includes thinking through and believing through how to manage land covenantally. In chapter 7 I discussed the decalogue and its foundational principles for a covenantal community.[16] It is telling that Israel's ten basic commandments begin in a statement about *the character of Yahweh* and end in *a statement about land*. Israel's foundational ethic runs from Yahweh to land, from obedience to Yahweh to egalitarianism in the land. Israel knows the negative alternative: idolatry (which violates the first commandment) to coveting (which violates the tenth commandment) (cf. Col. 3:5). The connections between the first and tenth commandments articulate the decisive connection Moses wants to make between the rule of Yahweh and the well-being of community.[17] Coveting land is a mode of idolatry.

The book of Deuteronomy is a remarkable set of statements about ordering the land in alternative, covenantal ways. Whether or not Deuteronomy is the first statement of covenant faith in Israel,[18] it is certainly the clearest and most important statement. Deuteronomy (the voice of Mosaic covenantalism) proposes that the land can indeed be ordered in covenantal ways, and need not be ordered in Canaanite ways.[19] Such a political and economic alternative requires a clear break with the Canaanite system, however, and with its ways of ideological legitimation, that is, Baalism.

Deuteronomy 7 provides a good point from which to consider Deuteronomic values of handling the land covenantally. Verses 1–5 are harsh, authorizing the destruction of all Canaanite symbols—pillars, altars, and images. The verses warn against making covenants with or showing mercy to the adherents of Canaanite monopoly: do not participate in their reading of reality or the covenantal social alternative will be domesticated. Verses 6–11, in contrast, voice no harshness and articulate Israel's status as a special people who are identified by Yahweh's passion and concern. It is possible (and conventional) to read this nation of Israel as Yahweh's "holy people" as an *ethnic* contrast of Canaan and Israel. However, Gottwald suggests that the contrast in both vv. 1–5 and 6–11 is better understood as a contrast between a society of oppressive stratification (called Canaanite) and egalitarianism (embraced as Israelite and Yahwistic). That is, the terms of the text are not at all ethnic, but concern social values, commitments, practices, and systems.

From this basic notion of a covenantal act of social relations, the derivative laws in the teaching of Deuteronomy then suggest an egalitarian social vision with considerable specificity:

- a practice of release of debt slaves (Deut. 15:1–11), canceling the very indebtedness upon which the urban monopoly was based
- a monarchy committed to torah (Deut. 17:14–20) that explicitly prohibits the king from seeking a monopoly or even an accumulation of arms or wealth[20]
- hospitality to runaway slaves (Deut. 23:6–16), which surely would subvert a slave-based economy
- prohibition of interest on loans within the covenant commu-

nity (Deut. 23:19–20), an alternative to the exploitative Canaanite system

- prohibition of kidnapping (Deut. 24:7), a second means of forcing people into bondage
- respect for a poor man concerning a loan (Deut. 24:10–13), which attempts to protect the modest economic claim of the poor
- prompt payment of hired help (Deut. 24:14–15), which prevents withholding of payment for the sake of investment
- justice for widows, orphans, and sojourners (Deut. 24:17–18, 19–22), providing value to those who had lost their value in the production-oriented system of the city-state
- limitation on brutal physical punishment (Deut. 25:1–3), thereby asserting that even the socially guilty are entitled to some respect.

There are no doubt other teachings in Deuteronomy that could be added to this impressive inventory of egalitarian proposals. Conversely, there are no doubt other legal provisions which would contradict this social vision, for the literature is not all of a piece. These citations, however, are enough to show that Deuteronomy is an impressive legal tradition that proposes in concrete ways humane and egalitarian social organization and conduct that are antithetical to the values and norms of the empire.

Moses understood that the vision of an alternative to Pharaoh's land system required more than an initial decision. It required the long, patient, determined development of social patterns and precedents for new kinds of social transactions that are not shaped by the rapacious policies of urban city-kings and do not use people in the service of royal ideology. The teaching of Deuteronomy, like that of the decalogue, worked powerfully against the uncriticized urban monopoly. Note well that this alternative is not a rural romanticism, but a genuinely alternative social strategy that proposes deep and concrete shifts in the allocation of goods, power, and land.

VOICES COUNTERING THE URBAN MONOPOLY

The Bible presents the covenantal alternative and the royal-urban monopoly as being in continual, profound, and unresolvable tension. The exodus narrative indicates that the covenantal alternative requires a decisive and nervy departure from the monopoly. Indeed Israel's emergence in the ancient political world is based precisely on the disclosure of Yahweh as an alternative God and Israel as embracing an alternative social vision in response to Yahweh.[21]

Both the covenantal and royal-urban systems offer complete and comprehensive views of reality. Both derive from and bear witness to the character of a god. The royal-urban system is not antireligious, as it embraces and practices Baalism. Nor is it irreligious. But it is profoundly anticovenantal and anti-Yahwistic. Both systems offer a foundational understanding of human personhood and human community. Both articulate a notion of what is socially permissible and what is socially possible. It is increasingly urgent for Christians to be able to read the Bible to see that our conversation about religion always carries with it a profound proposal for the shape of human power and human possibility.[22]

We do not yet fully understand the reasons, but the covenantal alternative of Moses and Sinai eventually proved problematic and unworkable for ancient Israel. The system of state control was reintroduced, even though the primal memories of Israel (which cluster around Moses) are profoundly resistant to such a system. First Sam. 8:5–20 indicates that the reintroduction of the royal-urban system was in response to a specific political-military threat from the Philistines, against which the covenantal system was deemed inadequate. The biblical tradition also suggests that the emergence of monarchy in Israel was a much disputed and much conflicted issue (1 Sam. 7—15). It is clear that the reformation of the royal-urban state, in profound tension with the covenantal foundations of Israel, was a very complex matter including new technologies, economic monopolies, and religious ideologies.[23] It is thus an oversimplification to credit the complete political renovation of Israel to the Philistine threat.[24]

The state system, especially under Solomon, constituted an important departure from the egalitarian vision of Moses.[25] The Solomonic enterprise featured an economics of incredible affluence and victimization, a politics of exploitation which sustained the economics of surplus, a liturgical conviction of God's absolute commitment to Jerusalem in the mode of imperial temple religion, and, with all of these, a new epistemology that had deep confidence in royal reason and royal legitimacy.[26] What emerged in Israel was a new rationality that lost touch with the old commitments of justice, steadfast love, and righteousness, and instead championed wealth, power, and wisdom (cf. Jer. 9:22–23).[27] It is not surprising that the Solomonic enterprise ended in social revolution (1 Kings 11—12) and a refusal, on the part of people with old tribal memories, any longer to submit to the urban monopoly and its oppressive, exploitative ways (1 Kings 12:4). In a sense, the revolt against the Solomonic rationality was a reenactment of the exodus event, in which peasant people disengaged from the centralized power (cf. 2 Sam. 20:1; 1 Kings 12:16).

The tension between covenantal alternative and royal-urban monopoly characterized the continuing life and faith of ancient Israel. On the one hand, the royal apparatus continued to have its way not only because it controlled technology, but also because it had a monopoly of imagination. That is, it was able to assert that the Jerusalem enterprise of "king and temple" was the will of God. That claim does indeed constitute a monopoly of imagination, for to think outside of those claims was perceived as a dangerous theological act of disobedience.

On the other hand, the prophets continued to sound the possibility of covenantal alternative.[28] They made their appeal not on the basis of personal, righteous indignation but on the insight that the royal-urban system inevitably brutalizes, oppresses, destroys, and leads to death. The prophets in ancient Israel continued to raise the Mosaic alternative of covenantal faith and covenantal relations. It is not possible here to comment in detail on this continued alternative voice, but I mention three characteristic dimensions of that alternative prophetic voice.

Micah and Resilient Peasant Hope

Hans Walter Wolff has shown that the poetry of Micah is the harsh, grieving voice of a village elder who sees that his village (Moresheth in Gath) is being pillaged and ruined by the tax laws of the royal economy of urban Jerusalem.[29] In 3:8, Micah appeals for *mišpaṭ*, the old egalitarian justice; and in 3:9–12 the poet envisions the destruction of Jerusalem because its leadership abhors justice, operates on bribes, and blindly perceives Yahweh as supportive of the temple ideology. What is important in Wolff's analysis is that Micah is not a lone voice but speaks for an embodied, identifiable, politically significant social group.

The most telling passage is 2:1–5, in which the poet harshly condemns those who "work evil on their beds," that is, who engage in land speculation, high finance, and government manipulation without working.[30] Such a nonworking enterprise signals a destructive disregard of the land. Thus "owning" the land is set against "working" the land.[31] The intent of such manipulators and speculators is to seize fields, oppress people, and take away the patrimony of the land. The patrimony is seized without attention to human cost because the land has come to be regarded by the urban managers as a mere commodity.

Micah 2:1–5 asserts that such practice can and will bring death to these usurpers. Those who usurp what is not theirs will eventually "wail with bitter lamentation" and will end up without land. Such greedy economic practices may lead to quick prosperity, but cannot ultimately succeed because they violate the intractable forces, realities, and values of community life. Partly this is the cry of resentment from the exploited. The canonical process has affirmed that this cry of resentment is the very truth of God.

Micah will not succumb to the ideology fostered in Jerusalem. No doubt he is persona non grata in the city-state. Because of his passion for his land and his people, however, Micah willingly risks his status in the city. In the end, he asserts, there will be a new apportionment of the land (perhaps a Jubilee) and the speculators will be excluded from the "assembly of Yahweh," that is, the assembly of those who will participate in the redistribution (v. 5). The poet is clear that Yahweh chooses the covenantal communities in the villages and tribes, and not the urban establishment as future possessors of the land.

Micah 5:2–4 sounds the positive alternative:[32]

But you, O Bethlehem Ephrathah,
who are little to be among the clans of Judah,
from you shall come forth for me
one who is to be ruler in Israel.

He shall stand and feed his flock in the strength of the Lord, . . .
And they shall dwell secure, for now he shall be great
to the ends of the earth.

This poetry provides a biting contrast between Jerusalem, where everything important happens, and the little village of Bethlehem, where history is never made. Mocking the royal-urban monopoly and its arrogant claims, the poet asserts that the real king will come from the village, not from the city. This caring king will remember the mandate of justice that is equally nonnegotiable for the vulnerable villagers and any real king. The threat to Herod so much later lay, not just in the fact that he did not know where the new king would be born, but that the new king was to appear outside the urban monopoly (Matt. 2:3–8).

Amos and the Sound of Harsh Criticism

The prophet Amos is known for his strictures against the distortion of justice. We usually have not understood, though, that Amos's concerns are not with incidental acts of injustice, but with the systematic economic distortion in which the royal-urban managers participate.

Bernhard Lang has analyzed the way in which "rent capitalism" has divorced market transactions from social care and responsibility.[33] When caring partnership and covenantal relationships are disregarded, the socially marginal are at the mercy of those who administer the monopoly. The harsh relationship between the marginal and the monopoly grows more and more insensitive; there is no care, only profit and use. Lang's thematization of Amos includes the following dimensions:[34]

1. The rich are townspeople who engage in shameless luxury (Amos 6:1–8; cf. Isa. 5:11–12; 56:12).
2. Landed property is often abused when small tenants liable to tax are ruthlessly exploited by landlords (Amos 2:8).
3. Peasants overburdened with debts must sell themselves into bondage to work off their liabilities. The bonded either become serfs who are endlessly in debt or are sold and become per-

manent slaves (cf. Amos 2:6; 8:6). Note the remarkable vocabulary of "buy . . . sell" used in terms of people.

4. Along with rent and interest, the corn trade is an important source of income for the upper class and further strengthens its position in the economy (Amos 8:4–6).[35] Economic forces required that farmers desist from the kind of agriculture that would enhance their own lives, in order to gear production to crops that served only the benefit of outside economic interests.[36]

According to Lang, Amos reflects an economic situation in which covenantal values have been completely disregarded and the profit motive operates at enormous human cost, without regard to Israel's covenantal commitments.

Jeremiah and the City's Ominous Future

Most relentlessly, the prophet Jeremiah desperately and passionately addresses a society that, unawares, lives close to and in the direction of death. Jeremiah's social analysis parallels Micah and Amos's.[37] Indeed in 26:18, Jeremiah is saved from execution precisely by appeal to the tradition and precedent of Micah. The poetry of Jeremiah includes this critique of the royal temple system:

> They have become great and rich,
> they have grown fat and sleek.
> They know no bounds in deeds of wickedness;
> they judge not with justice
> the cause of the fatherless, to make it prosper,
> and they do not defend the rights of the needy.
> (Jer. 5:27–28)

The prophet sees that the distortion in Jerusalem is not simply bad economic practice but economic practice rooted in a false and destructive religious ideology:

> Will you steal, murder, commit adultery, swear falsely, . . . go after other gods . . . and then come and stand before me in this house and say, . . . "We are delivered!" (Jer. 7:9–10)

Religion has lost awareness of the substance of Yahwism and imagines that Yahweh is like every other god and offers social well-being without critical requirement.

The alternative, urges the prophet, is to engage in covenantal practice:

> If you truly execute justice one with another, if you do not oppress the alien, the fatherless, or the widow, . . . if you do not go after other gods, . . . then I will let you dwell in this place, in the land that I gave of old to your fathers for ever. (Jer. 7:5–7)

Well-being in the land requires the practice of covenant in community. The land eventually will be forfeited if covenant is not practiced. The burden of Jeremiah is to assert that now is that eventual time of loss.

The alternative prophetic voice of Micah, Amos, and Jeremiah is singular: the royal-temple-urban policies of Jerusalem, rooted in false ideology, can only lead to death. And death came in the form of exile. Israel was put out of the land. Death came to the monarchy, to the temple, to the city. The city, the urban monopoly which imagined itself self-sufficient and immune, became even as Micah had anticipated:

> Zion shall be plowed as a field;
> Jerusalem shall become a heap of ruins,
> and the mountain of the house a wooded height.
> (Mic. 3:12; cf. Jer. 26:18)

In their lyrical, biting, caring way, the prophets understood precisely what is at issue. The land belongs to the social fabric of community life. It cannot be treated as a mere commodity, indifferent to human reality. Eventually, abusive and ruthless land policies cost too much in human terms. Then there will surely be a costly answering in a brutalized, exploited society. The cost is unavoidable.

To be sure, the prophetic assessment of the city is one-sided. It is one-sided, however, because nothing on the other side of the equation, nothing of culture and arts, of music, architecture, and business can balance this human distortion that leads to death. The prophets after Moses continue to voice this single, nonnegotiable reality.

Israel's faith comes to voice in bold statements, some of which are lyrical doxology, some indignant polemic:

The earth is the Lord's. (Ps. 24:1)

The land shall not be sold in perpetuity for the land is mine. (Lev. 25:23)

These foundational assertions take the land from its false owners and place it in its proper healing, promissory context of Yahweh's covenant. In that context the land is treasured, respected, and productive. But the land stays in dispute because the royal-urban ideology is ruthless and relentless.

Israel's faith begins in powerful doxology: "The land belongs to Yahweh." Sometimes the great doxology is silenced by abuse, displacement, and marginality. The great celebration is stilled, and it seems there is no more joy or celebration. Then into the midst of the hurt and alienation, Yahweh's claim comes not as doxology but as pathos-filled crying out. Israel, Yahweh, and the land cry in their hurt. At the beginning was joy and confidence. But by the time of Jeremiah at the end of royal dominance, the doxology grows tear-filled. Jeremiah in his grief can only say:

O land, land, land,
hear the word of the Lord.
(Jer. 22:29; cf. Zech. 12:12)

The poet continues, commenting on Jehoiakin, the last king, the pitiful boy-king, heir of the failed monopoly:

Write this man down as childless,
a man shall not succeed in his days;
for none of his off-spring shall succeed
in sitting on the throne of David,
and ruling again in Judah.
(Jer. 22:30)

That is the end of the royal-temple enterprise, destroyed by its own seduction. We witness and watch the collapse of the monopoly in grief, death, exile, failure, and finally despair. The premise endures. The land still belongs to Yahweh. Now the land is hurt, charred, abandoned. The premise holds, but now in grief, not in praise.

We hear the sadness and we are left with two questions. How could it happen that this great doxology runs out in a bitter and sad cry? What does this have to do with us, and our own season with the land?

OUR DEATHLY MONOPOLIES

There is an odd, agrarian dream in American society. This dream is rooted partly in the Bible, when "everyone shall sit under a vine and fig tree" (Mic. 4:4).[38] It is partly an odd, natural gift given by God to those who care for and respect the land. The dream is that the land is a partner to be loved and cherished, to be obeyed and honored, and to be taken seriously.[39] If honored, the land will yield its produce, not vast surpluses but enough for humanness. Such a view of land once authorized an agriculture that was a respected partner of the industrial enterprise. Those engaged in the industrial enterprise had no great will to distort this odd covenantal respect for the land. Those in business, commerce, and finance understood the delicate fabric of agriculture.

Something has happened in the city, however, that replicates the technology and ideology of Pharaoh. There is not only a breakdown of the social fabric but a failure to understand any longer the value of or need for a social fabric. One cannot tell what is cause and what is effect in the human failure of the urban monopoly. I submit that the breakdown has come with the powerful, aggressive emergence of a monopoly. We cannot therefore concentrate on the "farm crisis" as though it existed in a vacuum, as though farmers can be regarded as those who need help. Rather, we need to reflect on how we are trapped in and committed to alien monopolies that sooner or later will destroy us all.

1. We are trapped in a *monopoly of ideology*. The ideology is one of insatiable greed that goes under the name of "consumerism." That ideology urges that we must have more, and then, we imagine, we shall be happy or safe. The result is an endless pursuit of books, travel, dollars, stereos, wars, sexual partners, intimacy—and endless anxiety.

2. We are trapped in a *monopoly of technology* that tends to be largely a technology of militarism, in which the "more" of ideology yields more missiles, more intimidation, more secrets, more security. As our greed makes us endlessly anxious, our militarism makes us endlessly insecure. Agriculture becomes a sub-set for military policy; food, once a gift, is now a weapon. Indeed, everything is now a weapon, and our technology is a technology of insecurity and death.

3. We are trapped in a *monopoly of imagination* in which our ideology of anxiety and our technology of insecurity are united by the media.[40] Advertising tells us what to hope and what to fear. We reduce even deathly technology to happy, successful teamwork and seem not to notice that the team effort concerns killing.

Ancient and Modern Parallels

In the ancient world, ideology was fashioned by the priesthood of the temple and the scribes. In the ancient city, the temple was the media center. There ideology was articulated and enacted that justified the king and royal power, that is, the monopoly and concentration of goods and power.[41] In Israel as elsewhere, the temple and its myth-making was an appendage to the royal apparatus. The king was formally always the head of the priesthood.

The scribes, who generated wisdom, intellectual finesse, and secret knowledge, were the intelligence community that articulated facts and myths peculiarly useful to the king and the power elite.[42] In ancient Israel the strange scene of Hushai and Ahithophel (2 Sam. 17) shows the myth-making power of the scribes.[43] Priests, scribes, and wisdom teachers were on the payroll of the urban establishment and worked to legitimate the way the world is arranged.

Today, the media and the university are the places where "useful knowledge" is "generated" to enhance the technological monopoly. The media generate the greed and doubletalk that seduce people from human values enough to keep consumerism functioning.[44] That same consumerism in the ancient world took on a religious mode; the temple generated great festivals that functioned as an economic narcotic (Isa. 1:11–14; Amos 5:21–23; cf. Amos 6:4–6). For us the issues have not changed, though the medium of articulation has become secular.[45]

The university's "useful" knowledge is increasingly technical knowledge, managerial knowledge that raises no serious questions, and only contributes to the better working of the monopoly which goes uncriticized.[46] That the university tends in this direction is evident in its budget, which is weighted in science, engineering, and business, but lean on humanities. It is the humanities that characteristically provide enough distance from current assumptions to permit a serious critique, the very disciplines little prized in the power centers of modern life. The shriveling of the humanities as an educational priority encourages technical knowledge that can uncritically serve any ideology.

We live in a world shaped by the greed of consumerism, and new fearful imaginations. Everything becomes useful. Everything became exploitable. Everyone becomes dispensable. We need only be productive. And while productive, we lose our value. We end in a common despair.

The royal-urban monopoly in our time corresponds roughly to Pharaoh's or Solomon's. Land, agriculture, and farming are now part of the urban monopoly. The land must serve our fear, our greed, our endless drive for more. We insist that farmers produce more. We authorize schools of agriculture to do research to expand or refine production. Eventually farmers become like the rest of us. Lacking viable alternatives some embrace the ideology of greed, anxiety, "more"—and death stalks us all. Then we can no longer determine where the city stops and the farm begins, because we have all joined the monopoly, seeking to find a useful, safe place in it. Our focus then must be not on the land or on the farmers, but on the ideology and the monopoly in which we are enmeshed, which cannot give life and which is increasingly remote from humanness.

While the short-term issue may be political, the long-term issue is startlingly religious. It has to do with repentance, with a break with the values, hopes, fears, and ideology of the royal-urban monopoly which is an idolatry, which is loyalty to a god who cannot save. Through our false loyalties we embrace a distorted view of the world and we practice an anti-human society, powered by greed and fear.

The old reality of Israel's "withdrawal" from the imagination of the empire is a pertinent issue for us, to see whether we can disengage liturgically, psychologically, politically, and economically from the values of consumerism and militarism. From our memory of faith we remember an alternative. And in remembering we know better. The truth is that land is not a tradeable commodity. People are not tradeable commodities. Creation is not a tradeable commodity, not an endlessly exploitable property. Indeed, the Creator is not a commodity who is to be traded for a better God if one is available (cf. Jer. 2:9–13). In the end none of us is a tradeable commodity, not even our neighbor.[47]

The poison to death is deep within our system and consequently deep within our psyches, which have internalized the system. We mistake who we really are. The repentance required is not simply a repentance for farmers who have become too greedy or for bankers who have become too nervous. The repentance required is a common issue for all of us who are too heavily committed to the royal-urban monopoly and who too much benefit from that monopoly. After we have done our best social criticism, it remains to be seen if there are sacraments and liturgies powerful enough to permit and authorize disengagement, compelling enough to offer an alternative that is rooted in holiness and enacted as neighborliness. Finally we are asked about our baptism, about renunciation of the "vainglories" of the world, and about being heirs of a promised new life. The very question about common baptism frightens us. But what if this church focused on its baptism, stopped for a season the internal maneuvering and asked about a "more excellent way" in American society? The cost runs well beyond rhetoric. It probably runs toward trusting, and listening, and caring as we have not done lately.

OPTIONS BEYOND OUR CONVENTIONS

If we were to address this great issue of repentance and new possibility, we would need to stay very close to the biblical text. This live word of God is filled with riches and dangers that could change our life together. Let me comment on three texts.

1. The provision for the Jubilee year in Leviticus 25 embodies the most radical expression of an alternative, covenantal ethic of the land. The provision to return an inalienable birthright land to its rightful owner after forty-nine years is an extraordinary guard against monopoly. It is a clear statement that people matter more than property, that humaneness governs land management, that the fabric of the community is more crucial than accumulation. Most compelling, in Lev. 25:29–31, is the discerning social analysis of the difference between village and urban life. In walled cities the Jubilee does not apply and land may be sold to perpetuity, but houses in villages which have no wall are subject to Jubilee. In its realism, this text does not imagine that a Jubilee discernment of economic

reality will function in the great walled cities. Perhaps this particular text regards the royal-urban monopoly as beyond rescue, and urges Israel not to use its energy on such a hopeless cause. If so, it means we are not the first to despair about the reclamation of the city for covenant.

But I have another thought about Jubilee. The word Jubilee comes from *yabal*, ram's horn, a term that occurs frequently in Leviticus concerning the practice of Jubilee (Lev. 25:10, 11, 12, 15, 28, 30, 31, 33). The other word used is *shôphar*, also horn or trumpet (Lev. 25:9). These two words refer to the ram's horn that Israel used as a signal to execute its radical social vision in concrete economic ways by acting decisively against the monopoly for the sake of the human community.

In Joshua 6, a very different kind of narrative, the *yabal* is used in v. 6 and the *shôphar* in vv. 4, 5, and 20. That text reports the liturgical act whereby Israel goes around the great walled city of Jericho seven times—and the walls fall down. Jericho was a very old, powerful, and formidable city. Its archeological remains witness to a monopoly of wealth that must have been achieved and sustained by slave labor. It surely represented a concentration of military power against which Israel's social vision had little concrete chance. Is it coincidental that the sound of the Jubilee (*yabal, shôphar*) is the sound that destroys the walls, breaks the monopoly, and makes covenantal life possible? In the face of walled cities, Israel acts with a Jubilee, and the wall of monopoly comes tumbling down. In at least this one narrative, even the walled-in monopoly cannot resist the Jubilee of Israel's covenantal faith.

A young pastor in the farm belt told me of a local banker in his congregation who had loans out to farmers who could not pay, some of whom were members of this same church. The banker (who was free because his bank was not, like most banks, owned by the Chicago monopoly) decided to extend the mortgages without interest rather than force foreclosure. He said, "I want to live in this town a long time and these are my friends." It is important that the bank was not enmeshed in the urban monopoly. It is equally important that this banker had some sense of the preciousness of the human fabric. It is equally important that this banker and some of the farmers were in the same church. He let the farmers keep the

land. The pastor shrewdly observed, "The banker was practicing the
Jubilee, though he did not call it that." Israel had discerned that
none of us will be human very long if there are not occasions of
Jubilee among us, which have the strange power to break the deathly
monopolies.[48]

2. Jesus invites his disciples out of anxiety caused by fear and
greed. In Matt. 6:25–32, Jesus summons them to sort out their priorities because "you cannot serve God and mammon," you cannot
practice covenant and pursue capital at the same time. Finally they
will have to choose (cf. Luke 12:13–21).

That decision now faces us. Jesus says, "Do not be anxious." Quit
trying to have it both ways. Then, after his observance that spar-
rows and lilies live trustfully as a part of a rightly ordered yet
distorted creation, Jesus observes, "Not even Solomon with his great
urban monopoly was as well off as a bird or a flower." Not even
Solomon, the biblical model for self-sufficiency, who imagined he
could organize all of life around his greed and fear. Not even Solomon, for his great monopoly ended in a painful, angry social revolution (1 Kings 12). Not even Solomon could gather as much life
together as the heavenly Father, the caring Mother, will give on any
one day. Not even Solomon, not even us.

3. The tradition of Isaiah thinks about the city as much as anyone in the Bible. Isaiah knows that the city, in this case Jerusalem,
began with good intentions but lost its way. In the opening words of
Isaiah 1:21 and 23, the poet speaks of the city with the central
words of the covenant:

> The faithful city (*'amûnah*) has become a harlot, she that was full
> of justice (*mišpaṭ*)! Righteousness (*ṣedeq*) lodged in her, but now
> murderers.

> You princes are rebels, and companions of thieves. Every one
> loves a bribe and runs after gifts. They do not defend the father-
> less, and the widow's cause does not come to them.

The city has forgotten its mandate of care for the powerless, and
so comes punishment (Isa. 1:24–26). It finally cannot prosper in the
absence of faithfulness, justice, and righteousness. The royal-urban
monopoly cannot use up the world to sate itself. But then, astonishingly in vv. 26–27, the poet ends the poem with:

> Afterward [after the harsh judgment] you shall be called the city
>   of righteousness [*ṣedeq*],
>   the faithful city [*'amûnah*],
> Zion shall be redeemed by justice [*mišpaṭ*],
>   and those in her who repent, by righteousness [*ṣedeqah*].

In the end, after hurt, after the city is plowed as a field, it will become a place of humaneness, caring for widows and orphans. The city will be what it was initially summoned by Yahweh to be. When the royal-urban monopoly is transformed, the land will be healed and its children with it.

At the conclusion of the book of Isaiah, in 65:17–25, there is a matching poem, likely an intentional counterpart to 1:21–27.[49] In the most sweeping promise in the Old Testament, the poet has God say:

> I create new heavens and a new earth, . . . a new Jerusalem [a new city]. (vv. 17, 18)

Then the poem describes the new city. It has a new economics, wherein one will not plant and another eat the produce (vv. 21–22); a new medical policy, wherein there is no more infant mortality (v. 20); a new political policy, wherein people will no longer hurt or destroy (v. 25); and a new covenantal religion, wherein God will answer before they call (v. 24). In this new city there will be no more cries of distress, no more abandonment, no more terror (v. 19). There will be well-being in the very city. It is promised.

It may seem odd to begin by discussing the farm crisis and end talking about a transformed city. I have done so because it is clear to me that today the land will not be treated and managed differently until the ideology of the city is transformed, until the technology of the city is drastically revised, until the imagination of the city is opened to human possibility for the marginal. When the city practices justice (Ps. 96:11–12), then the fields and trees and farmers and bankers and all of us will sing and dance. We will be as glad and as free as Miriam and her sisters who departed the empire (Exod. 15:20–21). The old men and the young men will watch while the sisters and mothers in Israel take tambourines and dance and sing to the Lord, the God of exodus to whom the land belongs. That celebrative song is the song of the human community, human transformation, and human possibility that was begun at the edge of the empire. It is a song that runs from the waters of liberation in Egypt to the throne where angels sing:

> The kingdom of the world has become the kingdom of our Lord and of his Christ, and he shall reign for ever and ever. (Rev. 11:15)[50]

The angel will sound the trumpet. When the trumpet sounds in the last day—or tomorrow—the walls of monopoly will crumble, the land will be returned to its rightful place, the Jubilee will be practiced, and God will laugh. God will laugh at our odd Easter. We will laugh with God and with all the widows and orphans who have a part of the land.

NOTES

This chapter was initially delivered as an address at a conference on the urban dimension of the farm crisis at Riverside Church, New York, November 14, 1986, and later at the General Synod of the United Church of Christ, Cleveland, Ohio, June 28, 1987. Reprinted here by permission of A-R Editions, Inc., © 1991.

1. On the sociology of the city, see Lewis Mumford, *The City in History: Its Origins, Its Transformation, and Its Prospects* (New York: Harcourt, Brace & World, 1961). See also idem, *Myth of the Machine* (New York: Harcourt, Brace & World, 1970); and *Pentagon of Power* (New York: Harcourt, Brace & World, 1970). On the theme of city in the Bible, see Frank S. Frick, *The City in Ancient Israel* (Missoula, Mont.: Scholars Press, 1977).

2. Norman K. Gottwald, *The Tribes of Yahweh* (Maryknoll, N.Y.: Orbis Books, 1979). In my analysis, I follow Gottwald's model.

3. On Gen. 47 as an intentional piece of social criticism, see Walter Brueggemann, *Hope within History* (Atlanta: John Knox Press, 1987), 10–16.

4. In *Hope within History*, I have explored how the exodus narrative is constructed to nurture Israel in social resentment, so that from the outset Israelites are clear that their identity and historical vocation are in tension with the claims of the empire.

5. On "food as a weapon," see Wendell Berry, *The Unsettling of America* (New York: Avon Books, 1977), 37. Berry refers to agribusinesses as "the pornographers of agriculture" (p. 136).

6. On the claims of Egyptian religion, see Henri Frankfort, *Kingship and the Gods* (Chicago: University of Chicago Press, 1948). It is remark-

able that this famous analysis of Egyptian ideology largely ignored the enormous political and ideological implications of imperial religion.

7. On the *habirû* in light of sociological analysis, see David Noel Freedman and David Graf, eds., *Palestine in Transition* (Sheffield, Eng.: Almond Press, 1983).

8. Gottwald, *The Tribes of Yahweh*, 611–21.

9. Larry Jent has shared with me a report of a taped sermon by Peter Marshall that analyzes the progressive negotiations of Pharaoh, showing that Pharaoh in each case offers a choice to Moses that can be distorted by imperial interpretation. It is an exceedingly shrewd analysis.

10. On the term "withdrawal" in this context, see Gottwald, *The Tribes of Yahweh*, 85, 326, 408, 469; John M. Halligan, "The Role of the Peasant in the Arena Period," in *Palestine in Transition*, 17; and Marvin Chaney, "Ancient Palestinian Peasant Movements and the Formation of Premonarchial Israel," in ibid., 49, with his reference to Mendenhall's initial use of the term.

11. See Walter Brueggemann, *The Creative Word* (Philadelphia: Fortress Press, 1982), chap. 2.

12. Gottwald, *The Tribes of Yahweh*, 100–114.

13. Martin Buber, *The Kingship of God* (New York: Harper & Row, 1967).

14. Whether it is land in prospect or hill country land already held depends on whether the point of reference is Moses (in prospect) or Joshua (in hand). Gottwald's analysis and this general way of interpretation treat the two as parallel elements in a single program of social transformation.

15. Scholarly discussion of the theme of covenant has become sidetracked by historical questions and seems largely to have missed the sociological implications of Israel's vision, whether called by the name of covenant or not. Ernest W. Nicholson, *God and His People* (Oxford: Clarendon Press, 1986), chap. 10, has discerningly restated the main points of this radical vision.

16. See Walter Harrelson, *The Ten Commandments and Human Rights* (Philadelphia: Fortress Press, 1980).

17. Patrick D. Miller, Jr., "The Human Sabbath: A Study in Deuteronomic Theology," *Princeton Seminary Bulletin* 6 (1985): 81–97, has suggested ways in which the commandment on sabbath also holds together commands on neighbor and commands on God.

18. Lothar Perlitt, *Bundestheologie im Alten Testament* (Neukirchen-Vluyn: Neukirchener, 1969), proposed that covenant appears in Israel only in the seventh century with the work of Deuteronomy. That view is however too extreme, as Ernest W. Nicholson, *God and His People: Covenant and Theology in the Old Testament* (Oxford: Clarendon Press,

1986), and Dennis J. McCarthy, *Treaty and Covenant: A Study in Form in the Ancient Oriental Documents and in the Old Testament* (Rome: Biblical Institute Press, 1978) have shown.

19. Robert Polzin, *Moses and the Deuteronomist* (New York: Seabury Press, 1980), has forcefully suggested that the "voice" in this literature is much more complex than a single assignment of it to Moses. That analysis, however, does not vitiate the general claim made here.

20. Norbert Lohfink, *Great Themes from the Old Testament* (Edinburgh: T. & T. Clark, 1982), 55–75, has proposed that this law is a part of a larger corpus which seeks to guarantee covenantal order by a division of powers in the governing structure.

21. On the alternative social vision, see Freedman and Graf, eds., *Palestine in Transition*.

22. The book of Judges is a narrative account of a clear and dramatic contrast between these two socio-theological systems. Thus "doing evil in the sight of Yahweh" (3:7) and "crying out to Yahweh" are not mere religious statements, but are ways of participating in and/or criticizing social systems and social power arrangements.

23. See Frank S. Frick, *The Formation of the State in Ancient Israel* (Sheffield, Eng.: Almond Press, 1985).

24. See esp. Norman K. Gottwald, "The Participation of Free Agrarians in the Introduction of Monarchy to Ancient Israel," *Semeia* 37 (1986): 77–106. Internal tensions and developments are characteristically justified by the power elite in terms of external problems.

25. See George E. Mendenhall, "The Monarchy," *Interpretation* 29 (1975): 155–70.

26. The change in rationality in the time of Solomon has been presented by Gerhard von Rad, under the rubric of "Solomon's Enlightenment." See von Rad, *Old Testament Theology 1* (New York: Harper & Row, 1962), 48–55, 425–29. My impression is that James Crenshaw's criticism of the hypothesis does not reckon seriously enough with the sociological data that lies beyond the epistemological shift.

27. See Walter Brueggemann, "The Epistemological Crisis of Israel's Two Histories (Jer. 9:22–23)," in *Israelite Wisdom*, ed. John G. Gammie (Missoula, Mont.: Scholars Press, 1978), 85–105.

28. The connection between the covenant tradition and the prophets was programmatically presented by von Rad, *Old Testament Theology 2* (New York: Harper & Row, 1965), and was given careful treatment by Ronald E. Clements, *Prophecy and Covenant*, Studies in Biblical Theology 43 (Naperville, Ill.: Alec R. Allenson, 1965). Since then the high period of "covenantalism" has passed, and scholars are much more cautious about the connection. Nonetheless, it is difficult to dispose of the impression that the prophets continue to champion the egalitarian-

ism of the covenant against the urban monopoly. Since von Rad, a much more realistic sociological analysis is available and must be practiced. On the rootage of prophetic critique in the old traditions, see Michael Walzer, *Interpretation and Social Criticism* (Cambridge: Harvard University Press, 1987), 69–97.

29. Hans Walter Wolff, "Micah the Moreshite—The Prophet and His Background," in Gammie, ed., *Israelite Wisdom*, 77–84. More generally on the sociology of the prophets, see Robert R. Wilson, *Prophecy and Society in Ancient Israel* (Philadelphia: Fortress Press, 1980).

30. See the foundational analysis of the text by Albrecht Alt, "Micha 2:1–5," in *Kleine Schriften*, vol. 3 (Munich: C. H. Beck, 1959), 373–81. A wondrous contemporary commentary on this text may be found in Andrew H. Malcolm, *Final Harvest* (New York: Random House, 1986), in which Rudy the banker is perceived by the farmers with resentment because of his affluence. They recognize that he does not work the land with his hands. Concerning his murder, a witness reports: "As he was shooting Rudy, Jim Jenkins said to himself, 'How does it feel now, Mr. Banker, to be outside your own office with the fancy furniture and all them files and your money tricks? You're not in charge out here'" (p. 171). Malcolm's book is a journalistic account of an actual murder of a banker by a displaced farmer. It is enormously instructive for the social tensions present in the farm crisis.

31. John Steinbeck, *The Grapes of Wrath* (New York: Penguin Books, 1939), is eloquent about the distinction between owning and working the land. He writes: "Crops were reckoned in dollars, and land was valued by principal plus interest . . . all their love was thinned with money, and all their fierceness dribbled away in interest until they were no longer farmers at all, but little shopkeepers of crops, little manufacturers who must sell before they can make. . . . And it came about that the owners no longer worked on their farms. They farmed on paper; and they forgot the land, the smell, the feel of it, and remembered only that they owned it, remembered only what they gained and lost by it. . . . And the owners not only did not work the farms any more, many of them had never seen the farms they owned" (pp. 298–99).

32. It may well be that this poem does not originally come from Micah. Critical opinion is against assigning the poem to the prophet. I am more inclined to treat it as "genuine." But the important matter is that in the finished arrangement of the literature of Micah, this poem is surely intentionally juxtaposed to the earlier critical text. Thus the pattern of judgment and promise is what is important for our interpretation.

33. Bernhard Lang, "Social Organization of Peasant Poverty in Biblical Israel," *Journal for the Study of the Old Testament* 24 (1982): 47–63.

34. Ibid., 53ff.

35. Marvin L. Chaney, "Latifundialization and Prophetic Diction in Eighth-Century Israel and Judah" (SBL/ASOR Sociology of the Monarchy Seminar, 1985). Chaney has proposed that the concentration of land-wealth in the hands of a few led to the requirement of "demand crops" (grain, wine, oil) which were profitably entered into the international market but did not serve the small farmer well. See also D. N. Premnath, "Latifundialization and Isa. 5:8–10," *Journal for the Study of the Old Testament* 40 (1988): 49–60.

36. Wendell Berry's general argument is that agribusiness has not at all helped farmers economically but has only served the capitalist owners of business who are removed from and not interested in the farm. The parallel to the prophetic situation of Micah and Amos could hardly be more clearly drawn. Steinbeck offers an analysis that coheres well with Chaney's proposal. He writes: "And the farms grew larger and the owners fewer. And the crops changed. Fruit trees took the place of grain fields, and vegetables to feed the world spread out on the bottoms; lettuce, cauliflower, artichokes, potatoes—stoop crops. A man may stand to use a scythe, a plough, a pitchfork; but he must crawl like a bug between the rows of lettuce, he must bend his back and pull his long bag between the cotton rows, he must go on his knees like a penitent across a cauliflower patch" (*The Grapes of Wrath*, 298–99).

37. On the prophetic practice of social analysis, see Walter Brueggemann, "Blessed Are the History Makers," 65–67.

38. Cf. Walter Brueggemann, "Vine and Fig Tree: A Case Study in Imagination and Criticism," *Catholic Biblical Quarterly* (1981): 188–204.

39. Douglas Hall, *Imaging God* (Grand Rapids: Wm. B. Eerdmans, 1986), in his analysis of human "domination" has argued well for a covenantal relation with the nonhuman world. Hall does not explicitly focus on the land, but that is surely a crucial element in his nonhuman partnership with human agents.

40. Robert K. Merton, *Social Theory and Social Structure* (Glencoe, Ill.: Free Press, 1957), 157.

41. See John M. Lundquist, "What Is a Temple? A Preliminary Typology," in *The Quest for the Kingdom of God*, ed. Herbert B. Huffmon, Frank A. Spina, and Alberto R. W. Green (Winona Lake, Ind.: Eisenbrauns, 1983), 205–19.

42. On the social and political function of such scribes, see George E. Mendenhall, "The Shady Side of Wisdom," in *A Light unto My Path*, ed. H. N. Bream et al. (Philadelphia: Temple University Press, 1974), 319–34; and Glendon E. Bryce, *A Legacy of Wisdom* (Lewisburg, Pa.: Bucknell University Press, 1979), 135–88.

43. See William McKane, *Prophets and Wise Men*, Studies in Biblical Theology 44 (Naperville, Ill.: Alec R. Allenson, 1965), 55–62; and, more

generally, R. N. Whybray, *The Succession Narrative*, Studies in Biblical Theology 92 (Naperville, Ill.: Alec R. Allenson, 1968).

44. On the political function of propaganda, see Jacques Ellul, *Propaganda: The Formation of Men's Attitudes* (New York: Alfred A. Knopf, 1965).

45. The parallel seems obvious between the characterization of Amos 6:4–6 on the one hand, and contemporary slogans such as, "You owe yourself this," or "I want it all and I want it now," on the other hand.

46. On managerial modes of knowledge and their social function, see Alasdair MacIntyre, *After Virtue* (Notre Dame, Ind.: University of Notre Dame Press, 1981), 24–31, 70–83; and Robert Bellah et al., *Habits of the Heart* (Berkeley: University of California Press, 1985), 44–51 and passim. As relates to closed, technical education, see Allen Bloom, *The Closing of the American Mind* (New York: Simon & Schuster, 1987), albeit from a reactionary perspective.

47. Abraham Heschel, *Who Is Man?* (Stanford, Calif.: Stanford University Press, 1965), has most acutely and sensitively analyzed our social situation in which everything and everyone is reduced to a commodity. He has also argued that the sabbath is our most important protest against such a reduction of life to commodity.

48. On the importance of the Jubilee for biblical faith, see Sharon H. Ringe, *Jesus, Liberation, and the Biblical Jubilee* (Philadelphia: Fortress Press, 1985).

49. On the coherence of these texts as a part of the canonical design of the book of Isaiah, see Ronald Clements, "Beyond Tradition-History: Deutero-Isaianic Development from First Isaiah's Themes," *Journal for the Study of the Old Testament* 31 (1985): 95–113.

50. On the continuation of exodus motifs and exodus faith into the book of Revelation, see Jay Casey, "The Exodus Theme in the Book of Revelation against the Background of the New Testament," in *Exodus— A Lasting Paradigm*, ed. Bas van Iersel and Anton Weiler, Concilium 189 (Edinburgh: T. & T. Clark, 1987), 34–43.

13

Welcoming the Stranger

THE GOSPEL PERMITS AND REQUIRES a transformed
ethic. Paul presents that permit and requirement clearly and radically:

> Do not be conformed to this world, but be transformed by the
> renewal of your mind, that you may prove what is the will of God,
> what is good and acceptable and perfect. (Rom. 12:2)

In the words that follow that programmatic statement, Paul delin-
eates in some detail what this transformation of conduct would
look like. One pair of injunctions in Paul's inventory illuminates the
themes of conformity and transformation.

To be *conformed* in our society, I submit, is to "practice vengeance" (Rom. 12:19) against everyone who departs from our norm,
and therefore against every outsider who fails to conform. The failure to conform in our society may be expressed by personal morality, but it may also be expressed by political and economic postures
which are viewed as unacceptable. The inclination to vengeance is
now powerful among us, so that we who guard, honor, and benefit
from the norm become more and more exclusive.[1]

Paul's alternative to vengeance is hospitality. To "practice hospitality" (Rom. 12:13) is to receive and care for those who have been
excluded, that is, those who have been rejected because of their
violation of some norm. Thus as a starting point in this radical
Pauline urging, I juxtapose *conformity* as the embrace of *vengeance*
with *transformation* as the practice of *hospitality*. With such a

juxtaposition, the general theme of "conform–transform" becomes concrete and demanding.

For our time then I propose from Romans 12 a simple, rather obvious point. The ethical summons of the gospel is that in a world bent on vengeance, our vocation is to practice hospitality. In such a "thirsty" society as ours, that is, thirsty for blood, the practice of hospitality is not only odd and unusual but will often be perceived as subversive and counter-cultural.

THE PRODUCTION OF STRANGERS

Exclusion is the predictable outcome of certain social values and social policies. The stranger as "displaced person" is the product of a social system which displaces.

Among other things, the Bible is an exposé of social systems that thrive on estrangement, benefit from and depend on outsiders, and, in fact, produce outsiders. In the Old Testament, the outsider-producing systems are first of all the great empires, especially the Egyptian and Babylonian empires,[2] and the system of Canaanite city-states.[3] The empires are perceived critically in the Old Testament as social, economic, and political value systems that acquire and maintain monopolies of goods, money, technique, and land.

Because the dominant values are predictably the values of the dominant class,[4] those who have these monopolies also come to have a monopoly of legitimacy and virtue, and in the end a monopoly of imagination. They control not only every benefit in the present but every imaginable prospect for the future. The empires are not only concentrations of great power but come to be concentrations of society's norms. To be included "in" such a system is to live. To be "out," excluded, excommunicated, banished is to die, to be nullified, not to exist. To be "in" requires that one conform to the powerful norms of the system. The great empires in the Old Testament period inevitably were involved in the process of including people in and declaring people out.

In the ancient Near East, the classic embodiment of the outsider is the *ḫabirû*, an odd, nameless hovering mass of unnamed humanity mentioned often in the texts of the "insiders" as being at various times an inconvenience, a worry, and a serious threat.[5] The *ḫabirû* are the large mass of people who can find no right "place" in the system, perhaps because they do not sufficiently conform, and perhaps because the community needs some outsiders for the menial functions of society. In the texts, the *ḥabirû* are marginal people who in good times did menial work, in war times might have been hired cannon fodder, and in bad times lived by raids and terrorism, because they did not have any approved modes of access to land, power, or even food. While at times useful to the established social system of the empire, the *ḥabirû* were generally a threat. The empires used great energy to contain, administer, resist, and when possible nullify and eliminate them.

It is in the character of the empire to want to include everyone on its own terms, everyone who will accept the dominant norms, who will perform according to approved expectations, and who will accept a system of benefits which may be unequal but is nonetheless normative. While wanting to include everyone, however, it is also the case that the empire exists for and by the uneven distribution of goods. The necessary and inevitable social stratification dictates that some will have more, some much less, and perhaps some will have nothing.[6] That disproportion is what a socio-economic political monopoly is all about. The monopoly is not an accidental by-product, but the point of such power. Those who do not benefit from that disproportion are inherently a threat, because sooner or later, they notice the disproportion and want it adjusted. As they become a threat, the outsiders must be kept at a distance. One way of maintaining such social distance is by labeling as "stranger" the ones who do not conform enough to be included "in."

The Threat of the Outsider

For our purpose of understanding "the stranger" in biblical terms, it is important to acknowledge the likely connection between the general sociological term *"ḥabirû"* and the biblical term "Hebrew," which most scholars believe is simply an alternative rendering.[7] "Hebrew" apparently comes from the verb *'abar,* to "cross over." Thus the Hebrew is one who crosses over boundaries, who has no respect for imperial boundaries, is not confined by such boundaries, and crosses them in desperate quest of the necessities of life. The Hebrew is driven by the urgent issue of survival. Note that the term "Hebrew" is not, in this reading, an ethnic term but a sociological category referring to those who are not contained in or sustained by the social system but who must live outside the system and its resources and benefits. Thus we can conclude that the people who finally become the "people of God" in the Old Testament are some among those whom the empire had declared "strangers," "outsiders," "threat."

While the position of the outsider is often rooted in political and economic matters, there is a different distinction between insider and outsider in Gen. 43:32. In the midst of the Joseph narrative, it is written of Joseph:

> They served him by himself, and them by themselves, because the Egyptians might not eat bread with the Hebrews, for that is an abomination to the Egyptians.

The distinction between Joseph and the Egyptians is not ethnic but sociological. The Egyptians in the narrative are an embodiment of the Egyptian empire, the classic insiders. Joseph is a Hebrew, an outsider who does not qualify to eat with the imperial insiders. This verse provides important clues for our understanding of the stranger:

1. The text contrasts Egyptians and *ḥabirû*, those in the empire who control the monopoly and those who are disqualified outsiders.

2. The contrast concerns access to food and, therefore, to life, worth, security, and dignity. "Food" refers to the means of life. But it also concerns the most intimate of social transactions, where social distinctions are likely to be most rigorously observed.

3. The contrast concerns the issue of social power, but the matter of power is articulated as a religious-moral matter. The word "abomination" (*to'eveh*) suggests that the Hebrews are morally inferior, socially dangerous, and ritually impure. It is remarkable how sociological distinctions become reflected in ritual categories.

4. The biblical narrative notices the oddity of this arrangement of eating and therefore of social power. The narrator makes no explicit comment, but the fact that the eating arrangement is mentioned at all means that full notice is taken by the narrator of the discrimination. The biblical narrative is restless with this social arrangement of discrimination that the empire had come to regard as routine.

Creating outsiders is initially done to have a means of monopoly from which some are excluded. This monopoly of power is readily translated into a monopoly of sanctity and virtue, of holiness and righteousness.[8] In the Old Testament, this ritualizing of social distinction is carefully articulated in terms of laws of purity that concern food, the priesthood, and sexuality.[9] In Leviticus and Ezekiel especially, we find an intense sorting out of what is acceptable and unacceptable, the unacceptable being categories treated as morally inferior, socially dangerous, and ritually impure. But these "religious" categories are never far removed from the realities of social power and access to social goods.

In the New Testament, this way of identifying, categorizing, processing, and administering strangers shows up in Jesus' legal disputes with the advocates of the laws of holiness and righteousness (cf. Mark 7).[10] The practice of defilement and uncleanness turns out to be a labeling process with enormous social implications.

Landless and Not Belonging

I suggest now a third dimension of generating strangers that is intimately tied to the first two and may in fact be more foundational: strangers are those who do not have land, who are not judged as entitled to it, and who have no chance of acquiring any of the land.[11] Thus the "Hebrews" are those who "cross over" (*'abar*), trespass, do not respect the property or property rights of others because they are so desperate or resentful that they will not finally acknowledge present social settlements.

It is not accidental that strangers in our society are often experienced as *dis-placed* persons, that is, people without a place. They have no place (or have lost it) because the social system, with its capacity for inclusion and exclusion, has in fact assigned their place to another and so denied them any safe place of their own.[12]

Strangers are often those who are cut out of the history of the land, denied the fruit of the land, and therefore denied social power, social security, or social worth. Every society, including eventually the Israelite community itself,[13] has clear rules about who may own land, how to acquire land, and how to retain it. But the rules governing possession are made by those who have and know how to get land, so whenever those rules are made, some end up without land.[14] When some are excluded from the land, they do not belong, do not have voice or vote, do not know how to penetrate the closed systems of legislation and the courts.[15] Finally, they drop from view and no longer exist.[16]

Very often those denied land will settle for such a fate decreed by the landed. They become passive, docile, and hopeless; even then, however, they continue to be an unsettling presence, worrisome, and embarrassing. On occasion, those consigned to "nonexistence" refuse to accept their fate. They want in; they push, insist, and become a threat. Either way, in docile despair or hope-filled insistence, the outsider is always a threat to those who own, control, and administer land, goods, power, sanctity, and virtue.

SUBVERTING THE "INSIDENESS"

The biblical narrative is the story of the mystery of social power being given precisely among powerless outsiders. The empire believed that it had settled and resolved all questions of social power, and that the displaced people would eventually accept their lot in life as the intractable will of God. Every monopoly believes it has made a "final settlement" of the outsider.[17] Within the Bible, however, we encounter the story of this new, inscrutable, strangely given power that wells up upon the strangers, exactly where the empire thought such dangerous power could not appear. Indeed, Pharaoh believed that it was idleness that caused such fantasies about freedom and well-being, and that the recipe against such fantasies was a tougher work-schedule from the empire (Exod. 5:4–19).

The Bible makes the insistent affirmation that the power of imperial monopoly is not able finally to have its way. Those who have been categorized as "outsider" and "stranger" do not stay perpetually consigned to that role and identity. There is an "unsettling" which unnerves, threatens, and sometimes undoes the imperial system.[18] It is that unsettling that is a main storyline in the Bible, an unsettling that effects an inclusion of the outsider, a welcoming of the stranger, and the practice of hospitality within a system of vengeance.

We may identify three dimensions to those counterstories in the Bible that witness relentlessly against the monopolizing story of the empire.

1. The gift of power for life given outside the control of the

empire depends on the stranger bringing hurt, hate, and grief to public speech in the midst of a community. Public sharing of pain is the means whereby power and courage well up among the strangers. As long as the stranger docilely accepts the status of victim or believes that the status assigned by the empire is a fixed fate, nothing transformative or redemptive will happen. The empire will have its way. And the monopoly will continue its crushing, preemptive force as long as silence can be enforced.

The cry of protest and anguish is a daring, courageous assertion that this unequal arrangement is not right, will not be accepted or tolerated, and must be changed. In the Old Testament, we saw the beginning of outsideness in Egypt when the Hebrews were not permitted to eat as full members of the Egyptian community. Out of that initial discrimination, the daring act of a cry is undertaken in Exod. 2:23–25: "We groaned and cried out." At great risk the Hebrews, who were now state slaves, dared to speak against the monopoly. The cry is a risky act of hope whereby the outsider seriously engages the monopolistic system and refuses its absolute claim. In that moment of shrill speech, the imperial system is disclosed as a fraud that does not keep its promises and is not what it claims to be. In that dangerous moment of the cry, it is clear that the system is not the solution, but is in fact a large, painful problem. The cry insists that the empire must negotiate with a party that it does not even recognize as existing. The cry asserts that "we" are here as a serious social reality that cannot be pretended away.

2. The story of unsettling the empire is more than a daring act of protest. The second element in this biblical account is that there is one who hears and answers, who enters into powerful solidarity with the outsiders. One decisive form of the good news of the gospel is that "God has heard our cry," or, as it is more fully stated in Exod. 2:25: "God heard, God saw, God knew, God remembered," and in Exod. 3:8, "God came down to deliver." The wonder of the Bible is that the cries of the stranger reach the ears of this peculiar God who enters into solidarity, who intervenes, and whom the empire cannot contain or resist. The story includes this wonderment about Yahweh at its very center. It is a wonderment about the historical process that cannot be reduced or explained on any other terms.

According to this odd narrative, the intervention of this summoned God characteristically challenges, violates, and breaks up the exclusionary monopoly of the empire. When this "outsider God" commands, "Let my people go," the empire loses its terrible grip on those it has nullified.

This strange transaction of "crying out" and "being heard" is stylistically presented in Psalm 107. Repeatedly, the psalm names various crises, each of which is resolved in the strange and inexplicable experience of being heard and saved. The "cry–hear" structure of biblical faith is irreducible, even though it violates our attempts at reasonable discernment of the historical process. The outsider cries in order that help may come to those on the outside. The God of the Bible comes to those outside to bring them in to the land, into the full functioning of the landed, social process (cf. Exod. 3:8–9). The action of this God is portrayed and experienced as direct, powerful destabilization of the empire (cf. Exod. 11:4–6), an action that questions its foundational presuppositions and claims. This God who moves against exclusionary monopoly permits strangers and outsiders fresh access to land and to life, to sanctity and to righteousness.[19] The outsider, by this intervention, is rehabilitated. The rehabilitation of the stranger decisively changes the entire process of public life for everyone, the newly included and the always included. No one any longer has life on the old terms.

3 By the intervention of Yahweh, the God who hears the cries of the stranger, the outsider acquires a new status. This is the central affirmation of the biblical story aligned against the stranger-producing work of the empire. The outsider was nullified by the empire. Now, as a result of Yahweh's hearing and answering, that same stranger has a special identity, status, and vocation. The outsiders in solidarity with Yahweh are called to a new life in freedom that the empire cannot give or deny, in obedience that the empire cannot compel or prohibit. These same strangers are now called to a new life in solidarity with and allegiance to Yahweh who displaces Pharaoh as the sovereign over their lives. The covenant Yahweh makes with Israel becomes an alternative to the monopoly.[20] The covenant is with this God who ends the exclusion, reverses the nullification, breaks the monopoly, and gives land, goods, and power

to the reclaimed strangers so that they may live again. In making
this covenant the stranger becomes an insider. The ones who had
died (by the norms of the empire) now begin again to live.

The new status of the strangers is covenant partners with this
God and with each other. As allies of Yahweh, they have power,
possibility, and entitlement, so that the exclusiveness of the empire
is increasingly overcome. In the Old Testament, the new status as
an insider is commonly referred to as being "chosen." The classic
example is in Deut. 7:6:

> For you are a people holy to the Lord your God. The Lord your
> God has chosen you to be a people for his own possession, out of
> all the peoples on the face of the earth.

It is important that this people now formed in covenant was not
originally an ethnic community. They were in fact "no-people." Yahweh evoked and convened a community of people that did not exist
until that hour. They are, until then, only Hebrews, *ḥabirû*, socially
marginal masses without status or identity. Now they are given a
new social possibility.

In the New Testament the clearest text in this claim (with a direct
allusion to Exod. 19:5–6) is 1 Peter 2:9–10:

> But you are a chosen race, a royal priesthood, a holy nation,
> God's own people, that you may declare the wonderful deeds of
> him who called you out of darkness into his marvelous light.
> Once you were no people but now you are God's people; once you
> had not received mercy, but now you have received mercy.[21]

This strand of the Bible is the narrative account of the way in which
the socially excluded and nullified have, by the power of God's inter-
vening solidarity, been formed into a new community with social
hopes and possibilities that lie beyond the scope or horizon of the
empire.[22] Life is indeed possible outside the imperial monopoly!

A NEW COMMUNITY
OF HOME-MAKERS

Much of the Bible is a presentation of how this new community of
strangers has become a powerful force for "home-making" in the

world.[23] These strangers now become citizens of a new community and are given more than a new beginning. They have been invited into and authorized for a new way in the world. They are not to live primarily in relation to or in antagonism against the empire, but are to transform life where they are, so that the world may become a home and other strangers may also come to be at-home.[24] Four dimensions of this home-making enterprise are noteworthy.

1. This new community of strangers is able to *dream a different dream and hope a different hope*. People who own and manage the empire characteristically do not dream or hope. All their energy goes to maintaining the status quo. Strangers who can remember how unbearable it was in the imperial, excluding past can also anticipate how marvelous it will be in time to come. Their radical hope is not wishful thinking, but confidence that the God who initiated the transformation from outside to inside is the same God who is at work for the complete transformation of the world.

Because of this hope, the community refuses to absolutize the present. It trusts and knows that the present is open and unstable, in order that God's future may appear in the midst of the present. This community of dreamers has as a main task nurturing the dream of how this rescuing God has promised it will be. This hope-filled Israel waits for the transformation of the political process (Micah 4:1–4; Ezek. 34:25–31) and the natural process (Amos 9:11–15).[25] There will be a time of new covenant (Jer. 31:31–34), when all the nations shall be obedient to the purposes of Yahweh (cf. Isa. 19:23–25). This community refuses to let present realities negate the power of God's future.

2. This community of strangers is able to *endorse a different ethic*. This new ethic envisions a community that includes strangers, and therefore is a bold and radical alternative. This transformed community knows that strangers will never be at home until there is an ethic other than the empire's, for the ethic of the empire always produces more strangers. In the covenant, Israel embraces a social practice that the empire regards as subversive, treasonable, and foolish:

Do not oppress a stranger. (Exod. 22:21–24; 23:9)[26]

Do not exact interest from the poor. (Exod. 22:25–27)[27]

On the seventh day you shall rest; that your ox and your ass may have rest, and the son of your bondmaid, and the alien, may be refreshed. (Exod. 23:12)

When you make your neighbor a loan of any sort, you shall not go into his house to fetch his pledge. . . . If he is a poor man, you shall not sleep in his pledge. (Deut. 24:10–12)

You shall not oppress a hired servant who is poor and needy. (Deut. 24:14–15)

You shall not pervert the justice due to the sojourner or to the fatherless, or take a widow's garment in pledge. (Deut. 24:17)

When you reap your harvest . . . and have forgotten a sheaf in the field, you shall not go back to get it; it shall be for the sojourner, the fatherless, and the widow; that the Lord your God may bless you in all the work of your hands. (Deut. 24:19–22)

Love the sojourner. (Deut. 10:10)

The traditions of exodus and Deuteronomy shape the foundational ethical presuppositions of covenanted Israel.

That foundational material and memory provided the basis for continued critical reflection in ancient Israel, as it is preserved in the prophets.[28] The prophets constitute one important way in which the distinctive claims of this community continued to be valued and taken seriously. The prophets do not simply reiterate; they reinterpret the old materials.[29]

In the exilic community of the sixth century, after the disaster of 587 B.C.E., there was a dispute in the community of faith about inclusiveness and exclusiveness and an inclination to draw narrow norms that would exclude all those who were not holy and righteous. The exilic community was tempted to produce its own generation of unacceptable outcasts. In the face of that temptation, the material of Isaiah 56—62 provides an important alternative.[30] This poetic voice insists that the community be inclusive. Two texts show how this poet continued the tradition of radical inclusiveness, Isa. 56:4–8 and Isa. 58:6–7. Isaiah 56:4–8 concerns the inclusiveness of ritual practice. Rigorous norms would exclude both eunuchs and foreigners from worship, but here they are included. Isaiah 58:6–7 concerns right worship, and asserts that true worship is to bring the poor into your house, to practice social inclusiveness. This poetry remains very close to the initial radicalness of Moses and the Sinai ethic. Israel is here urged to be a community that transforms outcasts into members of the household—transforms "Hebrews" into covenanted Israelites.[31]

3. This community of strangers is able to *pray a different prayer.* If one always prays in the empire according to the modes of the empire, one learns to pray docile, passive prayers of resignation. Indeed the empire sponsors ritual activity that takes the dangerous edge off worship. These strangers now at home can still remember that they were strangers and that it was their shrill cry that evoked new social possibilities from God. The cry reported in Exod. 2:23–25 stands as a model for dangerous prayer that summons this transforming God. Thus Israel is still able to pray with shrillness and in protest. This community is not so docile or so reduced to conformity and despair that it accepts either the empire or the god of the empire as an eternal given.

This community practices hospitality, not vengeance. How peculiar it is that though this is a community summoned away from vengeance, its prayers can still articulate hope for vengeance directly from God.[32] Because Israel trusts Yahweh so intensely and believes God's promises of justice so deeply, its prayers impatiently demand intervention by God. In its prayer, Israel notices if God abandons and breaks promises:

> My God, my God, why hast thou forsaken me?
> Why art thou so far from helping me, from the words of my
>   groaning?
>
> (Ps. 22:1)

Israel has come out of forsakenness and does not want to be forsaken again, especially not by Yahweh. Israel notices if God is indifferent and does not answer:

> But I, O Lord, cry to thee;
>   in the morning my prayer comes before thee.
> O Lord, why dost thou cast me off?
>   Why dost thou hide thy face from me?
>
> (Ps. 88:13–14)

Israel notices if the neighbor maltreats:

For he did not remember to show kindness [*hesed*],
  but pursued the poor and needy
  and the brokenhearted to their death.
                                        (Ps. 109:16)

Israel expects that Yahweh will be faithful and intervene when a breakdown occurs in the home-making process because God is careless or a neighbor is ruthless. Israel is present in diligent ways to its own situation and experience. Israel is present, moreover, in abrasive prayers to be sure that this God of covenant does not sell out God's passion and become simply another lord of the empire. The radical ethic of Israel is matched and sustained by daring prayer. As Israel expects the world to be transformed, so Israel insists that God must be present in transformative ways. Israel has no patience for prayer that is not addressed against the stranger-generating realities all around.

4. This community of former strangers, so attentive to covenant, permits and credits in its midst the *abrasive prophetic voice of criticism and possibility*.[33] The presence of this voice of criticism and possibility prevents Israel from becoming simply another form of the empire, the kind at whose hands so much has been suffered. Thus Amos's abrasive strictures and Micah's shrillness, Jeremiah's desperation and Ezekiel's oddness keep insisting that there is for Israel, even royal Israel, an alternative way to be in the world. The prophets relentlessly assert that reliance upon a derelict monarchy, a sham temple religion, or the power of cynical affluence will finally end in death.

The astonishing thing about this assembly of former strangers is that they were never able to expel completely the disturbing voice of the prophetic. They understood that in the end, this voice is constitutive for a faithful community. It is this voice which keeps open the home-making prospect that would otherwise be terminated.

HOME-MAKING AS
PUBLIC WORK

Israel's home-making insistence, however, is not always the voice at the margin. Israel fully believes and trusts that the very empire of estrangement can and does become a hospitable home of covenantal justice. Justice is not to be confined to the edges of society but finally will become the practice and policy of the system. Israel will not let its abrasive passion be diminished. I cite four texts about this conviction of transformation of the power of the empire (see also my discussion of Isa. 1:21–23 in chap. 12).

1. Ezekiel 34 is a text about the transformed political community. Verses 1–10 voice a stinging indictment of the ruling authorities (shepherds), who have been endlessly exploitative. There will, however, be a new intervention by God who will introduce a new public policy. God asserts:

> I myself will be the shepherd of my sheep, and I will make them lie down, says the Lord God. I will seek the lost, and I will bring back the strayed, and I will bind up the crippled, and I will strengthen the weak, and the fat and the strong I will watch over; I will feed them in justice. (vv. 15–16)

The new ordering will be Yahweh's own administration of covenantal compassion. But then the text continues with a more specific political intent:

> And I will set up over them one shepherd, my servant David, and he shall feed them; he shall feed them and be their shepherd. And I, the Lord, will be their God, and my servant David shall be prince among them; I, the Lord, have spoken. (vv. 23–24)

There will be a new governance. It will be characterized by compassion and equity. God is the guarantor of that promise, and David is the instrument of its implementation.

2. The mention of David makes an easy transition to the New Testament and the new governance sponsored by this heir of David.[34] There is abundant evidence that Jesus' ministry was addressed precisely to those who had been excluded by the empire and the laws of holiness and righteousness. He related especially to the marginalized, who were nullified both politically and religiously.[35] His first announcement anticipates a new inclusion of the outcasts:

> The Spirit of the Lord is upon me,
>   because he has anointed me to preach good news to the poor,

He has sent me to proclaim release to the captives
  and recovering of sight to the blind,
  to set at liberty those who are oppressed,
  to proclaim the acceptable year of the Lord.
                              .   (Luke 4:18–19)

This quote from Isaiah 61 is a reference to the Jubilee year (Lev. 25).[36] That ancient proposal provides that those who have lost their land will have it restored to them so that they can resume life in society. Jesus here announces that his ministry is precisely to rehabilitate the marginal who have lost their land and their social power. In Luke 7:22 he announces to John that his intent has been actualized:

> The blind receive their sight, the lame walk, lepers are cleansed, and the deaf hear, the dead are raised up, the poor have good news preached to them.

Covenantal, stratified power arrangements are being overcome, and many "losers" are reentering the social system.

3. It is no wonder that Jesus' ministry finally clashed with the authorities, whose purpose it was to maintain the imperial advantage of some at the expense of others. Thus his ministry is perceived, at least in Luke, as highly partisan:

> And he was teaching daily in the temple. The chief priests and the scribes and the principal men of the people sought to destroy him; but they did not find anything they could do, for all the people hung upon his words. (Luke 19:47–48)

The contrast and social tension are clear. While Jesus is vigorously opposed by the religious-political authorities who guard the monopoly, he is dangerously popular with "the people," who share negatively in the grand disproportion of the authorities.

It is clear that welcoming the stranger is not a pious, easy act of generosity which will be uniformly approved. To welcome the stranger is to challenge the social arrangements that exclude and include. Thus any serious welcome of a stranger is a gesture that "unsettles" the power arrangements to which we have become accustomed. These texts from Luke indicate that Jesus did precisely that unsettling.

4. Finally, the Bible knows that the process of inclusiveness is not yet completed. The old patterns of exclusion and nullification still prevail in most places. The Bible, however, is resilient and bold in its conviction that God has resolved to stay with the question of inclusiveness until the old patterns are overcome and the new governance of God prevails. On the basis of God's resolve, the church sings in boldness and in hope:

> The kingdom of the world has become the kingdom of our Lord and of his Christ, and he shall reign for ever and ever. (Rev. 11:15)

Finally, those who act to welcome the stranger do so in hope, confident that in the end this way of community existence will come to fruition. We make caring, hopeful gestures along the way.

These texts so filled with hope know that a better way is promised and will be established. But in the meantime, the faithful struggle

to break the war system that produces homelessness;

to break the land system that displaces people;

to break the virtue system that nullifies some who do not meet the norm; and

to break every monopoly that excludes.

God is indeed a home-maker. God's work is precisely among the "aliens and exiles" (1 Peter 2:11) who are destined to be at home.[37]

The wonder of our present moment of faith and citizenship is that we, by our baptism, are invited to be a part of this story of inclusiveness in the face of alien powers and systems that exclude. This particular theological discernment of historical reality is not far removed in pertinence from our situation. The policies and practices of our present political order and economic arrangement are generating new waves of strangers every day. The obvious cases are in Lebanon, Latin America, and South Africa. But we can look much closer. Also displaced are the urban poor and farmers.[38] Increasing numbers of people are "extra," "redundant," "surplus," "dispensable." When they are no longer needed for the production or consumption machine, they are marginalized or even nullified.

Against such policies and practices, this biblical narrative issues a mighty protest and a powerful alternative. The hard work is to devise structures and systems of inclusiveness. The daily work is to make concrete, specific gestures of inclusiveness, each of which is a critical protest against and a challenge to the dominant system. That hard work and that daily work are set in the midst of God's work. We are very sure that God will not stop until all the displaced persons are brought to their proper place, in the midst of the community. In the midst of that cosmic resolve, our willingness to welcome the stranger constitutes an important witness to the stranger, to the empire, and to those who yearn for covenant and tremble excessively before the empire.[39]

NOTES

This chapter was initially delivered as an address to a convocation of the Sisters of Mercy in Rochester, New York, on June 21, 1986.

1. Attention to the problem of violence among us requires recognition of the connection between personal violence and a publicly approved policy of vengeance. On the one hand, a rising epidemic of child and spouse abuse indicates a breakdown of primary relationships. On the other hand, the insanity of the arms race and the "defense posture" that justifies it give credibility and legitimacy to other kinds of vengeance. The two, personal and public, are surely not unrelated.

2. Gen. 47:13–26, for all its stylization, is a shrewd description of how the monopoly-seeking empire generates more outsiders. The concentration of goods and power inevitably produces outsiders.

3. On the sociological reality of the Canaanite city-state feudalism and its commitment to social stratification, see Norman K. Gottwald, *The Tribes of Yahweh* (Maryknoll, N.Y.: Orbis Books, 1979), 391–98.

4. The dictum is from Karl Marx, "The ruling ideas of each age have ever been the ideas of its ruling class," *The Thoughts of Karl Marx*, ed. David McClellan (London: Macmillan, 1971), 46.

5. The textual evidence on the *ḥabirû* has been collected and judiciously assessed by Moshe Greenberg, *The Hab/piru*, American Oriental Series 39 (New Haven: Yale University Press, 1955). See more generally Frank S. Frick, *Formation of the State in Ancient Israel* (Sheffield, Eng.: Almond Press, 1985); and David Noel Freedman and David Frank Graf, eds., *Palestine in Transition* (Sheffield, Eng.: Almond Press, 1983), esp. the chaps. by Halligan, Gottwald, and Chaney.

6. On the decisiveness of stratification for social power, see Gerhard E. Lenski, *Power and Privilege: A Theory of Social Stratification* (New York: McGraw-Hill, 1966).

7. The linkage or equivalency of *ḥabirû* and Hebrew cannot be established with any certainty, but the connection has great plausibility.

See Frank A. Spina, "Israelites as *gerim*, 'Sojourners,' in Social and Historical Context," in *The World of the Lord Shall Go Forth*, ed. Carol L. Meyers and M. O'Connor (Winona Lake, Ind.: Eisenbrauns, 1983), 330–32. Note his reference to the work of Greenberg, Chaney, Borger, and Battero, and the important sociological work of Mendenhall, Gottwald, and Weippert. See also Gottwald, *Tribes of Yahweh*, 401–9.

8. Lenski, *Power and Privilege*, 50–58 and passim, has shown how a ruling group cannot finally rely on mere force, but must devise claims of legitimacy that include a dimension of religious, moral, or ritual legitimacy.

9. See Fernando Belo, *A Materialistic Reading of the Gospel of Mark* (Maryknoll, N.Y.: Orbis Books, 1981).

10. Belo, ibid., has shown how the Old Testament traditions of holiness and purity shape the disputes in which Jesus is engaged.

11. It is of course true that possession of land is a subpoint to the monopoly of political-economic power, a topic I have already mentioned. I judge land ownership to be so decisive and so peculiar, however, that I treat it as a separate item. Possession of land or denial of such possession is elemental and irreducible for understanding the stranger. Richard L. Rubenstein, *The Age of Triage* (Boston: Beacon Press, 1984), has argued that it is the practice of "enclosure" of land that eventuates in a disposal of "extra" people (see chap. 11, above).

12. On the cruciality of land as a "place" that permits dignity, community, and humaneness, see the moving, gentle novel of Wendell Berry, *A Place on Earth* (Berkeley, Calif.: North Point Press, 1983).

13. As Israel grew in royal power and wealth, there is no doubt it was seduced into the monopolizing, brutalizing practices of the Canaanite city states. It is against this "paganization" and "Canaanization" of Israel that the prophets protest. See George E. Mendenhall, "The Monarchy," *Interpretation* 29 (1975): 155–70, on this systemic distortion in Israel.

14. John Steinbeck, *The Grapes of Wrath* (New York: Penguin Books, 1939), 298, summarizes the matter with appropriate indignation: "And all the time the farms grew larger and the owners fewer. And there were pitifully few farmers on the land any more. And the imported serfs were beaten and frightened and starved until some went home again, and some grew fierce and were killed or driven from the country."

15. See Michael Ignatieff, *The Needs of Strangers* (New York: Viking Press, 1985), who stresses that strangers most need *membership* in the community, solidarity made possible by gestures and discourse of being publicly at home.

16. After a while the marginal are not reflected in government statistics, e.g., the unemployed appear in the statistics only as long as they

apply for relief. After they cease to apply or to be eligible for relief, they disappear from the vision of the state. The Reagan administration solemnly announced that there were no hungry people in the United States, and the Thatcher government has asserted that there are no homeless in Great Britain. Such assertions are perhaps not a matter of willful lies as much as the power of a horizon that makes such persons invisible.

17. I intend the phrase to be reminiscent of the German phrase, "The Final Solution." What the Third Reich acted out in most radical and pathological form is the aim of every monopoly that wants to eliminate or silence the voices of marginality, by having those voices safely placed where they cannot disrupt..

18. I am using the term "unsettling" in a way contrasted to the use by Wendell Berry, *The Unsettling of America: Culture and Agriculture* (New York: Avon Books, 1978). I do so deliberately. I am in complete agreement with Berry, but now mean to address a settled monopoly which needs to be "unsettled" if outsiders are to be included.

19. There is no doubt that Jesus' identification with the outsiders in his society constituted a critique of the laws of sanctity. Such a critique of law immediately has political implications, a point not lost on Jesus' opponents. See Belo, *A Materialist Reading of Mark*.

20. Thus "Israel" consists in "Hebrews" who have become covenanted. Gottwald, *Tribes of Yahweh*, has shown that the covenanted community of Israel was committed not only to this new God Yahweh (cf. Josh. 24:14–15) but also to a new egalitarian social vision. In the formation of the community from social "nonpersons," see the language of Exod. 12:38 and Num. 11:4.

21. For the sociological realism contained in this text, see John H. Elliott, *A Home for the Homeless: A Sociological Exegesis of 1 Peter, Its Situation and Stratagem* (London: SCM Press, 1981), 169 and passim.

22. The new social hopes and possibilities in this community beyond the horizon of the empire are sounded in a most poignant way in the Song of Hannah (1 Sam. 2:1–10), which anticipates the inversion of social power. The hopes of Hannah are echoed by Mary (Luke 1:46–55), in presenting some main themes for that Gospel narrative.

23. M. Douglas Meeks, *God the Economist: The Doctrine of God and Political Economy* (Minneapolis: Fortress Press, 1989), has argued that God is to be understood in the Bible through the metaphor of "home-maker," i.e., "economist." I understand my argument to be congenial to his thesis. It is this God who is a home-maker, and Israel in obedience to Yahweh takes on the same vocation of home-making. Meeks pays particular attention to the term "household" (*'óikia*), on which see Elliott, *A Home for the Homeless*, chap. 4 and passim.

24. On the problem of intellectual "homelessness" in the modern world, see Peter L. Berger et al., *The Homeless Mind: Modernization and Consciousness* (New York: Random House, 1974). Berger's argument (derivative from Max Weber) suggests that many whom we do not recognize as "strangers" are in fact estranged and in quest of an adequate "home."

25. On the range of hopes in Israel's faith, see Donald E. Gowan, *Eschatology in the Old Testament* (Philadelphia: Fortress Press, 1985).

26. On the sojourner, see Spina, "Israelites as *gerim*, 'Sojourners,'" 321–35. I have found this article most helpful in understanding our theme in the Old Testament.

27. Belo, *A Materialistic Reading of Mark*, proposes that it is "debt cancellation" that the Bible (and Jesus) opposes to the laws of ritual purity. Every teaching in the torah concerning interest, credit, and loans in effect concerns debt cancellation or recompense for a broad social injustice.

28. See Michael Walzer, *Interpretation and Social Criticism* (Cambridge: Harvard University Press, 1987), 67–94.

29. Walzer, ibid., has shrewdly seen that serious interpretation is an important mode of social criticism.

30. On the programmatic tension in this period as reflected in the texts, see Paul D. Hanson, *The Dawn of Apocalyptic: The Historical and Sociological Roots of Jewish Apocalyptic Eschatology* (Philadelphia: Fortress Press, 1979).

31. In the exilic period, of course, these terms are no longer used in this way. I use them only to suggest continuity with the older interpretive grid, and to suggest that while the labels change, the sociological realities persist.

32. George E. Mendenhall, *The Tenth Generation* (Baltimore: Johns Hopkins University Press, 1973), 69–104, has shown that the vengeance of God is not a capricious exercise of anger but the assertion of legitimate sovereignty. See Walter Brueggemann, *Praying the Psalms* (Winona, Minn.: St. Mary's Press, 1982), for a suggestion of how Israel relinquished its own thirst for vengeance to the vengeance (sovereignty) of Yahweh, over which Israel had no control.

33. For the prophetic expression of criticism and alternative, see Bernhard Lang, "The Social Organization of Peasant Poverty in Biblical Israel," *Journal for the Study of the Old Testament* 24 (1982): 47–63; Hans Walter Wolff, "Micah the Moreshite—The Prophet and His Background," in *Israelite Wisdom*, ed. John G. Gammie (Missoula, Mont.: Scholars Press, 1978), 77–84; James L. Mays, "Justice: Perspectives from the Prophetic Tradition," *Interpretation* 37 (1983): 5–17; and Michael Walzer, *Interpretation and Social Criticism*, chap. 3.

34. In making this connection, I do not suggest that the mention of David in this text leads necessarily or directly to Jesus. I mean only that this sort of expectation about David is easily adaptable for Christians in their effort to understand who Jesus is and what may be expected from him.

35. On Jesus' subversive attention to the marginalized, see Luke 7:31–35. See Belo, *A Materialist Reading of Mark*, 109–10 and passim.

36. For a general review of the connection of Jesus to the year of Jubilee, see Sharon H. Ringe, *Jesus, Liberation, and the Biblical Jubilee* (Philadelphia: Fortress Press, 1985).

37. Elliott, *A Home for the Homeless*, has shown in a convincing way that this language of exile and home in 1 Peter is not merely metaphorical but is reflective of the actual social situation of that community of Christians.

38. At a land conference in New York, I first heard the farm crisis and the displacement of "dispensable farmers" characterized as a policy of "triage." See n. 11, above. On the urban poor, see the pathos-filled account of Jonathan Kozol, *Rachel and Her Children: Homeless Families in America* (New York: Crown Publishers, 1988).

39. On the recovery of public life and the reality of the stranger in public life, see Parker J. Palmer, *The Company of Strangers* (New York: Crossroad, 1983). Particular attention should be called to the important work of Thomas W. Ogletree, *Hospitality to the Stranger: Dimensions of Moral Understanding* (Philadelphia: Fortress Press, 1985). Ogletree suggestively takes "hospitality to the stranger" as a metaphor for the whole of moral life and moral understanding. His acceptance of the radicalness of attentiveness to "the other" is congruent with my focus on hospitality as an alternative to vengeance.

PART
4

A COSMIC CONTEXT FOR INTERPRETATION AND OBEDIENCE

14

Cosmic Hurt/
Personal Possibility

Jer. 4:23–28; Isa. 45:18–22; Luke 6:21–31

SOMETHING IS GOING ON among us and it cannot be stopped. It cannot be stopped by reactionary politics and more arms. It cannot be stopped by orthodox theology or by stringent morality. It cannot be stopped by shrewd therapeutic strategies or even by wise exegesis. It cannot be stopped but must be faced.

What is happening is that the world is being dismantled before our very eyes. The world we have known is dying, withering, slipping through our fingers. Perhaps this is always so, because the old creation is being displaced. Whether or not it is always so, it is so now. It is so economically as the old powers tremble and the markets fall. It is so politically as the great nations cannot stop the new danger which we so piously label "terrorism." It is so intellectually as all kinds of new people do not accept our ways of knowing or the old conclusions we have drawn for so long. It is so very close to home. That the world is dying before our eyes is not idle speculation, but a daily experience of change so massive, of alienation so powerful, of anxiety so unending.

CRY NOW

The old world is dying because it has failed. The old world has been disobedient for so long, so unresponsive to God's dream of life, so hard-hearted, that God will sustain it in that form no longer. As leaders in the church, pastors, teachers, care givers, you face every

313

day those who know the world is dying—all it takes is one cancer diagnosis, one unmanageable financial notice, one daughter grown wretched in anorexia, and the world ends. At that moment there is no going home. It will never be the same again.

Because world-ending is so scary and so painful, we do not want to face it. Patients, clients, or parishioners do not want to face it. Our students do not want to face it. And in the end, neither do we. Therefore we face it piecemeal. At the worst we deny the world is ending and we find a target for displacement—communists, doctors, the welfare system, government managers of health care. We convince ourselves that the world must be defended and can be sustained, if we lean heavily enough. Or we can contain the danger by privatizing, by keeping the threat private, personal, contained, domesticated. The therapeutic community has conspired in this to reduce human experience to private, personal matters, to the neglect of the larger cosmic reality that the world is dying.

Serious theological thought shows us immediately that all our various pathologies are interconnected, reflecting our disorder at the center. The anorexic is linked to the larger crisis of consumerism. The abused child is not removed from the bombing of Libya which is, among other things, an act of acute child abuse. Cases of cancer rise from contamination by asbestos and the chemicals we must use to maintain our excessive standard of living. My little world is under assault, so I hold to orthodoxy or moralism or therapy in order to keep the questions small and manageable. The truth, however, is that the needy ones we serve and the bright ones we educate, and all of us, are in the midst of a world bent toward death.

Jesus said to his disciples who struggled for faithfulness in the midst of such a world, "Lucky are you that weep now" (Luke 6:21). Lucky if you are enough in touch with the deep multilayered death. Fortunate are you if you have noticed and let the fullness of the death enter your body.

Jesus summoned his disciples to grieve a full grief, to cry a full death, to let the private anguish touch the public, cosmic reality. We know the deception of not grieving. But we have yet to learn the equal deception of private grief that imagines my little hurt is isolated and not a piece of a full world of hurt. Jesus of course knew

how dangerous it is to weep the death of the whole world, how
seductively reassuring it is to celebrate our security, our standard of
living, our sound economy. He warns of the deception, "Woe to you
that laugh now" (Luke 6:25) . . . if you celebrate and take too much
comfort. "Woe" is promised here to those who settle comfortably
for the way things are.

Against the deception, seduction, and temptation of a culture
filled with self-congratulations, our faithful recognition is that the
world is dying. Jesus saw that, and before him Jeremiah saw it.
Jeremiah saw clearly that his people had chosen death. Jeremiah
gave his life to communicating this reality, so that his people might
know of their deathly choice. He did not engage in private pastoral
consolation, but in massive liturgical disclosure that resymbolized
the world. He uttered poetry inviting his people into the hard process of dismantling:

> I looked on the earth, and lo, it was waste and void;
>> and to the heavens, and they had no light,
> I looked on the mountains and lo, they were quaking,
>> and all the hills moved to and fro.
> I looked and behold, there was no human person
>> and the birds of the air had fled.
> I looked and lo, the fruitful land was a desert,
>> and all its cities were laid in ruins.
>> (Jer. 4:23–26)

Four times, "I looked . . . I looked, I looked, I looked." What I
saw is the world coming apart. This poem draws us back behind
Genesis 1, behind our capacity to manage, behind creation and
order, behind the serene confidence that it will all work out. For an
instant, life is shown in its raw formlessness and its dread void. It is
formless and void at the bed of a cancer patient. It is the same
formlessness and void in public places where there is no foreign
policy, only fear, and no economic policy, only greed. The poetry of
Jeremiah invites Israel to watch while creation recedes and retreats.
Our pastoral action is then to engage people in this cosmic hurt.
This cosmic hurt touches us so intimately, but at the same time it
touches public failure in which we are enmeshed . . . and we must
weep. Intimately and publicly, the eye of faith discerned that the old
world recedes to chaos.

Israel watched while Jerusalem turned back in death. The disciples grieved while they watched the Messiah die. Our deep quarrels are intensified by the end of a white, male world of competence and productivity. For some, it feels like all that is treasured is being taken away. We are empty-handed, void, formless, failed, beyond vitality. Yes we are. We either cry honestly, or, in our denial, we bomb and control and coerce in a wishful propping up of the failure, or we are numbed into resigned acceptance. In these various ways we are dulled into despair.

LAUGH LATER

But Jesus had another word, the word spoken precisely in the crater of destroyed Jerusalem, where there was none to comfort. He had said, Lucky are you if you practice the cosmic hurt and embrace the public death (see Luke 6:21). Then he said, "You shall laugh." Yes you shall. You shall celebrate. You shall rejoice. You shall watch while a new world is born, a new community is evoked, a new life is granted, precisely out of the ruin. Jeremiah, too, had another word. The same Jeremiah who saw chaos and void imagined what it will be like with life begun again:

> There shall be heard again the voice of mirth and the voice of gladness, the voice of the bridegroom and the voice of the bride, the voices of those who sing, as they bring thank offerings to the house of the Lord. . . . For I will restore the fortunes of the land as at first, says the Lord. (Jer. 33:10–11)

This hopeful word can be sounded only in the midst of the grief, only out beyond grief fully embraced, not before that, not anywhere else.

Our faith holds deep, central, and nonnegotiable the conviction that God will form new human persons and a new human community. We do not know how. In our present situation, as in every frightening situation, it is easier to think those promises of newness are simply old traditional promises that have now been outrun in our technological capacity for destruction. It is tempting to imagine that the loss may be true, but the promises are not operative. In our time, in an unprecedented way, it is easier to conclude that there will be no joyous afterward, no voice of bride and bridegroom.

There is nonetheless the powerful promise perched on the lips of Jesus, "You will laugh," because God's will works a new human community, we know not how. He countered the easy resignation of a closed world by saying tersely, "If you laugh now you will end crying." If you celebrate what is, you won't receive what will be. If you are deeply committed to the old world that is now ending, you won't be present or available for the new world God will put into the void of creation.

You will laugh. Long before Jesus, the poet we call Second Isaiah watched while his people struggled with the despair and alienation of exile. The poet watched while his people grieved a destroyed Jerusalem and feared a powerful Babylonian empire. He observed in anguish while they despaired and ended in resignation and defeat (cf. Isa. 49:14). Yet in the very situation where the world of the exiles had returned to void and to formlessness, the poet stood tall and spoke staggering poetry out beyond Jeremiah, replete with echoes of Genesis:

> For thus says the Lord,
> who created the heavens
>   (he is God!)
> who formed the earth and made it,
>   (he established it;
> he did not create it a chaos,
>   he formed it to be inhabited!);
> "I am the Lord, and there is no other.
> I did not speak in secret,
>   in a land of darkness;
> I did not say to the offspring of Jacob,
>   'Seek me in chaos.'"
>   (Isa. 45:18–19)

God did not say, "Seek me in chaos." Embrace the chaos, face it fully and acknowledge it, but do not be excessively fascinated by the loss, failure, and brutality. Do not linger there too long as if that is God's place of disclosure. Instead, watch for God to move powerfully out beyond the chaos to form a new world, a new community, new persons, new possibility.

The way to linger with chaos is to stay cozy with idols of nationalism, consumerism, professionalism, imperialism, autonomy. Chaos is shaped like our false excuses and our dishonest commitments.

But through this passionate, daring poetry there is a turn to a new world. The poet invites his exiled, despairing people to turn from the defeated idols of old-age denial to the powerful news of life given by the righteous savior who fashions a new world. The new world will not be old, tired Jerusalem revisited. The new world will not be a recurrence of old symptoms, old vicious cycles, old games people play, but a new mode of life marked by compassion, hospitality, justice, wholeness. And God will work it!

The community of disciples around Jesus had the irresistible conviction that

God works homecoming in the midst of exile,

God works creation in the midst of chaos,

God works resurrection in the face of crucifixion,

God works newness which is public, but only available to those who relinquish,

God works newness which is personal, new hearts and new possibility, in the face of despairing resignation.

Faced with the massive alienation in which we assume our lives are set, faced with the massive good news of the promise of God, we are drawn to see if the poets lied to us. Is it true that when we look, the earth is formless and void and the hills quiver and the world is emptied of people and beasts? Is it true that God said chaos is not the place of my action, but the power for life overrides to form a newness? Is it true that we will laugh as we watch the new world form? Is it true that letting go permits newness? Is it true that alluding to cosmic hurt permits personal possibility? Is it true that releasing old idols offers a way for the God of life who is beyond our control yet within our gift?

Yes, yes, yes. The church says yes. The new Jerusalem shouts affirmation. The cloud of witnesses verifies the poets. Life is not a syllogism of theology, a blueprint of morality, or a scheme of therapy, but an odd tale told by people who have stories of concrete transformation, of facing chaos and receiving new life, of laughing deeply at God's joy and God's gift and God's victory, and of daring to mock the chaos that has lost its power. The poets have not lied to us. They have presented us the only truth by which we can live. We are the liars when we turn our backs, close our ears, and harden our hearts to the truth of the poets, to the hope, joy, and promise of God's gracious future.

NEWNESS INEXPLICABLE

Of course I speak of matters faithful people know very well. I urge, on this basis, three things about our common practice.

1. We know the cruciality of grief, but we must find ways to let the grief touch our pain. Our deep ideological pathology forces us to contain grief in private realities of guilt and individual measures of hurt. The grief binds us all, oppressed and oppressor, victim and perpetrator, and we are driven to common tears that break beyond our private tears and cry for the whole world (cf. Rom. 8:18–23).

2. We must face the evangelical outcome of tears genuinely shed. Our grief work does not lead simply to a new "square one," unencumbered, as if now we will start again and determine the new configurations of our life. Rather our grief leads us to a newness given from the other side. The newness that comes out of grief is difficult for us to accept because it cannot be our work; it is the work of a God who acts for us and takes initiative beyond us. Newness is the work of a God who with rhetorical finality can say,

As I have resolved, so shall it be;
As I have purposed, so shall it stand.
(Isa. 14:24)

There is a deep cosmic silence in response to this sovereign assertion of God, for the defeated powers grow silent. God will out. We are privileged to act in the new space of this sovereign decree, wholly new people on our way rejoicing.

3. This cosmic drama of chaos and new creation will not be caught in our exegetical specifications or our therapeutic gestures. Our methods and categories contain, limit, and hence enfeeble God's staggering offer of newness. I urge you to think of this, that the linkages of cosmic hurt and personal possibility, of "laugh later" because of "cry now," can only come in imaginative liturgy, out beyond our management of healing and our social analysis. Jeremiah and 2 Isaiah are engaged in liturgic acts, moving well ahead of the data about a dying and a new living. We have emptied our common life of serious liturgy, and until we recover the power of our particular community metaphors we are left only with the liturgies of press conferences, professional football, and the 700 Club. Jeremiah and 2 Isaiah are struggling to reclaim Israel's imagination. It is only our shared imagination that lets us move into God's hurt

and God's hope and then be changed. When we abandon our characteristic shared imagination in the church, we succumb to the flat healings and the hopeless grieving of the world. We have been entrusted with more, with that which moves beyond our private, controlled habits to the great cosmic ache and the great magisterial gift of God.

I offer these thoughts to you as professional healers, those entrusted by the church with special responsibility for pastoral care. But I shall not stop until I cut a slice underneath that professional concern to acknowledge that you, too, are baptized, perhaps hurting, no doubt yearning, likely a little lonely. This text is for you as well as those with whom you work. This invitation of Jesus to cry now and laugh later is a promise to you as well as to the others. It is an invitation that you also should weep now, that you do the hurtful, scary relinquishment of the world you have arranged, that you live in, in dread or in delight, that you acknowledge the world you gather around you is in deep jeopardy. That you turn your heart and your eyes away from the contained private world of competence and congruence to the deep pain of the large world ending, that you face what it means in your very body that our criteria of certitude, our canon of competence, our trustworthy modes of explanation are now all exposed as tentative and called to a deep accountability. We are called to live at weighty risk toward a new world whose shape we cannot see but which is coming nonetheless.

The news is that God wills that strange chaos of exile. God wills the dismantling of our world, for that is where promise has a chance. The more decisive news, however, is that we will laugh later, the laugh of Sarah, the Easter laugh of Jesus, the cosmic laugh of God whose kingdom will have no end. We shall, along with our tired world, be remade for singing and praising and yielding, communing and obeying. We shall be remade along with our world which is now too prudent, too niggardly, too cunning, too coercive. We shall be remade according to God's powerful hope. We can in our fear and complacency resist the cry and so preclude the laugh, and hope for business as usual, world without end. But that way lies only killing and dying.

There is, though, this "other way" that leads us to say with our community:

Beloved, we are God's children now; it does not yet appear what we shall be, but we know that when God appears we shall be like God, for we shall see God as God is. (1 John 3:2)

We shall be like God,
  like God feasting,
  like God with fear finished,
  like God with bread abounding,
  like God, learning war no more,
  like God!
To be made like God we must begin in the way of the loss we cry, for the whole failed creation. Hope begins there in our crying and in our grief, but it ends in utter joy. It ends in a laugh that echoes the gracious, majestic laugh of God.

NOTE

This chapter was a sermon preached to the Association of Clinical Pastoral Educators in Atlanta, Georgia, October 10, 1986.

Scripture Index